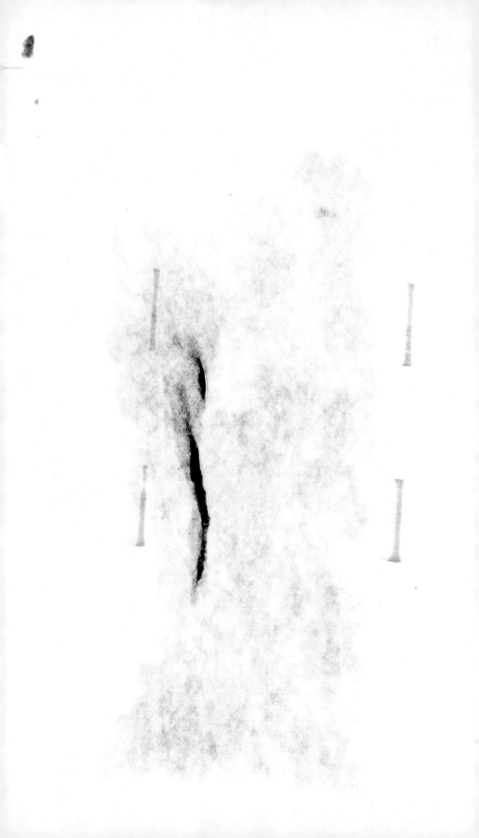

COUNSELING
ADULTS

THE BROOKS/COLE SERIES IN COUNSELING
PSYCHOLOGY
John M. Whiteley, University of California at Irvine
Series Editor

COUNSELING ADULTS
Editors: Nancy K. Schlossberg, University of Maryland
Alan D. Entine, State University of New York at Stony Brook

CAREER COUNSELING
Editors: John M. Whiteley, University of California at Irvine
Arthur Resnikoff, Washington University

APPROACHES TO ASSERTION TRAINING
Editors: John M. Whiteley, University of California at Irvine
John V. Flowers, University of California at Irvine

COUNSELING WOMEN
Editors: Lenore W. Harmon, University of Wisconsin—Milwaukee
Janice M. Birk, University of Maryland
Laurine E. Fitzgerald, University of Wisconsin—Oshkosh
Mary Faith Tanney, University of Maryland

COUNSELING ADULTS

EDITED BY

NANCY K. SCHLOSSBERG
UNIVERSITY OF MARYLAND

ALAN D. ENTINE
STATE UNIVERSITY OF NEW YORK AT STONY BROOK

BROOKS/COLE PUBLISHING COMPANY
Monterey, California

A Division of Wadsworth Publishing Company, Inc.

Production Editor: *Micky Lawler*
Interior Design: *Laurie Cook*
Cover Design: *Sharon Marie Bird*
Illustrations: *Katherine Minerva*

© 1977 by Wadsworth Publishing Company, Inc., Belmont, California 94002. All rights reserved. No part of this book may be reproduced, stored in a retrieval system, or transcribed, in any form or by any means—electronic, mechanical, photocopying, recording, or otherwise—without the prior written permission of the publisher: Brooks/Cole Publishing Company, Monterey, California 93940, a division of Wadsworth Publishing Company, Inc.

Printed in the United States of America

10 9 8 7 6 5 4 3 2 1

Library of Congress Cataloging in Publication Data

Main entry under title:

Counseling adults.
   (Brooks/Cole series in counseling psychology)
   Includes index.
   1. Adulthood. 2. Counseling. I. Schlossberg,
Nancy K., 1929-   II. Entine, Alan D.
BF724.5.C66   155.6   77-1041
ISBN 0-8185-0237-1

SERIES FOREWORD

The books in the Brooks/Cole Series in Counseling Psychology reflect the significant developments that have occurred in the counseling field over the past several decades. No longer is it possible for a single author to cover the complexity and scope of counseling as it is practiced today. Our approach has been to incorporate within the Brooks/Cole Series the viewpoints of different authors having quite diverse training and perspectives.

Over the past decades, too, the counseling field has expanded its theoretical basis, the problems of human living to which it addresses itself, the methods it uses to advance scientifically, and the range of persons who practice it successfully—from competent and skillful paraprofessionals to doctoral-level practitioners in counseling, psychology, education, social work, and psychiatry.

The books in the Brooks/Cole Series are intended for instructors and both graduate and undergraduate students alike who want the most stimulating in current thinking. Each volume may be used independently as a text to focus in detail on an individual topic, or the books may be used in combination to highlight the growth and breadth of the profession. However they are used, the books explore the many new skills that are available to counselors as they struggle to help people learn to change their behavior and gain self-understanding. Single volumes also lend themselves as background reading for workshops or in-service training, as well as in regular semester or quarter classes.

The intent of all the books in the Brooks/Cole Series is to stimulate the reader's thinking about the field, about the assumptions made regarding the basic nature of people, about the normal course of human development and the progressive growth tasks that everyone faces, about how behavior is acquired, and about what different approaches to counseling postulate concerning how human beings can help one another.

John M. Whiteley

PREFACE

The recognition that adulthood is not a period of sameness and constancy—that the process of development is an important normative movement throughout the adult years—is a rather recent one. Data show that adults experience the same conflicts, hopes, disappointments, and urges that other age cohorts experience. However, since the research is new and emerging, many adults continue to be uncomfortable with these feelings and to believe that they are not fully mature if they seek to share their anxieties with others.

The counseling profession, as a result, is faced with special challenges from this growing recognition of adult needs. This book is intended to aid helpers and helpers-in-service to understand the process of change that adults experience. Staff members of many human-services agencies and institutions will also find the book useful as they engage in providing services to their clienteles.

Counseling Adults is organized into four independent sections, each of which focuses on adult development from a different perspective. Section 1 deals with theory and includes articles on the male mid-life crisis, intimacy and crises in adulthood, issues involved in adaptation and the life cycle, early adulthood in men, and achievement patterns in adulthood.

The second section looks at adult development from the perspective of counseling interventions. Articles in this section examine the need for counseling adults, a developmental approach to counseling adults, and the question of age bias in counseling adults.

Sections 3 and 4 discuss programs that have been developed for counseling adults and for training counselors. The article by Walter F. Mondale has become particularly salient since his elevation to the Vice

Presidency of the United States, because it may provide a key to his thinking on desirable legislation. The final article offers a guide to further reading for students and practicing professionals alike.

Nancy K. Schlossberg
Alan D. Entine

CONTENTS

THEORETICAL CONSIDERATIONS 1

Theories of the Male Mid-Life Crisis[1]

ORVILLE G. BRIM, JR.
Foundation for Child Development

To have many middle-aged men in society is practically a modern phenomenon. In earlier times, 90 percent of the species were dead by age forty. Prehistoric man lived less than three decades. The lifespan of an ancient Greek or Roman was about four decades. Today more than a tenth of the population in this nation are males between the ages of forty and sixty, numbering nearly 25 million. These normbearers and decision makers, bill payers and power brokers have been the subjects of commentary and serious study for only a short time. In 1932 Walter B. Pitkin wrote *Life Begins at Forty,* and in the mid-thirties Charlotte Buhler (1935) and Elsa Frenkel-Brunswick (1968) had started their studies of personality changes during the middle years. But until a decade or so ago, most studies of adults were not developmental in perspective; most of the information we had about adults came from cross-sectional studies, as a by-product of other research interests. With few exceptions the dominant view was that nothing of significance takes place in

[1]Invited address to Division 20, at the 82nd Annual Convention of the American Psychological Association, New Orleans, September, 1974. Preparation of this paper was partially supported by the National Institute of Mental Health under Research Grant 1 RO1 MH25547-01.

the male personality during the mid-life period. People felt life ended at forty and there was nothing to do but wait around for retirement and death.

This is still the prevailing view, it seems. Robert R. Sears reports that in teaching his course at Stanford on human development through the life cycle, it comes as a surprise to many students to recognize that their parents may be having their own growth and adaptation crises. It is reminiscent of the story about Stalin's young son, before the revolution, who said to his mother, "Father should get out and do something; all he does is walk in the park with Lenin." Why this attribution of constancy of personality should occur for mid-life males, in the face of the experiences and evidence noted later, is a puzzle worth working on. We know that one attributes more trait consistency over time to others than to oneself, that lives seem more coherent from the outside than from the inside, but this should apply equally at all ages and to women as well as men, if it is a fundamental cognitive process in attribution. Could it be that society is heavily invested in this particular age-sex category and must count on conformity and stability? Is it motivated also by matters not quite so pragmatic, namely, that these men are fathers, and children, of all ages, desire a stable father figure? Or is it that they need to believe that somewhere, someone knows and can explain; but the fact that nobody knows, is one that nobody tells? Are middle-aged men rewarded for stoicism, and punished for expressions of uncertainty and suffering?

The body of scholarly work here under consideration challenges the premises that nothing happens to men in mid-life, and that middle-aged males need no help or attention. And, there is fiction (Bissell, 1965; Heller, 1974; Leggett, 1964; Stern, 1973); popular work (LeShan, 1973); self-help books (Bergler, 1967; Hills, 1973; O'Neill & O'Neill, 1974; Vorspan, 1974); mass media treatments (e.g., *True Story* magazine carried a lead article entitled "I am the Wife of a Man in a Mid-Life Crisis"), and the next season in television will see the launching, I am told, of a series on males at mid-life called "A Second Chance."

Because the concept of male mid-life crisis implies personality change, this work is germane. Here too there is fiction—the genre of work dealing with personality change, the stories and great legends of metamorphosis, e.g., *Dr. Jekyll and Mr. Hyde* (Stevenson, 1922) and *Seconds* (Ely, 1963). The popular, self-help literature is really vast on this topic, as we all know, and there are notable, serious, scholarly works, say Jerome Frank's (1963) *Persuasion and Healing* and John Mann's (1965) *Changing Human Behavior.*

COMPARATIVE ANALYSIS

In my analysis three authors and their colleagues receive most of my commentary: Daniel J. Levinson, Marjorie Fiske Lowenthal, and Bernice L. Neugarten. Levinson and his colleagues are completing their intensive study of forty males, about age forty, from four different occupational groups.[2] The methods involve intensive case studies, within the context of a comprehensive psychosocial developmental theory. Levinson uses a naturalistic and biographic research approach in his interviews with the forty males, and also draws heavily on fiction and biographical protocols. Lowenthal, Thurnher, and Chiriboga (1975) report on a major interview survey of California men and women at four different ages. This first volume presents descriptive baseline data, against which changes will be measured in a second field study in the next several years. Neither of these two research programs are longitudinal studies; e.g., the four groups delineated in the Lowenthal study represent an age span of some forty years, say between twenty and sixty, but cannot be viewed as points on an individual developmental process. Neugarten and her colleagues are represented by a large number of publications over the past two decades, some from the well known Kansas City research and some from other field studies (Coleman & Neugarten, 1971; Havighurst, Munnichs, Neugarten, & Thomae, 1969; Neugarten, 1968, 1973; Neugarten & Associates, 1964; Neugarten & Datan, 1973, 1974).

I have also drawn on Kenneth Soddy's (1967) *Men in Middle Life,* John Clausen's (1972) reports on the Berkeley growth study, and also several other observers and commentators with a less extensive data base than these, but with valuable thoughts about the male mid-life period. I should mention in particular David A. Hamburg (Note 1), Elliott Jaques (1965), Erik Erikson (1950), and Raymond Kuhlen (1964).[3]

The evidence shows and most agree that the individual as he moves through the adult years becomes transformed in appearance, social or life patterns, interests, relationships, and also with regard to inner qualities, for example, ways of experiencing and expressing emotions and motivations and preoccupations. There are hundreds of investigations which substantiate personality change in adulthood, in reactions to situations, in attitudes, in reference groups, in self-descriptive items, in sources of gratification, in dyadic relationships, in the objective descriptions by friends, and on psychological tests. The data come from self-reports, longitudinal studies, observational materials, individual protocols, personal descriptions attesting to the fact that "everybody is working on something," and, significantly, the inability to predict adult personality from childhood, or even adolescence. As

[2]This study will be published soon as a book. I have had the opportunity to read unpublished papers and parts of the book manuscript, and have had personal communications from Dr. Levinson, orally and by letter. The account presented here however is based on an early and partial version of his work. The final published version undoubtedly will differ in some respects.

[3]There are some visible omissions. Some simply are not utilized extensively, such as Jung, Maslow, and Fromm. Some are omitted, such as the Grant Study at Harvard, because the reports and interpretations are not well documented by the work of the study. As for others, such as the work of Roger Gould, Douglas Heath, Jerome K. Meyers, George Pollock, and Klaus Reigel, I have not given the time needed for a careful appraisal.

John Clausen observes, "the natural state of the organism (person) is to be in the process of becoming something different while remaining in many respects the same."

The classic criticism of this view of adult personality change is of course that of the psychoanalyst. (In contrast, Jung, 1933, and Erikson, 1950, both postulate changes, e.g., Jung commenting on the increase in introversion in middle and later life and the reorganization of value systems that characterizes adult change, and Erikson postulating a developmental task of stagnation vs. generativity.) But the psychoanalytic view is in opposition: the sense of identity is essentially established in adolescence and it produces consistency in behavior thereafter; character structure becomes fixed in early adulthood and the essential nature or personality remains unchanged (Neugarten, 1973). Previously I noted some other causes of the view that adult male personality does not change, namely, the mistaken attribution of continuity, the anxiety from perceiving the primary male figure in society as in uncertain change, and the normative pressure for stoicism. For these reasons, the burden seems to have been on behavior scientists to demonstrate change, rather than what seems more difficult, to demonstrate continuity.

Scientific documentation of change is difficult. As Neugarten (1973) points out, it is not the conviction that personality change occurs in adulthood, but the methods for measuring these changes that psychologists are lacking. Behavioral change is the ultimate criterion, but it cannot be measured except inferentially because it expresses itself variably over different situations. Therefore one needs various observers, in different situations over time, to capture the change as manifest in changes in either their responses or their ratings. Thus, it is difficult to demonstrate personality change except by this kind of summary of evidence from a variety of times and places.

Even the best of research is criticized as showing only phenotypic changes, leaving the genotypic personality underneath these surface manifestations still the same. The answer can be made as a three-fold challenge to the psychoanalytic view. First it is impossible for psychoanalysts to be convincing in moving from phenotypic behavior at time 1 to an accurate conceptualization of the genotypic trait that underlies it, and then to a conceptualization and measurement of the different phenotypical behavior appropriate at time 2.

Second, even if one says that traits like "ego strength" change little over time in contrast to other personality traits (e.g., interpersonal relationships or attitudes or self-esteem or social roles), one might be prepared to yield to the clinician the territory of "ego strength" and its durability, and move on to work with what is left, which in my view is effectively almost all of the adult personality.

Third, if one takes the position that it is the natural state of the male adult to be stable in personality, we must ask how much of the stability depends on an unchanging environment. In primitive, slow-changing environments there is likely to be continuity in personality, but in the United States, where both work and family situations are in rapid alteration, life span personality change may be increasing—coming to public attention compared to four decades ago—and continuity of personality increasingly difficult to demonstrate. Theorists of mid-life male changes have focused on different aspects of the person. Thus, Lowenthal et al. (1975) are concerned with the individual's goal domain, past, present, and future; with values; with aspects of psychological functioning such as morale and anxiety; with behavior trait changes and modes of adaptation.

Levinson and his colleagues use the concept of "life structure." It is meant to integrate traditional social structural perspectives with personality structure concepts. Levinson says it "requires first a clear distinction between role and personality and then a way of thinking about multiple roles in their patterning and their 'interpenetration' with personality" (Note 2). For the sociological component, one can think of life structure as containing a uniquely personal social system, with one's own set of unique statuses and roles, residences, the physical space one spends time in, his leisure, his travel, and the like. For the psychological component, one can think of it as consisting primarily of role behavior and related motives, attitudes, beliefs, both conscious and unconscious. Life structure can be viewed as separate from social organization, when one compares his specific unique arrangements with that of the larger order and contrasts his position with what he might become, wishes to be, or was.

Neugarten is the most eclectic in theory and variety of empirical problems studied. Her work over a twenty-year period has examined the lifespan development process with reference to many personality characteristics — values, preferences, attitudes toward death, definitions of and expectations for age grades, perspectives on time, to name a few.

These scholars and most others mentioned here use the term "transition." The transition concept clearly implies a change which moves the person from one position or stage to another. Hence, implicit in the word transition is the concept of stages or stable periods in personality. Lowenthal et al. (1975) use the concept of transition in connection with changes in statuses and roles, e.g., marriage, retirement; Levinson et al. use the term transition in connection with changes in stages of life structure, e.g., "getting into the adult world," "becoming one's own man." Even so the definition of transition for Levinson is difficult to pin down. Sometimes he says it is making something out of that which is new, but most often it is both death and rebirth, the best of the old along with the best of the new; in this way he speaks in allegory rather than using precise definition. Neugarten thinks of stages—whether social or psychological—much less formally, if at all, and hence speaks less often of "transitions."

As for "mid-life crisis," none of the three main theorists emphasizes crises in mid-life, although each recognizes that in some instances regular transitions can become crises. For example, Levinson says, "A transition may proceed relatively smoothly or with moderate or severe turmoil and disruption. In the latter case I speak of a developmental crisis" (Note 3). Other theorists agree. For instance, Clausen (1972) suggests that in the Berkeley growth study lowered aspirations and downward mobility are made with a smooth transition for a substantial number of the subjects. He goes on to add that those in transition often are not aware of it, that there are individual differences in how much and how often persons reflect on these matters— some subjects having undergone substantial change but thinking about it only when interviewed, while others seem to have mused about it almost every day.[4] The concept of "crisis," in mid-life and at other times, implies a rapid or substantial change in personality, and it is probably both rapid and substantial rather than either one alone, which is dislocating with respect to one's sense of identity—his usual reference groups, his role models, his principles, his values, his dyadic relationships, so that the whole framework of his earlier life is in question.

For some unknown number of men a mid-life crisis is a notable experience. An elusive concept to pin down, it reminds me of the story of the Southern mountain man who, when asked if he believed in baptism, said, "Believe in it, I've seen it." Elliott Jaques (1965) refers us to this theme in *The Divine Comedy*. This masterpiece of all time was begun by Dante following his banishment from Florence at the age of thirty-seven. In the opening stanza he created his setting in words of great power and tremendous psychological depth:

Nel mezzo del cammin di nostra vita
mi retrovai per una selva oscura
che la diritta via era smarrita.
Ah quanto a dir qual era e cosa dura
esta selva selvaggia e aspra e forte
che nel pensier rinova la paura!
Tant' e amara che poco e piu morte;[5]

CAUSES AND CONTENT

As one person has summed up the mid-life period, "The hormone production levels are dropping, the head is balding, the sexual vigor is diminishing, the stress is unending, the children are leaving, the parents are dying, the job horizons are narrowing, the friends are having their first heart attacks; the past floats by in a fog of hopes not realized, opportunities not

---

[4]We can also say that there are crises without transitions or personality changes, but this requires a different definition of crisis, namely, one of intense suffering, such as a temporary physical ailment, or extreme fear for an event that does not take place, neither of which need yield any significant durable change in personality.

[5]Translation: In the middle of the journey of our life I came to myself within a dark wood where the straight way was lost. Ah, how hard a thing it is to tell of that wood, savage and harsh and dense, the thought of which renews my fear! So bitter is it that death is hardly more.

grasped, women not bedded, potentials not fulfilled, and the future is a confrontation with one's own mortality" (Lear, 1973).*

The causes set forth for transitions—which may be crises—during the male mid-life period can be summarized in these concepts: (1) endocrine changes, (2) aspiration-achievement gap, (3) resurgence of "The Dream," (4) stagnation versus growth ("generativity"), (5) confrontation with death, (6) relationships within the family, (7) social status and role changes. I have not tried to order these theoretically, a point I consider shortly, but they are arrayed from the biological to the social structural.

Endocrine Changes

From about age thirty on there is a gradual decline in testosterone and cortisol and from thirty through the remainder of life there is a gradual decline in secretion of androgens for the male. There are other steroids identified, many of which are produced in large amounts and with greater age trends than the foregoing, but they are not as yet linked theoretically to physiological processes. There is much to be examined on this psychobiology frontier—in this unknown area of hormonal changes during the male mid-life period. To what extent the changes themselves contribute to individual self-reappraisals or vulnerability to stress we simply do not know at this time.

Aspirations and Achievements

Work still takes the largest single percentage of one's waking hours and constitutes for most a fundamental influence on the development and change in the sense of self through the life cycle. The search for self-esteem—to be valued by others who matter, and to be valued by oneself; to feel in control of the world, one's life course, time, and self in its values and behavior; to believe one is distinctive, unique even, that one counts for something special in the common pilgrimage of man; to sense personal growth and development so that one is something more than as of a week ago—the pursuit of these and other elements in the summary sense of self-esteem pervades the work of most people. (Note 4).

The aspirations in life that men set for themselves are primarily expressed through the institution of work. Over the course of the working life, from entry to the mid-life period, it is likely that although aspirations may be adjusted downward on occasion, one usually believes there is enough time left for the desired level of achievement to be reached in future years. But during mid-life most American males must adjust their career aspirations of earlier years downward to fit current reality. A man may be told that he has risen as

*From "Is There a Male Menopause?," by M. W. Lear, © 1973 by The *New York Times Magazine*. Reprinted by permission.

high as he can go in his place of work; that his present position must be accepted by him as the achievement level for his lifetime. In one of our best known studies Chinoy (1955) reports that automobile workers, comparing their career dreams with what they have actually accomplished, solved the problem of discrepancies by considering their work to be temporary and by maintaining their hopes of becoming an entrepreneur or farmer. Eventually, though, the worker faces a day of reckoning when he must recognize that he is "trapped," that his American dream of becoming his own boss will not be fulfilled.

This causative factor has been in the explanatory theories of many commentators on the mid-life period who make use of the aspiration-achievement gap and its reconciliation as the source and content of personality change. While many men may make this adaptation, in small steps, in a gradual alteration of one's self image, so that a transition to a new sense of self is accomplished without a crisis, for others depression emerges as one realizes he can no longer count on seemingly limitless years ahead. We note that moving toward old age there is cross-cultural evidence showing a decline in expressions of competition and risk (Gutmann, 1969) and a concern in the older age period not with reducing the aspiration-achievement gap but simply in holding on to what one has achieved, in protecting what one has from others, usually younger insurgent groups.

Resurgence of "The Dream"

Levinson and his colleagues most clearly set forth the view that maturation requires one to go through a period of suppression of certain aspects of the self in order to develop and commit to a given life structure, involving an occupation and a family, and that during middle age the suppressed aspects of the self push toward the surface and demand that the man reappraise who he is and what he has been doing. They use the concept of "The Dream" as a youthful aspiration, as an early image of the future self which never dies.

It seems to me that the major component of "The Dream" for males involves their work. It makes a sharp contrast, though, to the aspiration-achievement problem just described, because the middle-aged malaise may arise even though one achieves what he set out to do. The man may feel that he has attempted too little, not stretched himself, not seized opportunities. He may feel it is meaningless and ask, is this what I really wanted? Was it worth all I had to give up? Do I want to go on doing these things for the years I have left? What of those parts of myself that I had to neglect—to suppress—to sacrifice? There is a pervading sense of great sadness in these mid-life men of unfulfilled dreams, and it is the resolution of this crisis that is crucial to Levinson's theory. The man must give up the early adulthood life structure, allowing resurgence and expression of "The Dream," and work through the mid-life transition to the restructuring for middle adulthood.

Stagnation versus "Generativity"

Erikson (1950), in his work on stages of psychosocial development, sets one adult task as the resolution of the issue of stagnation versus generativity. The essence of a successful transition is to shift one's life interests and concerns to the development and achievements of the younger generation and to accept and value one's responsibility to care for this next generation of man.

The concept of generativity may describe the possible resolution of a mid-life crisis rather than its cause, but I include it here because it seems to me to be closest to the idea that a desire for a sense of personal growth is a deepseated characteristic of the human organism and that a failure of a sense of growth generates depression and leads to attempts to avoid this stagnation. (It may be that this developmental process is most important for gifted and successful men such as Erikson has studied and also may be of significance for men of early climax stories—e.g., Irwin Shaw's (1941) "The 80 Yard Run"—where one fears that he never again will do as much or as well in his career.)

Recently Helen Vendler (1974) in reviewing Allen Ginsburg's book *The Fall of America* describes the despair of Ginsburg's middle age: "Everything is already known, and everything has stopped happening . . . Friends are now what they will be for good: no one would change. Everything has been encountered: sex, love, friendship, drugs, even fame, even the boundary dimensions of self."

Confrontation with Death

Elliott Jaques (1965) in his influential paper "Death and the Mid-Life Crisis" says:

> Family and occupation have become established; parents have grown old, and children are at the threshold of adulthood. Youth and childhood are past and gone, and demand to be mourned. The achievement of mature and independent adulthood presents itself as the main psychological task. The paradox is that of entering the prime of life, the stage of fulfillment, but at the same time the prime and fulfillment are dated. Death lies beyond . . . I believe, and shall try to demonstrate, that it is this fact of the entry upon the psychological scene of the reality and inevitability of one's own eventual personal death that is the central and crucial feature of the mid-life phase— the feature which precipitates the critical nature of the period. [p. 506].

Signs to oneself that he is getting old—the hearing, the vision, the hair color, the body functions, the stamina, the teeth, the skin, the rate of healing wounds—are gradual in development and one recognizes that he has stopped growing up, and begun to grow old, that from here on out, everything is downhill. But these indices of aging are nothing compared to the vivid sudden confrontation with the fact of one's own mortality. One of Neugarten's (1968) several significant empirically-based observations about the personality change involves time orientation, and a change in mid-life when one stops counting "time since birth" and begins to think of one's life in reference to "time yet to live." Death represents to the middle-aged man the fact that he will not achieve what he thought he was going to achieve. He will not see those places he had planned to see, he will not explore those ideas he had on his future agenda.

One looks on with some pathos, and occasionally with a sense of tragedy, when the attempted mid-life solution to mortality is to intensify efforts and to engage in complicated attempts to master the use of time. It seems to me, as it must to you, that this is a clear expression of the actual or incipient confrontation with death in its fullest sense. Neugarten has suggested that the central task for middle age relates to the use of time and the essential polarities are between time mastery and capitulation; but this seems to me to pose the question or task too simply. We can say that one of the major psychological tasks for middle age is resignation to death and a permutation, a reordering, of life priorities. As Jaques shows in his many clinical cases, successful resolution liberates energy and leads on to self acceptance.

Relationships within the Family

As Anne Boedecker (Note 5) has written regarding the family, middle age is generally the time when a man's children are leaving the home for work and families of their own, his wife is readjusting to the role of housewife without children and perhaps entering or reentering the job market, and his parents may be aging to the point of becoming dependent on him. Some writers see this as a period of high tension and conflict within the family system and a period of high risk for the post-parental couple. On the other hand, there is a good bit of solid research reporting that couples rate the post-parental period as one of the best in their marriage, and have significant role changes only when family continuity is low. Lowenthal and colleagues are studying this empty-nest period as transition period, and we will know more later as a result.

In any event, two unusual points are noteworthy: Levinson and his colleagues point out that a man during his children's adolescence must inevitably compare a fantasy, his belief in his own power and influence to mold his child into some ideal being, with what is now becoming a reality, and accept the limited nature of his own influence. This reconciliation of aspirations to reality likely is taking place at the same time that his occupational aspiration-achievement gap is being worked through. We do not seem to have many facts about the expression of aspirations for children by parents at this older age level, although the work on earlier childhood aspirations with reference to certain character traits (e.g., Kohn, 1969) has been charted. The subtleties of the transference of the father's aspirations upon the children has been described, but not counted. Since blue collar and white collar workers "top out" at different ages, it might mean that the interaction with the adolescent would be different because the sons might differ in age as much as ten years. On the other hand, since blue collar workers marry earlier and have children earlier the age gap may not be as large. The actual facts here bear looking into because the problem may be more acute for the white collar worker with the older son.

As for husband-wife relations, I want to note the suggestion from Neugarten and the Committee on Human Development group, and specifically from David Gutmann's cross-cultural work (1969). It is that there are some concurrent age changes in the psychological stances of both men and women which bear on the male mid-life crisis. In essence, the older men are more diffusely sensual, more sensitive to the incidental pleasures and pains, less aggressive, more affiliative, more interested in love than conquest or power, more present than future oriented. At the same time, women are aging in the reverse direction, becoming more aggressive, less sentimental, and more domineering. While in the earlier years the husband tends to be dominant, during the aging process he comes to be more dependent. Apparently this comprehensive developmental event of middle and later life acts to reverse or at least equalize the domestic status of the partners, and tends to redistribute the so-called masculine and feminine traits among them, so that through these various sex-role changes there is ushered in the "normal unisex of later life."

What needs to be attended to here in regard to mid-life males—and Lowenthal and colleagues (Lowenthal et al., 1975; Lowenthal & Chiriboga, 1973) have made an excellent start—is that mid-life female personality changes and trajectories are outward, away from dependency on the husband, away from providing nurturance and support to him, so this source of his recognition, affection and sense of value becomes precarious, threatens to disappear.

Social Status and Role Changes

With this concept we move on to consider simply external events in male mid-life, where the theories of causation emphasize changes in position in social organization. It is the predictable sequence of changes in status and role through the lifespan that receives attention from Lowenthal and her colleagues (Lowenthal et al., 1975; Lowenthal & Chiriboga, 1973; Thurnher, 1974). Specifically, the volume reports on four populations facing imminent role gains or losses in transitions of adult life: high-school seniors before starting full-time work; newlyweds before the birth of their first child; parents whose youngest child will leave home within the year; and pre-retirement couples, leaving employment within a year or two. Now, Lowenthal, as noted, does not believe that such changes necessarily bring crises, but rather are occasions for both incremental and decremental changes, in which one stage is left behind, a phase of life over, but new growth and development ahead.

Neugarten also has considered the influence of status changes on mid-life personality and, although asserting personality does change, it is an inaccurate view that middle age constitutes a crisis period in the life-cycle any more than any other period of life. For most persons middle age brings with it the anticipated changes in family and work and health. Some of these changes are not necessarily interpreted as losses by the people who experience them. Whether perceived as losses or gains, the life events of middle age may produce new stresses for the individual, but they bring also occasions to demonstrate an enriched sense of self and new capacities for coping with complexity.

She says that since we have been socialized into a developmental view, the predictable on-time events when they arrive are not unsettling, "that the events are anticipated and rehearsed, the grief work completed, the reconciliation accomplished without shattering this sense of continuity of the life cycle" (Neugarten, 1970, p. 86). But, then she uses her concept of "on-time—off-time" in a new hypothesis about status changes causing mid-life crises and contends that it is the unanticipated, not the anticipated, which is likely to represent the traumatic event. Major stresses are caused by events that upset the sequence and rhythm of the expected life cycle, as when death of a parent comes in adolescence rather than in middle age; when the birth of a child is too early or too late; when occupational achievement is delayed; when the empty nest, grandparenthood, retirement, major illness, or widowhood occur off-time. We should note that there is another class of unexpected traumatic events, which must be viewed as stress events inducing crises which are not necessarily related to chronological age or to passage through the social structure. Instead these are cohort experiences, such as wars, depressions—and historically, plagues and holocausts. We do not find any major sociological analysis of the impact of these stress events on adult males in the United States since the work on the Great Depression of the 1930s, e.g., Bakke (1940) on unemployment, and more recently Studs Terkel's (1970) *Hard Times.*

By way of comment on these seven "causes," we see at the one extreme physiological theories of personality change which might stress the importance of hormonal shifts, while the other anchoring point is a strict sociological perspective which views the life cycle as a succession of social roles with personality change viewed as a product of life-long socialization experiences. Arrayed somewhere in between are the other propositions briefly reviewed above: e.g., the mid-life confrontation with death seems virtually unavoidable simply as one gets older, while the crunch of aspiration-achievement discrepancies, or the surfacing of the set-aside "Dream," lack the same inexorability, for both are partly dependent on external happenings.

Experience has shown that the extreme positions are not acceptable, alone, and that the study of adult personality change requires the conceptual ability to deal with both inside and outside determinants in interaction. Indeed, our three major figures in this review are distinguished by rare interdisciplinary perspectives.

Nevertheless, as must be evident from previous comments, they do differ in their emphases. Lowenthal and her colleagues are examining status changes—increments and decrements—on one hand, while Levinson and his colleagues, in spite of their concept of life structure, in my judgement lean toward a preference for intrapsychic changes.[6] Neugarten describes the influence of external social status changes, where they are off-time and hence disruptive, and the transition to a "time yet to live" orientation. But, most often she and her colleagues stress intrapsychic change from a developmental point of view. Her main theoretical position is that ego processes become increasingly important. In the first two-thirds of the lifespan the ego development is outward toward the environment, and for the last part of the lifespan inward toward the self.

She and Levinson are similar in viewing these changes as mainly internally paced, not triggered by outside events. She says (1973) that given the limitations of our methods and our variables, intrapsychic changes in middle and later life proceed in ways that do not necessarily parallel social interaction or levels of psychological well-being. She says that the direction of change is from outer to inner preoccupation and sees a major reason for these changes as primarily inherent or developmental, in that they seem to occur well before the "losses" of aging can be said to begin. In other words, the fact that these personality changes appear by the mid-forties in a group of well-functioning adults seems congruent with a developmental rather than a reactive view of personality.[7]

I must say that I find the various presentations by Levinson and Neugarten of their ontogenetic views incomplete. What still is missing is a clear specification of the causal process: we want to know both what are the mid-life changes, and also why they happen. If it is not mystical, beyond explanation, which it clearly is not in their views, and if it is not simply biochemically determined, which it also is not, in their views, then it would

---

[6]Levinsons says, "For me the term 'Life Course' refers to the phenomenal stuff of life over time—the ongoing events, the raw materials out of which biographies are written. 'Socialization' is one theoretical perspective from which a life course can be examined and analyzed. It deals primarily with the shaping of the life course by social institutions and groups. It is the usual orientation of sociologists and is well exemplified by Lowenthal (who uses personal characteristics mainly to explain the residual variance). The paradigm of development ordinarily refers to an unfolding from within and is the primary orientation of psychologists, especially in the study of pre-adult development. Erikson and I are similar in our conception of development as an unfolding that depends on both internal and external social factors. This is only partly explicit in our work and is a source of much confusion. To put it most simply: I see development as the evolution of Life Structure, which has both internal and external aspects; and the determinants of development are also both internal and external." (Personal communication)

[7]Neugarten says, "This isn't quite what I think. Changes *can* be triggered by outside events, but the outside event isn't a sufficient explanation of personality change. The problem is a semantic and a conceptual one, since 'personality' is such a poorly-defined term. But in my view there are changes which result from accumulated life experiences—some of these experiences are role changes, some are not. And personality changes can't be said to be 'caused' by any one type of thing." (Personal communication)

seem fair to ask them as behavior scientists to at least speculate about the causes. Contrast this to Lowenthal's approach, where the social-psychological meaning of the structural transitions and the role gains and losses can be made clear in clinical and learning theory terms. (In all fairness, though, this may be too facile. The concepts may be clear, but lack explanatory power. Lowenthal does not have a "developmental theory" in the usual sense.)

"AGES AND STAGES"

Does this bring reminiscences of the 1920s in developmental psychology? It may be that the field of adult development is similar to child development some fifty years ago in its exploration of age-linked developmental sequences. And, like child development then, it is in real danger from pop culture renderings of "life stages," from the public seizing on the idea of age-linked stages of development, such as the "male mid-life crisis," just as it seizes on astrology and tea-leaf reading. Certainly, the evidence does not justify linkage of crises either to stages, or to specific ages, during the mid-life period.

Considering "stages" first, in a succinct analysis Kohlberg (1973) states the distinction between three concepts of stages, namely, those consisting of age-linked social roles or developmental tasks; those consisting of biological maturational stages; and, third, a structural concept which is more advanced and sophisticated. In regard to the latter he says, after Piaget, that:

1. Stages imply distinct or qualitative differences which still serve the same basic function at various points in this development (e.g., modes of thinking in relation to intelligence).

2. These different structures form an invariant sequence, order or succession in individual development. While cultural factors may speed up, slow down, or stop development, they may not change its sequence.

3. Each of these different and sequential modes form a "structured whole."

4. Stages are hierarchical integrations. Accordingly, higher stages displace (or, rather, reintegrate) the structures found at lower stages.

> The characteristics of stages just mentioned, while defined by structural theory, are amenable to research examination. We can ask, "are they qualitative changes in adulthood forming an invariant sequence in any socio-cultural environment, which form a generalized structured whole and which hierarchically relate to earlier qualitative developmental change?" [p. 498].

Now, none of the major theorists under discussion advance a theory of stages in the true structural sense just described. Levinson's work deals with the psycho-social periods in the development of men from age 18 to 45, and these are: leaving the family; getting into the adult world; age 30 transition; settling down; mid-life transition; and restabilization—entry into middle adulthood. The important view of the developmental sequence is that it starts early, and one cannot understand the mid-life transition, or the advent of any crisis, as a stage in the developmental history without knowing the position one is in vis-a-vis the prior stages. He says one must remember that it has not all been smooth up to that point of age 40, from adolescence on, for there have been four intervening stages to work through with varying degrees of success. At this point it is too early to say more than that the stages that he postulates are intriguing, and that biographical analyses to be presented in the forthcoming volume will attempt to link the stages to each other, so that we can see if the theoretical case is convincing. Levinson writes, "Kohlberg's view of stages does not hold either for me or for Erikson. I explicitly do *not* present the psychosocial developmental periods in adulthood as forming a hierarchical progression. They are more in the metaphor of seasons in the year: they follow an invariant order and each can be seen as arising out of the previous one and leading to the next one, but they do not differ in value and all are necessary" (Note 6).

Considering "ages" now, three types of evidence do not support the existence of age-specific crises. The first is the epidemiological. Probably the fundamental symptom of a mid-life crisis is depression. As David Hamburg notes, the usual presenting symptoms or "depressive equivalents" are physical complaints, and verbal self-descriptions involving hopelessness, helplessness and worthlessness. He observes that these characteristics of depression set it off from the "ubiquitous sad moods" of day-to-day life which are not incapacitating, and from "grief experiences" which focus on a temporary loss—but do not necessarily correlate with any personality change or crisis. Studies of the incidence of depression find it high in adolescence and common again in mid-life, but with no age specificity.

As for the secondary symptoms themselves, such as the attempts by men at self-medication for depression, with alcohol—or chronic fatigue, loss of energy, impotence, agitation, social withdrawal—a recent review by Morton Kramer (Note 7) for the SSRC Committee on Work and Personality in the Middle Years summarizing mid-life epidemiological data does not show any specific ages of high incidence within the mid-life passage, e.g., the 8 million alcoholics and the 25 million heavy drinkers in the United States show no notable age clustering throughout the male middle years.

Secondly, clinical data and inferences from fiction or biography cannot document age links. While there certainly are many novels, many personal protocols, they are not admissible because of the missing cases. The data simply demonstrate that some males at the age of 40 report for others, or themselves, a mid-life crisis. Maybe most 40 year olds do not have this experience; maybe more 50 year olds do.

Nor do we have, thirdly, any set of major field studies linking personality crisis to chronological age. On the one hand, Neugarten and colleagues do not believe in age-specific changes, and, moreover, report that when attempts were made to operationalize concepts of ego development or concepts of psychological crises, subject differences were not age related. In the near future though, this picture may change because of forthcoming publication of national survey data in which specific attention is given to relationships between age and the sense of loss of personal control over one's life. Two still unpublished studies by Gerald Gurin and Patricia Gurin at the Institute of Social Research (Ann Arbor, Michigan), and by Daniel Yankelovich, Inc., (New York City) show a decline in the sense of personal control beginning about age 50 to 55. More such studies will be valuable in our understanding of age-linked crises.

IN CONCLUSION

Six statements seem to me to follow from this brief review:

First, the mid-life male is likely to be undergoing some profound personality changes.

Second, these changes will have more than one cause, along the lines delineated above.

Third, a "male mid-life crisis" will occur for some men if there are multiple, simultaneous demands for personality change; if, for instance, during the same month or year the man throws off his last illusions about great success; accepts his children for what they are; buries his father and his mother and yields to the truth of his mortality; recognizes that his sexual vigor and, indeed, interest, are declining, and even finds relief in the fact.

Fourth, these challenges may be stretched out over ten or twenty years. Some men are obsessed about their achievements, but not yet confronting the fact of death; other men are sharply disappointed in their children's personalities but not yet concerned about sexual potency. The events come early for some men, much later for others. There is no evidence that they are related to chronological age in any but the most general sense, e.g., "sometime during the forties."

Fifth, there is as yet no evidence either for developmental periods or "stages" in the mid-life period, in which one event must come after another, or one personality change brings another in its wake. The existence of "stages," if proved true, would be a powerful concept in studying mid-life; meanwhile there is a danger of our using this facile scheme as a cover for loose thinking about human development, without carrying forward the necessary hard-headed analyses of the evidence.

Sixth, the "growing pains" of mid-life, like those of youth and of old age, are transitions from one comparatively steady state to another, and these changes, even when they occur in crisis dimensions, bring for many men more happiness than they had found in younger days.

REFERENCE NOTES

1. Hamburg, D.A., & Hamburg, B. Occupational stress, endocrine changes, and coping behavior in the middle years of adult life. Unpublished paper, 1974.

2. Levinson, D.J. Personal communication, July 2, 1975.
3. Levinson, D.J. Personal communication, July 2, 1975.
4. Social Science Research Council. Description of proposed activities, Committee on Work and Personality in the Middle Years. New York, June, 1973.
5. Boedecker, A. The impact of career success or failure on the male mid-life crisis: A proposal for research on adult development. Unpublished paper, Pennsylvania State University.
6. Levinson, D.J. Personal communication, July 2, 1975.
7. Kramer, M., & Redick, R.W. Epidemiological indices in the middle years. Unpublished paper.

REFERENCES

Bakke, E.W. *The unemployed worker.* New Haven: Yale University Press, 1940.

Bergler, E. *The revolt of the middle aged man.* New York: Grosset & Dunlap, 1967.

Bissell, R. *Still circling Moose Jaw.* New York: McGraw-Hill, 1965.

Buhler, C. The curve of life as studied in biographies. *Journal of Applied Psychology,* 1935, *19,* 405-409.

Chinoy, E. *Automobile workers and the American dream.* New York: Doubleday, 1955.

Clausen, J. The life course of individuals. In M. W. Riley, M. Johnson, & A. Foner (Eds.), *Aging and society* (Vol. III). New York: Russell Sage Foundation, 1972.

Coleman, R., & Neugarten, B. L. *Social status in the city.* San Francisco: Jossey-Bass, 1971.

Ely, D. *Seconds.* New York: Signet Books, 1963.

Erikson, E. *Childhood and society.* New York: W. W. Norton, 1950.

Frank, J. *Persuasion and healing.* New York: Schocken Books, 1963.

Frenkel-Brunswik, E. Adjustments and reorientation in the course of the life-span. In B. Neugarten (Ed.), *Middle age and aging.* Chicago: University of Chicago Press, 1968.

Gutmann, D. The country of old men: Cross-cultural studies in the psychology of later life. In W. Donahue (Ed.), *Occasional papers in gerontology.* Ann Arbor: University of Michigan, 1969.

Havighurst, R., Munnichs, J. M., Neugarten, B., & Thomae, H. *Adjustment to retirement: A cross-national study.* Assen, Netherlands: Van Gorcum & Co., 1969.

Heller, J. Something happened. *New York Times Book Review,* October 6, 1974, p. 1.

Hills, L. R. *How to retire at 41.* New York: Doubleday, 1973.

Jaques, E. Death and the mid-life crisis. *International Journal of Psychoanalysis,* 1965, *4,* 502-514.

Jung, C. G. *Modern man in search of a soul.* New York: Harcourt, Brace, & World, 1933.

Kohlberg, L. Stages and aging in moral development: Some speculations. *Gerontologist,* 1973, *13,* 497-502.

Kohn, M. L. *Class and conformity: A study in values.* Homewood, Illinois: Dorsey Press, 1969.

Kuhlen, R. G. Developmental changes in motivation during the adult years. In J. E. Birren (Ed.), *Relations of development and aging.* Springfield, Illinois: Charles C. Thomas, 1964, 209-264.

Lear, M. W. Is there a male menopause? *New York Times Magazine,* January 28, 1973.

Leggett, J. *The Gloucester branch.* New York: Harper & Row, 1964.

LeShan, E. *The wonderful crisis of middle age.* New York: David McKay, 1973.

Lowenthal, J. F., & Chiriboga, D. Social stress and adaptations: Toward a life-course perspective. In C. Eisdorfer & M. P. Lawton (Eds.), *Psychology of adult development and aging.* Washington, D.C.: American Psychological Association, 1973, 281-310.

Lowenthal, M. F., Thurner, M., Chiriboga, D., & Associates. *Four stages of life: A comparative study of women and men facing transitions.* San Francisco: Jossey-Bass, 1975.

Mann, J. *Changing human behavior.* New York: Charles Scribner's Sons, 1965.

Neugarten, B. L. (Ed.). *Middle age and aging: A reader in social psychology.* Chicago: University of Chicago Press, 1968.

Neugarten, B. L. Dynamics of transition to old age. *Journal of Geriatric Psychiatry,* 1970, *4,* 71-87.

Neugarten, B. L. Personality change in late life: A developmental perspective. In C. Eisdorfer & M. P. Lawton (Eds.), *Psychology of adult development and aging.* Washington, D.C.: American Psychological Association, 1973, 311-335.

Neugarten, B. L., & Associates. *Personality in middle and late life.* New York: Atherton Press, 1964.

Neugarten, B. L., & Datan, N. Sociological perspectives on the life cycle. In P. B. Baltes & K. W. Schaie (Eds.), *Life-span developmental psychology: Personality and socialization.* New York: Academic Press, 1973, 53-69.

Neugarten, B. L. & Datan, N. The middle years. In S. Arieti (Ed.), *American handbook of psychiatry.* New York: Basic Books, 1974.

O'Neill, N., & O'Neill, G. *Shifting gears.* New York: E. M. Evans, 1974.

Pitkin, W. B. *Life begins at forty.* New York: Whittlesey House, McGraw-Hill, 1932.

Shaw, I. The eighty yard run. In C. Grayson (Ed.), *New stories for men.* New York: Doubleday, 1941.

Soddy, K. *Men in middle life.* New York: Lippincott, 1967.

Stern, R. *Other men's daughters.* New York: E. P. Dutton, 1973.

Stevenson, R. L. *The strange case of Dr. Jekyll and Mr. Hyde.* New York: J. H. Sears & Co., 1922.

Terkel, S. *Hard times.* New York: Pantheon, 1970.

Thurnher, M. Goals, values, and the life evaluations at the pre-retirement stage. *Journal of Gerontology,* 1974, *29,* 85-96.

Vendler, H. Review of Allen Ginsburg's book *The fall of America. New York Times Book Review,* February, 1974.

Vorspan, A. *Mazel Tov! You're middle-aged.* New York: Doubleday, 1974.

Intimacy and Crises
in Adulthood

MARJORIE FISKE
LAWRENCE WEISS
Human Development Program
University of California, San Francisco

ABSTRACT

Even though interpersonal intimacy has been proposed as a vital developmental task in the achievement of adulthood (Erikson, 1963) there has been little systematic study of intimate relationships as a psychological resource in transactions and crises of the adult life course, including those resulting from sociohistorical change. Both the high degree of complexity and relativity of the concept of intimacy, as well as the American male's traditional flight from intimacy, contribute to its lack of exploration. It is the thesis of this article that in the absence of overwhelming external challenge, most individuals find the motivation to live autonomous and satisfying lives only through one or more mutually intimate dyadic relationships. Some preliminary evidence in support of this thesis is presented showing marked life stage and sex differences. In addition a theoretical framework for the study of psychosocial change in adulthood focusing on areas of commitment, juxtaposed with some evidence, suggests a more flexible life stage theory than that proposed by Erikson (1963). The implications of intimacy as a resource are discussed for two adult risk groups: middle-aged women in the post-parental stage of life and middle-aged men who are "overwhelmed" by life stresses.

BACKGROUND

With a few exceptions, notably the psychoanalytic theorists, psychological and social scientists have left the concepts of love and intimacy to philosophers, poets, novelists, artists, and the humanists. The assumption seems to be that such essentials to life and growth, both individual and

Research data reported within this article supported by Grant No. AG00002, National Institute of Aging (formerly HD03051 and HD05941, National Institute of Child Health and Human Development).

societal, cannot be studied scientifically. The exceptions are notable, including Freud and many of the neo-Freudians such as Spitz and Wolf (1946). More recently, Bowlby and his colleagues (1969), Chevalier-Skolnikoff (1971) and Harlow (1971) have conducted important work with animals. The bulk of this theoretical and empirical work, however, was on the relationship between mother and infant, and its implications for future relationships and other dimensions of development.

Erikson (1963) and Sullivan (1953) have made the capacity for intimacy a vital component of their developmental theory, identifying it as the critical developmental task in the transition from adolescence to adulthood. In classical analytic theory, the assumption is that such a developmental stage could not be successfully negotiated without the firm underpinnings of a satisfactory infant-mother relationship. Erikson's work is not quite so dogmatic on this point. While brilliantly illuminated in case studies, and in his biographical works (1958, 1969, 1975), Erikson's developmental theory and the role of intimacy within it have proven difficult to define succinctly, and to put to empirical test (Gruen, 1964). Many clinicians, on the other hand, have found his insights "true" in a therapeutic relationship, and among others, the case studies of healthy people as well as of patients by Robert Coles reveal Erikson's strong influence (Coles, 1967).

Research has been done on the process of acquaintanceship, affiliation, courtship and marriage on the one hand, and social networks on the other. There have been very few systematic studies of the significance of intimate dyadic relationships across the adult life course, however, even though sensitive adults are aware of their importance for growth in adulthood, and as a rich psychological resource in the inevitable transitions and crises of the life course.

Interpersonal intimacy is a complex concept, both theoretically and operationally. The major components contained in an intimate relationship, as reported in our earlier work, include similarity, reciprocity, and compatibility (Weiss & Lowenthal, 1975). These components are in turn manifested through various verbal, nonverbal, and physical modalities. Verbal manifestations of intimacy range from the sharing of intellectual ideas, similar attitudes (Byrne, 1971) and guarded exchanges of information to totally free, open, and spontaneous interchanges and self-disclosures that involve reciprocal expressions of affection and love. Nonverbal manifestations of intimacy range from the similarity of behaviors such as gestures or dress, to sustained eye-contact (Argyle & Dean, 1965) as well as spatial distancing or positioning (Hall, 1966; Kiesler & Goldberg, 1968), to an occasional and often totally unexpected sense of being pleasurably shaken by the presence of another. Physical manifestations of intimacy range from a casual handshake or hug, to the kind of "earth-moving" sexual encounter described by Hemingway in *For Whom the Bell Tolls*. Morris (1971) describes 12 stages necessary for a man and a woman to pass through in order to establish an intimate "bond," which in turn is necessary for survival. In his schema, (which we feel needs more rigor), sexual intercourse is the final stage, and itself in turn strongly influences the depth of the "bond." As reflected in the above ranges, there are a variety of degrees or levels that may exist in an intimate relationship. Of particular importance here are those qualities within a relationship that emphasize emotional support or dependability, trust, and mutual empathy or understanding. Dahms (1969) reports a study in which he asked university students to whom they would turn for help with severe crises. The majority of the students took their problems to their peers, faculty, or others rather than to helping professionals. It appears, then, that in times of extreme crises, one's close friends or significant others may be an important resource in the adapting process. The degree of resourcefulness that various levels of intimacy may have on the adaptation process is an intriguing question that clearly needs additional exploration.

Close dyadic relationships consist of varying mixes of all the above forms or manifestations of intimacy, sometimes one far outweighing the others. In our opinion and based on what little evidence is available, the question of the conceptual usefulness of scales or levels of intimacy, contrary to Dahms (1972), should be left open. For example, from a subjective point of view, the concept of intimacy is a highly relative one. As some of our earlier work has shown (Lowenthal & Haven, 1968), one person's confidant is another's casual acquaintance. Jean Paul Sartre, in a recent "Sartre at Seventy" interview (Sartre & Contat, 1975), spends considerable time ruminating about such complexities. He discusses the subtleties of non-verbal, non-sexual physical intimacy, on one hand, and verbal on the other, and centers his hopes for the future of mankind around an increased willingness of individuals to yield their subjective selves to others, above and beyond any expectation of reciprocity. The relativity of the concept of intimacy is further reflected in our work on friendship patterns across the life-course (Weiss & Lowenthal, 1975). The middle and lower middle-class people in our sample of various life stages, when asked to describe the nature of their relationship with their three closest friends, not only attributed different functions to each (reflecting a heterogeneous pattern), but also often expressed a desire for closer, more reciprocal and emotionally laden relationships than they actually had.

In the four adult life stages studied, these needs were expressed much more frequently among women than among men. This comes as no surprise to those familiar with our cultural, and especially our literary tradition. From *Moby Dick* and *Huckleberry Finn* to *Death in the Afternoon* and *The Great Gatsby* (and beyond), a main theme has been the urge (or necessity) to escape from what is construed as a yoking intimacy with women, to escape into parallel work, parallel play, or fighting with men. Intimacy between men is warded off as though in fear of homosexuality, and the exploration of intimacy between men and women is left to the women, writers and otherwise. This fear of intimacy is found much less often among English and European writers of earlier and concomitant vintage. Flaubert, Stendahl, the early

Tolstoy, and the great poets and essayists of Nineteenth Century England did not leave themes of "sense and sensibility" entirely to the insights and gifts of the Austens. Nor have they written only about the nuances of intimacy between sexes: from Shakespeare on, male friendships, homosexual or otherwise, have been subjects for literary homage, with no noticeable signs of guilt. Indeed, even today, it is frequently observed (though to our knowledge not empirically studied) that close friendships among European men are as frequent as among women. In some strata of our own society, relationships among men are qualitatively different from that of women (Lowenthal, Thurnher, Chiriboga, & Associates, 1975).

It remains to be seen whether Sartre is a true prophet, but he does seem to be holding a sensitive finger to the winds of change. Research, the mass media, and, in between, the popularizers of "psychology," share an increasingly pervasive theme of complaint: lack of "real" communication between the sexes, between the generations, and among humankind in general. Indeed, the remarkable, if not frightening, proliferation of various kinds of encounter groups is perhaps the most dramatic consequence of the pervasive and tragic emotional frustration, if not malaise, among middle-class Americans. Some recent research done at Stanford on the impact of encounter groups on its participants found that 13% of the participants could be deemed "casualties" or entered into psychotherapy as a result of the experience, as compared to 3% of the controls, signifying a high risk situation. On the other hand, however, most of the participants were satisfied (61%) with their experience and reported positive change with respect to inner understanding and sensitivity to others, but with negligible effect on one's social networks, including degrees of intimacy (Lieberman, Yalom, & Miles, 1972). This latter finding seems somewhat contradictory to alleged objectives of most encounter groups, namely to facilitate interaction with others on a more meaningful, open and intimate level. It may be that the often rather forcefully arranged possibilities for "instant intimacy" are so overwhelming that they actually inhibit the usually slow-growing development of a close relationship under less artificial circumstances.

The striving for interpersonal intimacy is not, in our opinion, the result of nostalgia among the various generations and age cohorts making up our current population. Rather, it seems to be a conscious or preconscious realization that the traditional norms of our society, and the frontier atmosphere within which these norms developed and continue to influence our educational and familial systems, as well as our communications media, have resulted in the repression or suppression of what, next to the dire necessities of life, is perhaps the basic human need. Except for such groups as the New England Brahmins and their Southern counterparts, our culturally varied ancestors, of whatever generation American, were so caught up in the challenges and grueling work of Western expansion, power dreams, and women having yet more children to till the soil and later build the factories, that they had no time or inclination for introspection.

It is our thesis that in the absence of overwhelming external challenge, most "average" men and women find the energy and motivation to live autonomous, self-generating and satisfying lives only through one or more mutually supportive and intimate dyadic relationships. In addition, we suspect that the development of "crises," both personal and societal, could, under optimal circumstances, have a unifying effect and facilitate the further development of existing intimate relationships. Such crises may also provide the setting for the initiation of new close relationships among persons directly involved in them. At our present stage of evolution (as Maslow's, 1954/1970, search for self-actualizing people indicates), a relatively small proportion of the population (including, but not only, the geniuses) are born with or develop early the capacity for living autonomous, self-actualizing lives. We agree with Sartre (Sartre & Contat, 1975) that many others may become autonomous if our social institutions and norms begin to loosen up the sanctions against the expression of subjective experience, especially interpersonal, and each finds his own way of giving and yielding to others.

There is, as we have noted, relatively little research on the subject of intimacy, and even less from the perspective of the adult life course through old age. The Human Development Program on this campus more or less stumbled onto its importance as a critical intervening resource between life stress and adaptation many years ago. In reviewing the research literature, we will therefore be drawing somewhat immodestly on our own work. At the same time, we are in a position to know and are pleased to report that there is something like a groundswell of theoretical and research interest in the subject among young, as yet unpublished, psychologists, sociologists, and anthropologists.

After a brief review of what is known in this relatively new field, we shall then sketch out some relevant aspects of a conceptual framework which we are developing, primarily for research purposes. We believe that this framework may, as it becomes refined with empirical data, be useful for clinicians, and will therefore conclude with some suggestions in regard to its implications for counseling psychologists.

Insights from Research

Almost none of the relatively little research literature on intimacy has been devoted to close relationships as a resource in life crises as these are usually defined. On the other hand, all of us, from clinical, personal, and observational experience, and from the reading of life histories and case studies, could supply a wealth of anecdotal material about how the availability of an intimate other can help ease one through the stressful periods of life. One of our few research-based observations is that widowerhood is often more traumatic for men than widowhood for women (Lowenthal, Berkman, & Associates, 1967), and we explain this on the basis that men are less likely to have other persons with whom they are intimate. In fact, men name their spouses as their confidantes far more often than women do (Lowenthal & Haven, 1968). In addition, Jourard (1964) and Taylor (1968) elaborate on these sex differences and claim that man's inability to disclose himself intimately contributes to his shorter life expectancy. The process of disclosing oneself to another during particular periods of crises may be the only "therapeutic" action necessary, whether it be "cathartic" in the Aristotelian sense, or self-validating (Sullivan, 1953) in form.

In any case, it has long been established within the research literature on animals that the "herding instinct," or the tendency for affiliation among the same species, serves as a definite survival mechanism (Lorenz, 1966), and directly reduces fear or anxiety (Latané & Glass, 1968). Schachter (1959), performing several experiments with humans dealing with anxiety and affiliation, found that people preferred to affiliate with others when presented with an anxiety-provoking situation—not just anyone, but others in a similar plight. He interpreted his findings in terms of the need not only for anxiety reduction, but also for self-evaluation and social appraisal. In other words, people are attracted to those who fulfill their needs and desires, and provide them with protection and security. This, however, is true only to a certain degree. When the crises are overwhelming, then reactions may sometimes be just the opposite, with the individual seeking privacy and isolation. An extreme example of this would be the retreat into a psychotic depressive reaction under a serious loss, or even worse, a catatonic state with total blockage of external reality and communication.

It has long been traditional among the medical profession to ignore the need for closeness with others among sick or dying patients. Some psychiatrists, primarily geriatric, recognize this need and are able to transcend the classical Freudian "do not touch" code and employ the therapeutically important modality of touch. Physical manifestations of intimacy, such as the holding of hands, the stroking of the patient's head, or even an arm around the shoulder is extremely important in helping the older person deal with severe crises, including the prospects of dying (Simon, Note 1). In fact, in a recent doctoral dissertation (Weiss, 1975), it was found that the importance of touch was not just in the frequency of the act, but in the quality of the touching experience, as reflected through its location, duration, intensity, sensation, and the extent of the body touched. In addition, the differences between men and women in the quality of touching were quite marked, reflecting different tactile needs for men and women. These differing tactile needs have to be taken into consideration not only in the helping relationships, but also in other social relationships that are closer or involve more intimate interaction.

While it is clear that some animals may prefer to be sick and die in solitude, or, conversely, that some die as a result of the tremendously strong desire to flock together (Lorenz, 1966), we know far too little about the needs of human beings in this respect. Indeed, it may well be that even people who have been undemonstrative all their lives have a very deep-seated need for the physical warmth of human contact when their defenses are weakened by being critically ill or dying—a need which family and friends may or may not sense, and which medical staff are explicitly trained to disregard along with any other verbal or physical signs of "emotional involvement" with patients. These needs, however, have to be recognized and incorporated into the health care of the ill, as well as those significant others who are affected by the stress. How often does one see a situational crisis where the only focus of the "helping" personnel is on the patient, totally ignoring the mother, spouse, or friend who may also be present? They too need support to overcome the burden of the stressful situation.

In the case of death or even divorce, the loss of the significant person creates a void, resulting in a strong need to replace the intimate. The proliferation of "singles" groups all over the country, many geared specifically to the needs of the recently widowed and divorced of all age groups, provides dramatic testimony to the growing acceptability of the acknowledgement of the needs of men, as well as women, for the replacement of a lost intimate.

Before shifting our attention to the more ordinary stresses of the adult life course, and how the presence of, or capacity for, an intimate relationship affects them, we first have to emphasize that intimacy, as we have defined it, goes beyond Schachter's (1959) concept of selective affiliation. In fact, as our earlier work on friendship reflects (Weiss & Lowenthal, 1975), the important qualities in a close relationship are more reciprocal or mutual in form, involving trust, support, understanding, and the sharing of confidences. We are still working on this defining process in our present research. Nonetheless, in a preliminary longitudinal analysis of our data of the role of the capacity for intimacy or mutuality as a mediator between the stresses of normative life course transition (leaving home, having or planning for the first child, having the youngest child leave home, and retiring), we have found that there are marked life stage and sex differences. This was also true of the baseline data reported in Lowenthal, et al. (1975) where, for example, the capacity for mutuality proved a greater resource for highly stressed but well-adapted middle-aged men than for anyone else. Five years later, when nearly three-fourths of the sample as a whole had undergone the anticipated transition, we find that the happiest people and those having the fewest psychological (and physical) symptoms are those with a high baseline rating on mutuality, in this instance, intrafamilial. This is the kind of generalized finding that usually gets reported in studies of adults.

There are, in fact, notable variations by stage and sex which make the overall correlation relatively meaningless. Among the former high school seniors there was no relationship between mutuality and these indicators of adaptation at any of the three periods of interviewing, possibly because they had not yet reached Erikson's postulated intimacy stage. This interpretation is partially confirmed by the fact that, at the initial contact, newlywed women ranking high on both intra- and extrafamilial intimacy were significantly happier than those who had low ratings. That this was not true eighteen months and five years later, when the majority had at least one child, may well be due to the often-noted alteration in the marital relationship with the advent of the first child—or, equally plausible, that the glow of the honeymoon phase had worn off. Interestingly, newlywed men, who were noted at the baseline as having a surge of exuberant energy and often were involved in a phrenetic range of activities, revealed no relationship between the assessed capacity for mutuality and our adaptive measures at any of the three periods of contact.

On the other hand, among men who were anticipating the empty-nest stage at the initial contact, there was a high correlation between intrafamilial mutuality and happiness eighteen months later when the youngest child had left home, perhaps because they felt they would now get more attention from their wives. Women at this stage resembled the men in this respect. This relationship between mutuality and happiness among the middle aged does not hold, however, five years later. Possibly the effects of a *second* honeymoon had worn off. Our interpretation, however, based on in-depth analysis of intensive life histories of these subjects, is rather different. During these baseline interviews, men and women had hoped for a closer relationship with their spouses after the youngest child had left home, and perhaps had attained it when the house first became free of the distractions caused by the presence of an adolescent. The longer-range goals of these men and women, however, were often on a collision course, many women hoping to become committed to some activity or interest beyond the family, and many men hoping to be yet more pampered by their wives, to ease them through another ten or fifteen years of boredom on jobs to which they had relatively little commitment, and even less hope of changing (Lowenthal, 1975).

This original detailed analysis (Lowenthal et al., 1975) also showed that mutuality was a significant resource for certain types of "challenged" men, those who were having or had had much stress, but were not preoccupied or obsessed by it. Thus we are not surprised to find that eighteen months later the happiest men among those facing retirement were those with a high initial mutuality rating. That this was not true five years after the initial contact may well be due to the already mentioned disparate long-term goals of men and women at this life stage, as if, in support of Jung's (1933) thesis, to make up for what each of them had missed in earlier life stages. The implications of these findings for the interpretation of research data which do not take into account variations between the sexes at various ages or stages of adulthood are self-evident.

Toward a Conceptual Framework

For the early phases of life, psychologists have emphasized the developmental task of the establishment of same-sex dyadic relationships in the pre-puberty and early puberty stages. And we have already noted Erikson's formulation of intimacy with a member of the opposite sex as the critical developmental task of late adolescence and early adulthood. Scholars studying later phases of adulthood, however, have tended to by-pass dyadic relationships in favor of research on participation in social networks, familial and otherwise (Lowenthal & Robinson, in press). The emphasis is on behavioral involvement and activity patterns, rather than on the quality of interpersonal relationships.

As a result of our previous empirical work, we are beginning to develop a theoretical framework for the study of psychosocial change, centered around four areas of commitment. Shifts from one type of commitment to another may prove functional for adaptation in various stages of the adult life course (Lowenthal, in press). The four foci of commitment are interpersonal; mastery or competence; creativity; moral and self-protective. In our concept of interpersonal commitment, we steer a middle course between nineteenth century romantic ideas of lifelong commitments to dyadic heterosexual and same-sex relationships, and the predictions of Lifton 1967/1969 of an emerging new human type who will make many smooth and fluid transitions across the life course, with inconsistency in self-image and commitments the norm, rather than, in Lecky's (1969) terms of self-consistency, the exception. Nor do we completely abjure nineteenth century romanticism—on the contrary, we strongly suspect that former intimate relationships, disrupted by death, distance or interpersonal conflict, may continue to be a resource in terms of crisis, chronic and acute, throughout the life course, such as is described by Sartre (Sartre & Contat, 1975) in discussing his earlier relationship with Camus. Knowing through past experience that one is capable of having an intimate relationship, romantic or otherwise, may prove nearly as important a resource in difficult life situations as actually having an intimate at the time of crisis: a former relationship is reinforcing, and at the same time sustains hope for a future one.

The proposed framework for studying psychosocial change in adulthood includes coping not only with the inevitable crises of life, but with the more insidious psychological and social changes involved in the growing awareness of becoming mature, then, as is the norm in our culture, becoming obsolete, and finally confronting the imminence and inevitability of death. Incidentally, and relevant to the theme of this paper, we are convinced, though we cannot yet demonstrate, that individuals who have worked through the death of an intimate other between late childhood and early adulthood are better equipped to cope with the prospective loss of the most intimate of intimate others, the self, than are those who have not.

Implicit in Erikson's (1963) stage theory is that there is a main task for each stage, and that, once mastered, one is then free to go on to the next. While he states (1975) that each mastered capacity has continuing importance throughout adulthood, he has not as yet elaborated on the nature of their significance. Nor does Erikson explore differences between the sexes in great detail (much of his work has focused on men), which in many areas of life, including intimacy, we have found to be more important than life stage differences within the same sex. High school boys resemble pre-retiree men more than they resemble high school girls, for example, and on many counts.

If we juxtapose the aforementioned evidence from our longitudinal study into a theoretical commitment framework, we seem considerably to modify Erikson's (1963) stage theory. While he focuses on a sequence of tasks for successive life stages, our findings, as those of other adult longitudinal studies (e.g., Britton & Britton, 1972), strongly suggest that one must simultaneously examine several "tasks" or commitments, how they periodically wax and wane, and how these rhythms differ, and possibly conflict, between the sexes. Erikson's formulations relate essentially to interpersonal commitments, from dyadic (intimacy) to the more broadly interpersonal implied in his concept of generativity, to an almost pan-human level ("integrity"), a sense of being at one with one's fellow men and one's place in human history. In other words, he tends to focus on one commitment per life stage, which, with successful completion, enables one to move on to the next.

Highly relevant to our concept of intimacy as a continuing and vital necessity for a satisfying and growth-oriented existence through old-age (an essential component of intimacy, as we see it, is concern with growth of the other) are one's concept of self and the feeling of hope. It has generally been accepted, at least since the work of George Herbert Mead (1934), Harry Stack Sullivan (1953), and to some extent since the earlier inception and development of classical psychoanalytic theory, that close interpersonal relationships are essential not only to the beginnings of a concept of one's self, but to its continuing change across the life course, for better or for worse. An exception to this would be the person who never experienced any, or enough, of the types of intimacy we have suggested in infancy, adolescence, or young adulthood, and whose self-concept seems to be sustained only through a more or less random kind of social feedback. Indeed, this may well be a common personality configuration in our culture, people whose energies are devoted almost exclusively to the procuring of indiscriminate feedback (and they might well resemble Lifton's Protean Man). So all-absorbing is the need for the reinforcement provided by adulation that there is no room for the kind of interpersonal commitment that intimacy requires, or for the genuine substantive concerns involved in commitment to competence, mastery, creativity, or to moral, spiritual or religious values.

We have called these people, whose sheer survival depends on constant generalized reinforcement, a variant of the life-long self-protective. This is to be distinguished from the self-protectiveness that often develops with age and its concomitant dependencies, as well as from that of lifelong isolates, who, were they to allow themselves to be "caught" by a psychotherapist, a circumstance from which their very isolation protects them, might well be labeled schizoid (Lowenthal, 1964). The kind of narcissistic self-preservation we are referring to also differs from what we have elsewhere (Lowenthal et al., 1967) called the *marginally isolated,* individuals who keep trying, but continuously fail to establish intimate relationships. Unlike the narcissistic self-protective, both the life-long and marginally isolated may have commitments to competence or mastery, and to moral or religious precepts and faiths which are sustaining. They have no need to manipulate the adulation of others to survive.

As to hope, while we have good evidence for its being closely related to time perspective, that is, preoccupation with past, present or future, and the individual's projection of his or her lifespan, at this point we can only say that we are convinced that, for many people, intimacy is a sine qua non for the sustainment of hope. The exceptions are the life-long self-protectives who for whatever reason are incapable of it. We know from the work of Spitz and Wolf (1946) that infants and children deprived of a close relationship become withdrawn, unenterprising and despondent. Some die. We know that schizophrenics long confined to mental hospitals increasingly withdraw and grow old there, unless they sustain relationships with family, friends, or staff. We know that people in nursing homes, which are generally not distinguished by personal warmth on the part of staff, become rapidly depressed, enclosed in a cocoon, and some die without known cause. In fiction and autobiography we also can read about the liberating, hope-inspiring effect of a new close friendship or of falling in love. From the same sources, as well as from our own lives, we know that this kind of renewal is not limited to one stage of life—it can happen, even for the first time, in old age.

Implications for the Counseling of Adults

One of the generalizations we should like to draw from this paper is that one cannot generalize about counseling adults past the age of 30, any more than one can assume that every disturbed young woman is a hysteric, or that every disturbed child grew up in a "schizophrenic family." The day may come when longitudinal research, extending throughout adult life, will enable us to locate various populations at risk and provide some inkling of the psychological, social and cultural-historical factors involved. At this stage of our knowledge, we can venture to suggest only two such risk groups, both middle-aged. From our own research, we have learned that one such group at risk is made up of middle and lower middle-class women facing, or actually in, the early phases of the post-parental stage. Most of these women, who have mainly been family-centered, can anticipate another 25 or 30 years of reasonably healthy life. Many have not very clearly thought through the urge to find commitments, beyond the family sphere. Yet they are caught in a bind, because they also yearn for a renewal of intimacy with their spouses, often expressed in terms of "better communication." Many of their husbands, increasingly dependent, are demanding more of their wives' time, mainly in pampering to their own physical comfort, and such men are often jealous of any actual or potential outside interests on the part of their spouses. Further, the social milieu in which these women live still places many obstructions in the way of those who want to "do" something, whether educational, creative, voluntary, or paid. It is all too easy for these women to use their husbands' demands as an excuse for not taking any initiative. Over and above this conflict, as we are beginning to see in the follow-up material, many of these women are reaching the age when they have increasingly dependent parents, sometimes their own, sometimes their spouses', and occasionally all four. It is, of course, the women in our culture who primarily bear the burden of the psychological and physical needs of the dependent parents, at least while their husbands are still working. Altogether these women facing the empty nest stage were the most poorly adapted of our eight age and sex subgroups. For reasons of their socioeconomic class, and perhaps its accompanying prejudices, few would voluntarily seek counseling.

The second high risk population are the middle-aged men. As current statistics show, they have a high rate of heart attacks and other cardiovascular problems, as well as mental health problems, dramatically reflected in the upward swing of the suicide percentages. It is precisely this group in which we found that the existence or absence of close interpersonal relationships was an important factor in the extent to which men were preoccupied with their stressful experiences. In addition to the fact that men in general do not have, but want, more emotional qualities within their close relationships, the middle-aged men who are "overwhelmed" rate themselves low on the capacity for intimacy and mutuality. These findings support the proposition presented here: close interpersonal relationships serve as a resource against life's crises. Therefore, this risk group, the middle-aged men, needs special attention in counseling in the form of focusing in on their interpersonal milieux as a resource. It is our intention to explore this resource area further to bring more knowledge and understanding to bear on its clinical application.

In addition to the above fairly well-supported suggestions, we can only summarize impressions which we as yet can only tentatively suggest may have important implications for the counseling of adults, and hope that they will be supported in future research.

Perhaps most important among these is the promise of a more flexible life stage theory than that initially formulated by Erikson. First, there may be marked cultural and class differences in the developmental stages of adulthood. Second, even among the largely privileged individuals whom he clinically or biographically studied in depth, presumably drawing on this experience in the development of his important theoretical contribution, there may be additional or more pertinent developmental tasks. For example, Berezin (1963) offers the possibility of a consultative stage as a late extension of the stage of generativity, one involving less responsibility than Erikson's concept implies. We are also willing to venture the hypothesis, with less hesitancy, that within each socioeconomic group in each culture, the developmental trajectories of men and women differ. For example, among some of the middle and lower middle-class women we are studying longitudinally, a generative stage (in Erikson's sense) seems to develop after the more literal generative phase of childbearing and rearing. Erikson's (1968) essay on women strongly implies, in true Freudian tradition, that the former is the principal if not the only form of generativity available (and satisfying) to women. His afterthoughts on this subject (1975) since the advent of the women's liberation movement are more open, but his thesis about psychological sex differences being to a considerable extent determined by biology (with which the authors of this article have no quarrel) remains intact.

Even more important, we believe, is flexibility about the stage concept and its implication that each successive stage must be attained before the next can be reached. We suggest more attention to the simultaneous examination of the individual's commitments to all of Erikson's stage-tasks (and some other forms of commitment as well) at each successive stage of the adult life course. For example, we suspect either for developmental or circumstantial reasons that many people may achieve true intimacy only long after young adulthood. We also have some evidence which leads to a firmer conclusion: that the salience of intimacy waxes, wanes, and waxes again across the life course and that the rhythms vary between the sexes, often with disruptive consequences. At the same time, we may, in our culture at least, be experiencing sociohistorical change toward more self-revelation among both sexes, which may eventually mitigate such disruption.

REFERENCE NOTE

1. Simon, Alexander, personal communication.

REFERENCES

Argyle, M. & Dean, J. Eye contact, distance, and affiliation. *Sociometry,* 1965, *28,* 289-304.

Berezin, M. A. Some intrapsychic aspects of aging. In N. E. Zinberg & I. Kaufman (Eds.), *Normal psychology of the aging process.* New York: International Universities Press, 1963, pp. 93-117.

Bowlby, J. *Attachment and loss.* Vol. I. New York: Basic Books, 1969.

Britton, J. H., & Britton, J. O. *Personality changes in aging.* New York: Springer, 1972.

Byrne, D. *The attraction paradigm.* New York: Academic Press, 1971.

Chevalier-Skolnikoff, S. *Ontogeny of communication in Macaca Speciosa.* Unpublished doctoral dissertation, Dept. of Anthropology, University of California, Berkeley, 1971.

Coles, R. *Children of crisis.* Boston: Little, Brown, 1967.

Dahms, A. Preferred sources of help in time of crisis as related to conceptual systems of college students (Doctoral dissertation, University of Northern Colorado, 1969). Ann Arbor, Mich.: University Microfilms, No. 69-15, 720.

Dahms, A. *Emotional intimacy.* Denver, Colorado: Pruett, 1972.

Erikson, E. H. *Young man Luther: A study in psychoanalysis and history.* New York: W. W. Norton, 1958.

Erikson, E. H. *Childhood and society.* (2nd ed.) New York: Norton, 1963.

Erikson, E. H. Womanhood and the inner space. (Ch. 7) *Identity: Youth and crisis.* New York: Norton, 1968, pp. 261-294.

Erikson, E. H. *Gandhi's truth.* New York: Norton, 1969.

Erikson, E. H. *Life history and the historical moment.* New York: Norton, 1975.

Gruen, W. Adult personality: An empirical study of Erikson's theory of ego development. In B. L. Neugarten & Associates, *Personality in middle and late life.* New York: Atherton Press, 1964, pp. 1-14.

Hall, E. T. *The hidden dimension.* New York: Doubleday, 1966.

Harlow, H. F. *Learning to love.* San Francisco: Albion, 1971.

Jourard, S. *The transparent self.* Princeton: Van Nostrand Reinhold, 1964.

Jung, C. G. The stages of life. In *Modern man in search of a soul* (trans. by W. S. Dell & C. F. Baynes). New York: Harcourt, Brace and World, 1933, pp. 95-114.

Kiesler, C. A. & Goldberg, G. N. Multidimensional approach to the experimental study of interpersonal attraction: Effect of a blunder on the attractiveness of a competent other. *Psychological Reports,* 1968, *22,* 693-705.

Latané, B. & Glass, D. Social and nonsocial attraction in rats. *Journal of Personality and Social Psychology,* 1968, *9,* 142-146.

Lecky, P. *Self-consistency: A theory of personality.* Garden City, N.Y.: Doubleday Anchor, 1969.

Lieberman, M. A., Yalom, I. D., & Miles, M. B. *Encounter groups: First facts.* New York: Basic Books, 1972.

Lifton, R. J. *Boundaries: Psychological man in revolution.* New York: Random House (Vintage Books), 1969. (Originally published, 1967.)

Lorenz, K. *On aggression.* New York: Harcourt, Brace, and World, 1966.

Lowenthal, M. F. Social isolation and mental illness in old age. *American Sociological Review,* 1964, *29*(1), 54-70.

Lowenthal, M. F. Psychosocial variations across the adult life course: Frontiers for research and policy. *The Gerontologist,* 1975, *15*(1), Part 1, 6-12.

Lowenthal, M. F. Toward a sociopsychological theory of change in adulthood and old age. In J. E. Birren & K. W. Schaie (Eds.), *Handbook of the psychology of aging.* New York: Van Nostrand Reinhold, in press.

Lowenthal, M. F., Berkman, P. L. & Associates. *Aging and mental disorder in San Francisco: A social psychiatric study.* San Francisco: Jossey-Bass, 1967.

Lowenthal, M. F., & Haven, C. Interaction and adaptation: Intimacy as a critical variable. *American Sociological Review,* 1968, *33*(1), 20-30.

Lowenthal, M. F. & Robinson, B. Social networks and isolation. In R. H. Binstock & E. Shanas (Eds.), *Handbook of aging and the social sciences.* New York: Van Nostrand Reinhold, in press.

Lowenthal, M. F., Thurnher, M., Chiriboga, D., & Associates. *Four stages of life: A comparative study of women and men facing transitions.* San Francisco: Jossey-Bass, 1975.

Maslow, A. H. *Motivation and personality.* New York: Harper, 1970. (Originally published, 1954.)

Mead, G. H. *Mind, self, and society* (C. W. Morris, Ed.). Chicago: University of Chicago Press, 1934.

Morris, D. *Intimate behavior.* New York: Random House, 1971.

Sartre, J. P., & Contat, M. Sartre at seventy: An interview. *New York Review,* Aug. 7, 1975, 10-17.

Schachter, S. *The psychology of affiliation.* Stanford, CA.: Stanford University Press, 1959.

Spitz, R. A. & Wolf, K. M. Anaclitic depression. *Psychoanalytic study of the child,* 2. New York: International Universities Press, 1946, pp. 313-342.

Sullivan, H. S. *The interpersonal theory of psychiatry* (H. S. Perry & M. L. Gawel, Eds.). New York: W. W. Norton, 1953.

Taylor, D. A. The development of interpersonal relationships: Social penetration processes. *Journal of Social Psychology,* 1968, *79,* 75-90.

Weiss, L., & Lowenthal, M. F. Life-course perspectives on friendship. In Lowenthal, M. F., Thurnher, M., Chiriboga, D., & Associates, *Four stages of life: A comparative study of women and men facing transitions.* San Francisco: Jossey-Bass, 1975, pp. 48-61.

Weiss, S. *Familial tactile correlates of body image in children.* Unpublished doctoral dissertation, School of Nursing, University of California, San Francisco, 1975.

Adaptation and the Life Cycle

BERNICE L. NEUGARTEN
University of Chicago

A life history can be understood only by considering its historical setting. The life cycle of a man born in 1910 differs from that of a man born in 1950. Any historical, economic, or political event varies in personal significance according to the point in the life cycle at which the event occurs. For example, the effects of the Great Depression or the Vietnam War on a young man just finishing school and entering upon economic adulthood differ greatly from those on a middle-aged man at the height of his occupational career.

The interweaving of historical time and life time occurs in the context of a third dimension, that of socially defined time. Every society is age-graded, and every society has a system of social expectations regarding age-appropriate behavior. The individual passes through a socially regulated cycle from birth to death as inexorably as he passes through the biological cycle: a succession of socially delineated age-statuses, each with its recognized rights, duties, and obligations. There exists a socially prescribed timetable for the ordering of major life events: a time in the life-span when men and women are expected to marry, a time to raise children, a time to retire. This normative pattern is adhered to, more or less consistently, by most persons within a given social group — although the actual occurrences of major life events are influenced by various contingencies and although the norms themselves vary somewhat from one socioeconomic, ethnic, or religious group to another. For any social group it can easily be demonstrated that norms and actual occurrences are closely related. Age norms and age expectations operate as a system of social controls, as prods and brakes upon behavior, in some instances hastening an event, in others, delaying it. Men and women are aware not only of the social clocks that operate in various areas of their lives but also of their own timing; and they readily describe themselves as "early," "late," or "on time" with regard to the major life events.

From this perspective, time is at least a three-dimensional phenomenon in charting the course of the life cycle, with historical time, life time (or chronological age) and social time all intricately intertwined.

This is a slightly revised version of a paper originally titled Dynamics of transition of middle age to old age, *Journal of Geriatric Psychiatry,* 1970, 4, 71-87.

The social change that occurs with the passage of historical time creates alterations in the rhythm and timing of the life cycle, leading in turn to changes in age norms and in expectations regarding age-appropriate behavior. Within the family cycle, there are points at which the individual moves from "child" to "adolescent" to "adult" and where, after physical maturity is reached, social age continues to be marked off by relatively clear-cut biological or social events: marriage, the birth of the first child, the departure of children from the home, and the birth of grandchildren. At each of these points, the individual takes on new roles in the family and his status in relation to other family members is altered.

Changes in timing of the family cycle have been dramatic over the past several decades: age at marriage has dropped; children are born earlier in the marriage; longevity has increased, thereby increasing the duration of marriage. Marriage and parenthood imply adulthood within the family cycle, so it may be said that adulthood is reached earlier than before. The average modern woman marries before her twenty-first birthday, gives birth to her first child within the first year or so thereafter, bears all her children in the next six to eight years, and sees her last-born child in school by the time she reaches 35. Active parenthood is becoming shorter, for children are leaving home at an earlier age. It follows that grandparenthood also comes at an earlier age now than in preceding generations. At the same time, widowhood tends to occur later.

The historical trend, therefore, has been toward a quickening of events through most of the family cycle, followed by an extended postparental interval (now some 15 to 17 years) in which husband and wife are the remaining members of the household.

Marriage, although it defines maturity within the family, is no longer synchronous with the attainment of economic maturity. With the increasing needs of the American economy for technical and professional workers, the length of time devoted to education has increased for young people, but without a comparable delay in marriage.

Changing sex-role patterns with regard to the timing of economic maturity are reflected in the rising proportion of young married women in the labor force. In 1890, only six per cent of married women aged 14 to 24 were working; by 1970 it was over 40 per cent. While the percentages reflect marriages in which husbands are working, as well as those in which husbands are still in school, they reveal in both instances that young wives are increasingly sharing the economic burdens of new households and that they are doing so at younger and younger ages. Economic maturity is being deferred for men, but not for women.

The new rhythms of social maturity impinge, of course, upon other aspects of family life as well. Parent-child relationships are influenced in many subtle ways by the fact that half of all new fathers are under 23 and half of all new mothers under 21. Changes in parental behavior, with fathers reportedly becoming less authoritarian and with both parents sharing more equally in tasks of homemaking and child-rearing, may be reflections of this trend. The relative youth of parents and grandparents may also be contributing to the complex patterns of help between generations that are now becoming evident, including the widespread financial help that flows from parents downward to their adult children. Similarly, with more grandparents surviving per child and with an extended family system that encompasses several generations, new patterns of child-rearing are emerging in which child-grandparent relations take on new significance.

In a recent study of three-generation families in which various styles of behavior by grandparents were delineated, we found that younger grandparents (those under age 65, as compared with those over 65) more often followed what we called the *fun-seeking* pattern. The *fun-seeker* is the grandparent whose relation to the child is informal and playful and who joins the child for the specific purpose of having fun, somewhat as if he were the child's playmate. Grandchildren are viewed by these grandparents as a source of leisure activity, as an item of "consumption" rather than "production," and as a source of self-indulgence. The relationship is one in which authority lines are irrelevant and where the emphasis is on mutual satisfaction.

Another new trend among the middle-aged is for women to go back to work. The proportion of working women in their early 20's is high; it drops off somewhat from age 25 to 35 and then rises again. More than 50 per cent of all women aged 35 to 44 are now in the labor force and more than 50 per cent of those aged 45 to 54. The young child is likely to have his mother at home but his grandmother out working; the adolescent, to have both mother and grandmother working.

A few generations ago, with children spaced further apart, the last child married and the nest emptied when women were in their mid-50's. Today, this event occurs when many women are in their late 40's, at about the same time they experience the menopause and the biological climacterium. This is the same age when the census data show the number of women on the labor market taking its sharpest upturn.

These are but a few examples of the way in which historical time and social change are affecting the course and rhythm of the life cycle, affecting in turn social expectations with regard to age-appropriate behavior.[1]

Although there have been many changes in the life cycle, there also remain many regularities and continuities. While it is true that the rapidity of social change is unprecedented and that the explosion of knowledge occurring in the social, psychological, physical, and biological sciences may upset many of our present assumptions about human nature, people's lives in the next few decades are not likely to be transformed as drastically as some of our newspaper writers would lead us to believe. Despite the contraceptive pill and the increased freedom with regard to the occurrence and timing of

---

[1]The effects of social change upon the timing of major life events and the creation of new age norms are described at greater length in an earlier paper (Neugarten & Moore, 1968).

parenthood, despite the organ transplants and the promise of greater control over death, and despite space travel, the human life cycle is likely to retain its major features for some time to come. Biologists seem to believe, for instance, that the human life-span is relatively fixed by genetic factors; and even as they begin to separate the effects of aging from those of injury or disease, and as greater proportions of the population live to the biological limits, it is likely to be a long time before the life-span itself can be lengthened.

New methods of biological engineering may alter the genetic composition of the human species, yet for the foreseeable future we are likely to deal with human organisms who will grow and develop to biological maturity in the first third of the life-span, who will continue to change psychologically and socially in the second and third parts of the life-span, and who will age and die. Accordingly, men and women will continue to experience many of the same biological, social, and psychological regularities of the life cycle.

Some of these regularities will continue to arise from the social controls related to age-norms and age-appropriate behavior. Because individuals live in contact with persons of all ages, they learn what to anticipate. There is a never-ending process of socialization by which the child learns what facets of his childhood behavior he must shed as he moves into adolescence; the adolescent learns what is expected of him as he moves from school to job to marriage to parenthood; and the middle-aged learn approved ways of growing old. Thus the social ordering of age-statuses and age-appropriate behavior will continue to provide a large measure of predictability.

There are certain other regularities of the life cycle which may be said to arise more from within the individual than from without. To draw a dichotomy between "inner" and "outer" is, of course, merely a heuristic device, given a transactional view of personality. As the result of accumulative adaptations to both biological and social events, there is a continuously changing basis within the individual for perceiving and responding to new events in the outer world. It is in this sense that orderly and predictable changes occur within the personality as well as in the social environment.

People change over time as the result of the accumulation of experience. As events are registered in the organism, human individuals inevitably abstract from their experiences and create more encompassing and more refined categories for interpreting new events. The mental filing system not only grows larger but it is reorganized over time, with infinitely more cross-references and classifications. Not only do middle-aged parents differ from their adolescent children because they, the parents, were born in a different historical period and were therefore subject to different formative experiences, but they differ also because of the effects of having lived longer, of having therefore a greater apperceptive mass or store of past experiences (or, again, a more complex filing system) by which to evaluate any event.

(It is not being cynical to suggest that young people who demonstrated on college campuses all over the world are subject to the same imperatives of change that stem from the course of the life cycle. This is not to say that people as they age become more conservative politically, for the evidence on this point is moot, but rather that with increasing age, perspectives inevitably lengthen and, as a consequence, attitudes and behavior change. Only a few hippies have remained hippies into their 30's and 40's, not only because the social issues have changed and hippie culture itself has altered, but because there are internal pressures to change that stem from movement through one's own life cycle.)

A few such alterations that occur with age can be illustrated from some of our studies carried out in the Committee on Human Development at the University of Chicago over the past decade, where we have been making studies of personality, of adaptational patterns, of career lines, of age-norms and age-appropriate behavior in adults, and of attitudes and values across social class and generational lines. While this set of inquiries has not involved longitudinal research on the same subjects (except for one group of 300 older persons who were followed over a seven-year period), it represents a related set of investigations in which the number of men and women participating now totals well over 2,000. Each study is based upon a relatively large sample of normal people, none of them volunteers, all living in metropolitan communities in the Midwest.

In one set of investigations of persons aged 40 to 70 from varied walks of life, based upon both interviews and projective data, we found that different modes of dealing with impulse life become salient with increasing age. In middle age, there is an emphasis upon introspection and stocktaking, upon conscious reappraisal of the self. There is conscious *self-utilization* rather than the self-consciousness of youth. Preoccupation with the inner life seems to become greater; emotional cathexes toward persons and objects in the outer world decreases; the readiness to attribute activity and affect to persons in the environment is reduced; there is movement from outer-world to inner-world orientation. A constriction seems to occur in the 60- and 70-year-olds in the ability to integrate wide ranges of stimuli and in the willingness to deal with complicated and challenging situations in the environment. We have referred to this increased saliency of the inner life as an increased "interiority" of personality. We regard it as reflecting certain intrinsic as well as responsive processes of change, since it was measurable in well-functioning adults by the mid-40's, well before the social losses of aging occurred and well before there was any measurable change in competency of performance in adult social roles.

In the present context this increased interiority is to be regarded as one of the "inner" psychological regularities of the life cycle. Interiority seems, however, to be relatively independent of adaptation or *purposive* behavior. Our studies suggest that interiority is age-related and adaptation is not (Neugarten et al., 1964). In more general terms, adaptational abilities are to be distinguished from age-related personality changes.

A related finding appeared in a different sample of middle-aged adults. In this instance we interviewed at length 100 highly placed men and women concerning what they regarded as the most salient characteristics of middle-adulthood. These persons were university graduates: business, professional, and artistic leaders, some of whom appeared in *American Men of Science* and *Who's Who in America*. Both men and women talked of the difference in the way time is perceived. A particularly conspicuous feature of middle age is that life is restructured in terms of time left to live rather than time since birth. Not only is there a reversal in directionality but also an awareness that time is finite. Middle-aged people look to their positions within different life contexts — changes in body, career, family — rather than to chronological age for their primary cues in clocking themselves. It was at first a surprise, then a commonplace, that middle-aged persons when asked their age could not immediately give their exact age but stopped to think, often saying, "Let's see . . . 51? No, 52. Yes, 52 is right."

Yet responses like the following were characteristic. "Before I was 35, the future just stretched forth. There would be time to do and see and carry out all the plans I had . . . Now I keep thinking, will I have time enough to finish off some of the things I want to do?" Or, "Time is a two-edged sword. In some of my friends, it brings anxiety that there won't be time enough. To others, it adds a certain challenge in seeing how much pleasure can still be obtained. But all of us figure backward from the end . . . and estimate how much time we can expect."

The change in time-perspective is intimately related to the personalization of death. Death in middle age becomes a real possibility for the self, no longer the magical or extraordinary occurrence that it appears in youth. In women there is the rehearsal for widowhood which becomes characteristic (one which rarely occurs in men); and in men there is the "sponsoring" issue with regard to young associates as well as with regard to one's children, an issue we called "the creation of social heirs."

Increased interiority, changed time perspective, and personalization of death are only a few of the psychological changes which have emerged from our own studies and which we regard as characteristic of men and women as they move through adulthood.

The fact that regularities of change through the life cycle are demonstrable along biological, social, and psychological dimensions leads to the questions of adaptation and the concept of the "normal, expectable life-cycle."

Adults carry around in their heads, whether or not they can easily verbalize it, a set of anticipations of the normal, expectable life cycle. They internalize expectations of the consensually validated sequences of major life events — not only what those events should be but when they should occur. They make plans, set goals, and reassess those goals along a timeline shaped by these expectations.

The individual is said to create a sense of self very early in life. Freud, for example, in describing the development of the ego, and George Mead, in describing the differentiation between the "I" and the "me," placed the development of self very early in childhood. But it is perhaps not until adulthood that the individual creates a sense of the life cycle, that is, an anticipation and acceptance of the inevitable sequence of events that will occur as men grow up, grow old, and die. Adulthood is when he understands that the course of his own life will be similar to the lives of others and that the turning points are inescapable. This ability to interpret the past and foresee the future, and to create for oneself a sense of the predictable life cycle, presumably differentiates the healthy adult personality from the unhealthy.

From this point of view, the normal expectable life events do not themselves constitute crises, nor are they trauma producing. The end of formal schooling, leaving the parents' home, marriage, parenthood, occupational achievement, one's own children growing up and leaving, menopause, grandparenthood, retirement — in our society, these are the normal turning points, the markers or the punctuation marks along the life cycle. They call forth changes in self-concept and in sense of identity, they mark the incorporation of new social roles, and accordingly they are the precipitants of new adaptations. But in themselves they are not, for the vast group of normal persons, traumatic events or crises that trigger mental illness or destroy the continuity of the self.

That we often err in construing a normal life event as a crisis can well be illustrated in one of our own recent studies of middle age. Wishing to study patterns of adaptation, we began with a study of women, reasoning that women's lives in the middle years were characterized by two major crises: the biological climacterium evidenced by the menopause and the change in roles that follows upon children leaving home. We felt that these two crises for women in their 40's and 50's might have measurable effects upon their psychological well-being.

Accordingly we selected a population of 100 normal women aged 43 to 53 from working-class and middle-class backgrounds, all of whom were in good physical health, all married and living with husbands, all mothers of at least one child, and none of whom had had hysterectomies. Five to six hours of interviewing and projective testing were carried out, and we obtained data on a large number of psychological and social variables, including measures of anxiety, life satisfaction, and self-concept. Because this period of life has been relatively unexplored by psychologists, and because psychiatrists have shown special interest in the menopause and in questions of the possible relation to so-called involutional depressions, this study perhaps warrants relatively full description.

Like puberty and pregnancy, the climacterium is generally regarded as a significant turning point in a woman's psychosexual development — one that reflects profound endocrine and somatic changes and one that presumably involves a variety of psychological and social concomitants. Because it signifies that an important biologic function, woman's reproductive life, has come to an end, the menopause has often been described as one of the most critical events of the middle years — as a potential threat to a woman's identity.

Although there is a large medical and popular literature on the climacterium, there is a conspicuous lack of empirical research with normal, or nonclinical women. While an estimated 75 per cent of women experience some disturbance or discomfort during the climacterium, only a small proportion receive medical treatment, suggesting that conclusions about the menopause drawn from clinical observations can not be generalized to the entire population.

In the present study, several approaches were employed in exploring the menopause as a focus of concern. Women were asked about their expectations regarding menopause, what they had heard or read about it, what they had observed in other women. Each woman was asked also whether she regarded herself as premenopausal, menopausal, or postmenopausal; what was the basis of her assessment; and what, if any, were the symptoms and reactions she had experienced.

We first divided the 100 women into three groups: those who reported no changes or irregularities in their menstrual patterns and were evaluated as premenopausal; the menopausal; and those who had stopped menstruating for at least two years, the postmenopausal. We discovered at once that menopausal or climacteric status was an insignificant variable: that is, it did not differentiate among these women with regard to any of our other variables.

Moving on, we found that these women as a group tended to minimize the significance of the menopause and to regard it as unlikely to produce much anxiety or stress. For instance, when asked to select those which worried them most from a list of possible events or sequelae of middle age, only four women of the 100 regarded menopause as a major source of worry. (More than half indicated that "losing your husband" was the greatest concern; "just getting older" and "fear of cancer" were also frequent responses.) When asked, at another point in the interview, what was disliked most about middle age, only one of the women mentioned the menopause. When questioned further, at still another point in the interview, about the best thing and the worst thing about menopause, only 12 women could not mention anything good about menopause but 30 could not think of anything bad about it.

These women were unusually cooperative and eager to talk about themselves, yet even after considerable time was given to the topic on two different interview occasions, only one-third could think of any way that a woman's physical or emotional health was likely to be adversely affected by the "change of life." Some expressed the view that the menopause served to improve a woman's state of health. A majority maintained that any changes in health or emotional status during the climacteric period were caused by idiosyncratic factors or individual differences in capacity to tolerate stress generally. "It depends on the individual. Personally, I think if women look for trouble, they find it." Similarly, when asked about how the menopause affects sexuality, 65 per cent maintained there was no effect and that any alteration in a woman's sexual life during climacterium must be a function of her attitudes prior to the menopause. (Of the 35 women who thought there was change in sexual activity associated with climacterium, half thought sexual activity becomes less important and half thought sexual relations become more enjoyable because menstruation and fear of pregnancy were removed.)

In a specially devised checklist of attitudes toward menopause (Neugarten, Wood, Kraines, & Loomis, 1963), the overwhelming majority (over 80 per cent) attributed little or no change or discontinuity in a woman's life to the menopause. About three-fourths took the view that, except for the underlying biologic changes, women have a relative degree of control over their symptoms and need not have even symptomatic difficulties.

In addition to studying attitudes, we devised a checklist of menopausal symptoms based on a careful review of the medical literature (the 28 most frequently reported somatic, psychosomatic, and psychological symptoms — hot flashes, paresthesia, vertigo, headache, insomnia, irritability, depression, and so on) and asked women to report the frequency and intensity of their symptoms (Neugarten & Kraines, 1965). We found that overall these women held relatively favorable views of the menopause and did not regard it as a major loss of feminine identity, irrespective of the severity of their symptoms.

We obtained also from each woman a brief psychosexual history, then assessed the degree to which each reported physical or emotional difficulty regarding the first sex information, menarche, menstrual periods, first sexual experience, pregnancy, and childbirth. The result was that difficulties with menarche, menstrual periods, and pregnancy were related to severity of menopausal symptoms. Those women who reported the most symptoms and who viewed the menopause as disturbing, unpleasant, and unpredictable were those who expressed more negative affect regarding their earlier psychosexual experiences.

Our general conclusions were, then, that there was little evidence in these data to support a "crisis" view of the climacterium and that the crisis theory in the literature probably reflects basic differences between clinical samples and a community sample.

We then moved further in the analysis. To measure psychological well-being, we used several different measures: a set of ratings of life-satisfaction, a self-cathexis scale and a body cathexis scale, the Taylor Manifest Anxiety scale (taken from the MMPI), the IPAT Anxiety Questionnaire (from Cattell's 16-factor test), and a set of measures based on the TAT. The correlations between climacteric status, menopausal symptoms, and attitudes toward menopause, on the one hand, and each of the various measures of psychological well-being, on the other, were very low (most ranged from 0.11 to 0.35). We concluded, just as we had from the first part of this study, that the menopause was not a crisis event; for if it were, it should have shown a significant relation to the psychological well-being or mental health of these women.

With regard to our second presumed "crisis," the empty nest, our findings were similar. We divided the women according to family stage: the intact stage, in which none of the children had left home; the transitional stage, in which one or more had left, but one or more remained; and the empty nest, or postparental stage, in which all the children were living outside the home. We looked also at those women who had children under age 14 at home, as compared with those whose youngest child was 15 or older. We worked out a set of life-styles or role orientations and separated the sample into those who were primarily home-oriented, community-oriented, work-oriented, or mixed home-community-oriented. We studied these women also for *change* in pattern of role activities, assessing the extent to which each woman had expanded or constricted her activities in family roles (wife, mother, homemaker, grandmother, daughter) and in nonfamily roles (worker, church member, club member, citizen, friend, user of leisure time) over the past five to 10 years and grouped the women into "expanders," "shifters," "statics," and "constrictors."

The relationships among these social role variables and our measures of psychological well-being were all low and showed again that our initial hypothesis was wrong. Rather than being a stressful period for women, the empty nest or postparental stage in the life cycle was associated with a somewhat *higher* level of life satisfaction than is found among other women. Evidently for women in this sample, coping with children at home was more taxing and stressful than having their children married and launched into adult society. Neither was life satisfaction correlated with *role-change* patterns — although the latter finding may be an artifact of our data. (It was of some interest that in this sample life satisfaction was highest in the home- and community-oriented women, and lowest in the work-oriented.)

Now that the study is completed, we wonder that we should ever have formulated such naive hypotheses; yet it seemed tenable enough to predict that women who showed high symptomatology at menopause and whose children had left home would be those women who would have shown lower levels of life satisfaction than the other women in the sample.

That this was not so is evidence for the normal, expectable life cycle. Women in their 40's and early 50's expect the menopause to occur and see it, therefore, as a normal and natural event. They may have listened to old wives' tales and may have some mild anxieties which they project on other women, but they know the climacterium is inevitable; that all women survive; and they take it in stride or, as one of them put it, regard it merely as "a temporary pause that depresses." Many welcome it as relief from menstruation and fear of unwanted pregnancies.

The normal, expectable life event too superficially viewed as a crisis event can be illustrated in the researches of other investigators as well as in our own. For example, to an increasingly large proportion of men, retirement is a normal, expectable event. Yet in much of the literature on the topic, it is conceptualized by the investigator as a crisis, with the result that the findings from different studies are at variance, with some investigators unprepared for their discovery of no significant losses in life satisfaction or no increased rates of depression following retirement. The fact is that retirement is becoming a middle-aged phenomenon, with many workers, for instance, now offered the opportunity to withdraw from work at age 55. The latest national survey indicates that a surprisingly large proportion of workers in all industries are choosing to retire earlier and earlier, with the main, if not the single, determining factor being level of income — as soon as a man establishes enough retirement income he chooses to stop working. Even more pertinent is the fact that nearly 70 per cent of persons who retired *as planned* were content in their retirement, compared with less than 20 per cent of the unexpected retirees — those who retired unexpectedly because of poor health or loss of job (Barfield & Morgan, 1970).

Death, too, becomes a normal, expectable event to the old, and there are various studies which describe the relative equanimity with which it is anticipated (Munnichs, 1966). The fact that old people do not necessarily fear death comes to the young graduate student as a surprise — evidence of an age-graded perception — but the surprise disappears when he discovers that old people more often than not talk calmly and freely about death once the interviewer himself overcomes his reluctance to discuss it. Judging from the many interviews with old people that are now in our files at Chicago, the crisis is not death, but for some, *how* one will die, whether in the accustomed home and family environment or elsewhere. Some recent findings (Lieberman & Coplan, 1970) are of interest on this point. They studied matched groups of old people (matched for age, health, ethnic background, education), one group living in their homes in the community; the second, persons on a waiting list to be admitted to a home for the aged; the third, a group who had survived relocation and who had been living in the institution for two years or longer. Each group was divided into those who were near death and those who were not — or "death-imminent" and "death-distant." This determination was made by following the groups over a three-year interval to see who died and who survived and then going back and studying their interviews and test performances. Among the death-imminent, it was the second group who showed evidence of fear of death, not the first nor the third group, that is, neither of the groups who were living in familiar and stable surroundings. It would appear that it is the prospect of dying in a *non*-normal, *un*expected circumstance that creates the crisis.

The situation with regard to widowhood is more equivocal; yet even here, as shown in a study by Parkes (1964), while somatic symptoms increased somewhat for both younger and older widows in the months following bereavement, consultation rates for psychiatric symptoms were very high for women under 65 but not in women over 65. Is this because by the time a woman reaches old age, death of a husband — a husband several years her senior, in most cases — moves into the category of the expected? On this same point, Baler and Golde (1964), in reviewing some of the epidemiological data regarding the widowed as a high-risk group in terms of mental illness, physical illness, and mortality, indicate that there is excess risk at younger rather than at older ages for both sexes.

All these findings are not to deny that the expectable life event precipitates crisis reactions in some persons, especially in those who come to the attention of the mental health professional; but this reaction is probably true for the minority, not for the majority. Even for the minority, it is more often the timing of the life event, not its occurrence, that constitutes the salient or problematic issue. This observation is not a denial, however, of the fact that the major life events in middle age and old age are losses to the individuals concerned or that grief is their accompaniment. It is to say, rather, that the events are anticipated and rehearsed, the "grief work" completed, the reconciliation accomplished without shattering the sense of continuity of the life cycle.

In drawing the distinction between illness and health, between the clinical and the normal, the psychology of grief is not synonymous with the psychology of mental illness. The relationships between loss, grief, physical illness, and mental illness are complex, although "loss" itself is a multidimensional factor. Some of Lowenthal's work (Lowenthal, Berkman, & Associates, 1967) seems to support the point being made here; old persons who had experienced retirement or widowhood in the three years prior to being interviewed were not more frequently diagnosed by psychiatrists as mentally ill, nor did they find their way into mental hospitals with any greater frequency than others. Mental illness, on the other hand, was associated with self-blame, with reports of having missed one's opportunities, of having failed to live up to one's potentials; in short, with intrapunitiveness.

In summary, then, there are two distinctions worth making: first, that it is the unanticipated life event, not the anticipated — divorce, not widowhood in old age; death of a child, not death of a parent — which is likely to represent the traumatic event. Moreover, major stresses are caused by events that upset the sequence and rhythm of the life cycle — as when death of a parent comes in childhood rather than in middle age; when marriage does not come at its desired or appropriate time; when the birth of a child is too early or too late; when occupational achievement is delayed; when the empty nest, grandparenthood, retirement, major illness, or widowhood occur *off-time*. In this sense, then, a psychology of the life cycle is not a psychology of crisis behavior so much as it is a psychology of timing.

REFERENCES

Baler, L.A., & Golde, P.J. Conjugal bereavement: Strategic area of research in preventive psychiatry. In *Working papers in community mental health*. Vol. 2, No. 1. Boston: Harvard School of Public Health, Department of Public Health Practice, 1964.

Barfield, R.A., & Morgan, J.N. *Early retirement: The decision and the experience*. Ann Arbor, Mich.: Institute of Social Research, University of Michigan, 1970.

Lieberman, M.A., & Coplan, A.S. Distance from death as a variable in the study of aging. *Developmental Psychology*, 1970, *2*, 71-84.

Lowenthal, M.F., Berkman, P.L., & Associates. *Aging and mental disorder in San Francisco: A social psychiatric study.* San Francisco: Jossey-Bass, 1967.

Munnichs, J.M.A. *Old age and finitude: A contribution to psychogerontology.* Basel: Karger, 1966.

Neugarten, B.L., & Associates. *Personality in middle and late life.* New York: Atherton Press. 1964.

Neugarten, B.L., & Kraines, R.J. Menopausal symptoms in women of various ages. *Psychosomatic Medicine.* 1965, *27,* 266-273.

Neugarten, B.L., & Moore, J.W. The changing age-status system. In B.L. Neugarten (Ed.), *Middle age and aging.* Chicago: University of Chicago Press, 1968.

Neugarten, B.L., Wood, V., Kraines, R.J., & Loomis, B. Women's attitudes toward the menopause. *Vita Humana,* 1963, *6,* 140-151.

Parkes, C.M. Effects of bereavement on physical and mental health: A study of the medical records of widows. *British Medical Journal,* 1964, *2,* 274-279.

Periods in the Adult Development of Men: Ages 18 to 45

DANIEL J. LEVINSON
CHARLOTTE N. DARROW
EDWARD B. KLEIN
MARIA H. LEVINSON
BRAXTON McKEE
Yale University

ABSTRACT

This is a preliminary statement of a theory of psychosocial periods in the development of men from the end of adolescence to the middle 40's. The theory has emerged from a study of 40 men currently in the mid-life decade (age 35-45). The method was biographical: through a series of interviews we constructed the adult life course of each man and looked for a sequential order underlying the highly diverse, unique individual biographies. (a) The first period, *Leaving the Family,* is a bridge between adolescent life and full entry into the adult world. (b) *Getting into the Adult World* extends from the early 20's until 27-29; its major developmental tasks are to build an initial life structure, to form an occupation, and to work on the ego stage of Intimacy vs. Aloneness. (c) This is followed by the *Age Thirty Transition* which lasts for some four to six years and provides an opportunity to modify or drastically change the provisional first structure. (d) *Settling Down* extends from the early 30's until age 39-41. Its tasks are to build a second and more stable early adult life structure and, in the late 30's, to "Become One's Own Man." (e) The *Mid-Life Transition* involves the termination of early adulthood and the initiation of middle adulthood, and is part of both. Its tasks are to

This project is carried out by the Research Unit for Social Psychology and Psychiatry at the Connecticut Mental Health Center, and the Department of Psychiatry, Yale University. This is a slightly revised version of a paper originally published in *Life History Research in Psychopathology,* Volume 3, edited by D.F. Ricks, A. Thomas, and M. Roff, University of Minnesota Press, 1974.

reappraise and modify the late 30's' life structure, to rediscover important but neglected parts of the self and, toward the end, to make choices that provide the basis for a new life structure. (f) The Mid-Life Transition ordinarily gives way in the mid-40's to a period of building and living within a first provisional life structure for middle adulthood. Though our study ends at this point, we assume that there is a further evolution, involving periods of transition and of relative stability, throughout the life cycle.

This is a progress report on a study of forty men, all of whom are currently aged 35-45. There are ten men in each of four occupational groups: blue- and white-collar workers in industry; business executives; academic biologists; and novelists. Each man was seen six to ten times for a total of ten to twenty hours over a period of two to three months. We had a single follow-up interview with most of the men about two years after the initial interviews. Our aim is to construct a theory of adult male development over the age span of about 20-45.

DEVELOPMENTAL PERIODS IN THE ADULT LIFE COURSE

We have found it convenient to distinguish several gross chronological periods in the adult life course: early adulthood, roughly ages 20-40; middle adulthood, ages 40-60; and late adulthood, age 60+. We are studying early adulthood and the "mid-life transition"—that is, the several years on either side of 40 that constitute a transitional period between early and middle adulthood.

These are descriptive time units that we use to begin making developmental distinctions within adult life. Something even as simple as this is necessary because of the tremendous neglect of development and socialization in the main adult years, roughly 20-65, in psychology, psychiatry, sociology, and so on. In the past people have spoken as though development goes on to age 16, or perhaps to age 18; then there is a long plateau in which random things occur; and then at around 60 or 65 "aging" begins.

There is little work in sociology on adult socialization. In psychology there are the concepts and "psychohistorical" approach of Erikson and the extensive work of Jungian depth psychology, which is almost totally ignored by the academic disciplines. Like Jung and Erikson, we assume that there is something we can call adult development, that there is a psychosocial evolution just as in pre-adult life, and that we won't understand adults and the changes they go through in their lives if we don't have a conception of what is intrinsic to adulthood. We can then see how derivatives of childhood operate to facilitate or hinder certain kinds of development.

One of our chief theoretical aims is to formulate a sociopsychological conception of the life course and the various developmental periods, tasks, structures, and processes within it. There are, of course, wide individual and group differences in the concrete life course, as our findings show. At a more conceptual level, however, we are interested in generating and working with hypotheses concerning *relatively universal, genotypic, age-linked, adult developmental periods* within which variations occur. As we conceive of these periods, their origins lie both in the nature of the individual as a biosocial and biopsychological organism and in the nature of society as an enduring multi-generational form of collective life. The periods do not represent simply an unfolding of maturational potentials from within; they are thus different from the Freudian or Piagetian stages of childhood development, which are seen largely as an internal unfolding. Nor do they simply represent stages in a career sequence as shaped by an occupational, educational, or familial system. The periods are thus not simply a function of adult socializing systems, although these systems play an important part in defining timetables and in shaping one's course through them.

We are trying to develop an embracing sociopsychological conception of male adult development periods, within which a variety of biological, psychodynamic, cultural, social-structural, and other timetables operate in only partial synchronization. It is an important further step to do similar studies of women and to learn about similarities and differences between the sexes under various social conditions. The remaining sections of this paper set forth our theoretical conception of these periods from roughly age 20 to 45. Within the framework of this overall theory we shall note some illustrative concepts, findings, and areas of exploration. Again, we emphasize that this is a report of work in progress (as of May 1972) and by no means a final statement.

Leaving the Family (LF)

We conceive of Leaving the Family (LF) as a period of transition between adolescent life, centered in the family of origin, and entry into the adult world. In our sample, LF ordinarily occupies a span of some three to five years, starting at age 16-18 and ending at 20-24. It is a transitional period in the sense that the person is half in and half out of the family: he is making an effort to separate himself from the family, to develop a new home base, to reduce his dependence on familial support and authority, and to regard himself as an adult making his way in the adult world.

The separation from the family proceeds along many lines. In its external aspects, it involves changes such as moving out of the familial home, becoming financially less dependent, and getting into new roles and living arrangements in which one is more autonomous and responsible. In its internal aspects, it involves an increase in self-parent differentiation and in psychological distance from the family. Of course, these processes start earlier and continue well beyond the LF period. We say that someone is in this period when there is a roughly equal balance between "being in" the family and "moving out." From the point of view of ego development, the young man is in the stage that Erikson has identified as Identity versus Role Diffusion.

LF ordinarily begins around the end of high school (graduation or dropping out). Those who enter college or the military have a new, institutional life situation that is in many respects intermediate between the family and fully adult life in the community. The institution constitutes a home base providing some degree of structure, control, support, and maintenance. It also provides spheres of autonomy and privacy in which the young person is largely responsible for himself and can strike out in new paths. He has increasing opportunities to form relationships, as a compeer, with adults of various ages and thus to begin experiencing himself as an adult who is part of that world (rather than an adolescent standing reluctantly at the edge of it).

Those who move directly from high school into the labor force—and this is most often the case within the working-class population—have no institutional matrix to shape the transition. They may continue to live at home for several years on a semi-boarder status, "leading their own lives" and yet remaining in some ways subject to parental authority and integrated within the family network. This is a common pattern among ethnic groups with strong communal and extended family bonds. Often the young man works with his father or relatives during this period. If he marries during LF, the couple may live for some time with one spouse's parents or relatives. The initial work history has the same transitional character. For several years (in some cases, permanently) the young man has no genuine occupation. He works at various jobs and acquires a variety of skills. But, lacking seniority, influence, and broader competence, he tends to be given the worst jobs on the worst shifts and to have the least job security. Even though a young man in this position may be economically self-sufficient and living on his own, he is still on the boundary between the family and the fully adult world; and getting across this boundary is his major developmental task.

The LF period ends when the balance shifts—when one has for the most part separated from the family (though further work on separationconnectedness in relation to family continues for many years, if not forever) and has begun to make a place for himself in the adult world.

Getting into the Adult World (GIAW)

The period we call Getting into the Adult World (GIAW) begins when the center of gravity of one's life shifts from the family of origin (or an equivalent authoritative-protective social matrix) to a new home base and an effort to form an adult life of one's own. This period ordinarily starts in the early 20's and extends until roughly age 27-29. It is a time of exploration and provisional commitment to adult roles, memberships, responsibilities, and relationships. The young man tries to establish an occupation, or an occupational direction, consistent with his interests, values, and sense of self. He begins to engage in more adult friendships and sexual relationships, and to work on what Erikson has termed the ego stage of Intimacy versus Aloneness.

The overall developmental task of the GIAW period is to explore the available possibilities of the adult world, to arrive at an initial definition of oneself as an adult, and *to fashion an initial life structure* that provides a viable link between the valued self and the wider adult world. The concept of life structure is of central importance in our thinking. In its external aspects it refers to the individual's overall pattern of roles, memberships, interests, condition and style of living, long-term goals, and the like—the particular ways in which he is plugged into society. In its internal aspects, life structure includes the personal meanings these have for the individual, as well as the inner identities, core values, fantasies, and psychodynamic qualities that shape and infuse one's engagement in the world and are to some degree fulfilled and changed by it. Traditional behavioristic and sociological approaches tend to emphasize the external aspects and to ignore the internal. Conversely, depth psychological approaches tend to emphasize the internal dynamics without taking sufficiently into account the nature of the sociocultural world and the individual's actual engagement in it. Our approach is to use concepts such as life structure to provide an initial focus on the *boundary between individual and society;* from this base, we can then move outward to a fuller examination of the social world and inward to a fuller examination of the personality.

GIAW is, like all entry periods, a time of exploration and initial choice. It involves, to varying degrees and in varying sequences, the processes of exploratory searching, of making provisional choices, of further exploratory testing through which the rightness of an initial choice is assessed and alternatives are considered, of increasing commitment to certain choices and the construction of a more integrated, stable life structure.

There are wide variations in the course, duration, and outcome of this period. These are a few of the patterned sequences we have found:

a. Perhaps the most frequent pattern we find is that of the man who makes a provisional commitment to an occupation and goes through the initial stages of a career. During his 20's he is establishing a tentative structure, including an occupational choice and the beginnings of commitment to an occupational identity. Then, somewhere in the interval between age 28 and 32, he enters a transitional period in which he works on the questions: Shall I make a deeper commitment to this occupation and build a stable life structure around it? or I still have a chance to change; shall I take it? There is a kind of bet that's being made here, at around age 30. Many of our subjects remain in the occupation initially chosen in their 20's; they get married or reaffirm the existing marriage, and they enter a new period, Settling Down.

b. In some cases, the man at around 30 decides that his initial occupational choice was not the right one—that it is too constraining, or that it is a violation or betrayal of an early Dream which now has to be pursued, or that he does not have the talent to succeed in it—and he makes a major shift in occupation and in life structure, sometimes including marriage. In this pattern the man makes a provisional structure in his 20's and then makes a moderate or drastic change at about 30.

c. Still another variant is that of the man who during his 20's lives a rather transient, unsettled life. He then feels a desperate need at around 30 to get more order and stability into his life. It is our tentative hypothesis that if a man does not reach a significant start toward Settling Down by about age 34, his chances of forming a reasonably satisfying life structure, and one that can evolve in his further development, are quite small. A number of movies in the last few years have depicted this particular kind of Age 30 Crisis. One is *Five Easy Pieces.* Another is *Getting Straight,* which is about an ex-college radical who has been in a transient, wandering stage during his 20's. Around 30 his tentative occupational choice is to become a high school teacher, and he makes an effort which he and the educational establishment collude to destroy.

A concept of great value in the analysis of the GIAW period is the *Dream.* Many men, though certainly not all, enter adulthood with a Dream or vision of their own future. This Dream is usually articulated within an occupational context—for example, becoming a great novelist, winning the Nobel Prize (a common Dream of our biologists), contributing in some way to human welfare, and so on. Where such a Dream exists, we are exploring its nature and vicissitudes over the life course. Major shifts in life direction at subsequent ages are often occasioned by a reactivation of the sense of betrayal or compromise of the Dream. That is, very often in the crises that occur at age 30, 40, or later a major issue is the reactivation of a guiding Dream, frequently one that goes back to adolescence or the early 20's, and the concern with its failure. We are also interested in the antecedents and consequences of not having a Dream, because the Dream can be such a vitalizing force for adult development.

A second, crucial concept is that of the *transitional period.* The time around ages 28-32 seems to be a transitional period, a link between the termination of GIAW and the onset of the next period. We are trying to be very specific about age-linkages in order to counteract the strong tendency to assume that in adulthood very little is age-linked because development isn't occurring. We pursue tenaciously the possibility that the age-linkages are stronger than has been recognized. The *Age 30*

Transition, and others like it at different points in the life course, may occasion considerable turmoil, confusion, and struggle with the environment and within oneself; or it may involve a more quiet reassessment and intensification of effort. But it is marked by important changes in life structure and internal commitments, and presages the next stage in development.

Settling Down (SD)

The next period is Settling Down (SD). As noted above, this period ordinarily begins in the early 30's. The individual now makes deeper commitments; invests more of himself in his work, family, and valued interests; and within the framework of this life structure, makes and pursues more long-range plans and goals.

The imagery and meaning of Settling Down are multifaceted. One aspect of this period involves *order,* stability, security, control. The man establishes his niche in society, digs in, builds a nest, and pursues his interests within the defined pattern. This aspect may be stronger or weaker in a given case. A second, contrasting aspect has more the quality of *making it.* This involves planning, striving, moving onward and upward, having an inner timetable that contains major goals and way stations and ages by which they must be reached. The executive has to get into the corporate structure by age 40 or has to be earning at least $50,000 by 40; the assistant professor has to get tenure by 40; and so on.

So these are two aspects of SD. One has more to do with *down, in, order;* the other has more to do with *up, mobility, ambition.* Antithetical to both of these is the disposition to be free, unfettered, not tied to any structure no matter how great its current satisfaction nor how alluring its future promise, always open to new possibilities, ready to soar, wander, quest in all directions as the spirit moves one. We see the surgence of this disposition in the present state of society. This disposition is usually not predominant during the early SD period, but this does not mean it is necessarily absent nor that it may not in time reassert itself. Indeed, it frequently reappears toward the end of SD.

The SD period lasts until the late 30's or early 40's, when various internal and external changes bring on new developments. We shall note just a few major characteristics of this period. In creating an integrated life structure, one can utilize only parts of one's self, and this means that important parts of the self are left out. A myth supported by most theories of pre-adult development is that at the end of adolescence you get yourself together and, as a normal, mature adult, you enter into a relatively stable, integrated life pattern that can continue more or less indefinitely. This is a rather cruel illusion since it leads people in early adulthood to believe that they are, or should be, fully adult and settled, and that there are no major crises or developmental changes ahead. The structure one creates in early adulthood cannot fulfill or reflect all of oneself. Parts of the self are repressed or simply left dormant. At some point the life structure must be enlarged, reformed, or radically restructured in order to express more of the self.

One reason the SD structure must change is that it is based to some degree upon illusions—illusions about the importance and meaning of achieving one's occupational goals, about one's relationships with significant others, about what it is one truly wants in life, and so on. A *de-illusioning* process—by which we mean the reduction or removal of illusions and not a cynical disillusionment—is an important aspect of post-SD development. For example, the man in the early SD period tends to regard himself as highly autonomous. He is making his own way, he is not a child anymore, his parents are not telling him what to do, he is on his own. One of his illusions is that he is, in fact, freed of what he would call tribal influences. In actuality, however, the ambitions and the goal-seeking of the 30's are very much tied in with tribal influences. We seek to a large extent what the institutions and reference groups important to us are helping to define. We may be free of our parents, but we find or invent others who guide us, protect us, tell us what to do. Toward the end of SD, a new step is taken.

Becoming One's Own Man (BOOM)

The next step is Becoming One's Own Man (BOOM). Calling this the BOOM time has a certain metaphorical rightness. We are now inclined to regard BOOM not as a separate period but as a time of peaking and culmination of the Settling Down period and a connecting link to the Mid-Life Transition.

BOOM tends to occur in the middle to late 30's, typically in our sample around 35-39. It represents the high point of early adulthood and the beginning of what lies beyond. A key element in this period is the man's feeling that, no matter what he has accomplished to date, he is not sufficiently his own man. He feels overly dependent upon and constrained by persons or groups who have authority over him or who, for various reasons, exert great influence upon him. The writer comes to recognize that he is unduly intimidated by his publisher or too vulnerable to the evaluations of certain critics. The man who has successfully risen through the managerial ranks with the support and encouragement of his superiors now finds that they control too much and delegate too little, and he impatiently awaits the time when he will have the authority to make his own decisions and to get the enterprise really going. The untenured faculty member imagines that once he has tenure he will be free of all the restraints and demands he's been acquiescing to since graduate school days. (The illusions die hard!)

The sense of constraint and oppression may occur not only in work but also in marriage and other relationships. We have been greatly impressed by the role of the mentor, and by developmental changes in relationships with mentors and in the capability to be a mentor. The word *mentor* is sometimes used in a primarily external sense—an adviser, teacher, protector—but we use the term in a more complex psychosocial sense. The presence or absence of mentors is, we find, an important component of the life course during the 20's and 30's. The absence of mentors is associated with various kinds of developmental impairments and with problems of individuation in mid-life.

The mentor is ordinarily 8 to 15 years older than the mentee. He is enough older to represent greater wisdom, authority, and paternal qualities, but near enough in age or attitudes to be in some respects a peer or older brother rather than in the image of the wise old man or distant father. He may be a teacher, boss, editor, or experienced co-worker. He takes the younger man under his wing, invites him into a new occupational world, shows him around, imparts his wisdom, cares, sponsors, criticizes, and bestows his blessing. The teaching and the sponsoring have their value, but the blessing is the crucial element.

The younger man, in turn, feels appreciation, admiration, respect, gratitude, love, and identification. The relationship is lovely for a time, then ends in separation arising from a quarrel, or death, or a change in circumstances. Following the separation, the personality of the mentee is enriched further as he makes the valued qualities of the mentor more fully a part of himself. In some respects the main value of the relationship is created after it ends, but only if there was something there when it was happening. This is probably true of psychotherapy as well.

The number of mentor relationships in an individual's life does not vary widely. Few men have more than three or four, and perhaps the modal numbers are none and one. The duration of the intense mentor relationships is also not extremely variable, perhaps three to four years as an average and ten to twelve years as the upper limit. When this relationship ends, the pair may form a more modest friendship after a cooling-off period. The ending of the mentor relationship may take a rather peaceful form, with gradual loss of involvement. More often, however, and especially during the 30's, termination is brought about by increasing conflict or by forced separation, and brings in its wake intense feelings of bitterness, rancor, grief, abandonment, and rejuvenation in the mentee.

The final giving up of all mentors by those who have had them tends to occur in the middle or late 30's. One does not have mentors after 40. One may have friendships or significant working relationships after this, but the mentor relationship in its more developed form is rare, at least in our sample and in our life experience. It is given up as part of Becoming One's Own Man. The person who was formerly so loved and admired, and who was experienced as giving so much, comes now to be seen as hypercritical, oppressively controlling, seeking to make one over in his own image rather than fostering one's independence and individuality; in short, as a tyrannical and egocentric father rather than a loving, enabling mentor.

There are clearly irrational elements in this process, such as the reactivation and reworking of Oedipal conflicts, which have their origins in childhood. To focus solely on these, however, is to restrict our vision and to miss the adult developmental functions of the relationship and its termination. Whatever its Oedipal or early childhood-derived meanings, the relationship with the mentor has crucial adult meanings as well. It enables the young man to relate *as an adult* with another man who regards him as an adult and who welcomes him into the adult world on a relatively (but not completely) mutual and equal basis.

The young man must in time reject this relationship, but this is largely because it has served its purpose. He is ready to take a further step in Becoming His Own Man: to give up being a son in the little boy sense and a young man in the apprentice-disciple-mentee sense, and to move toward assuming more fully the functions of mentor, father, and peer in relation to other adults. This kind of developmental achievement is of the essence of adulthood and needs to be studied. It is probably impossible to become a mentor without first having been a mentee.

The importance of mentors in the adult development of women is just beginning to be recognized. To take but one example, Epstein (1970) has shown that the lack of a mentor has been a major obstacle in the professional development of women. It would serve crucial developmental functions, for male as well as female students, if there were more female faculty members in our graduate schools and professional schools. Among other things, this would help to overcome the tremendous polarization of masculine and feminine that now exists in professional training and in our society generally. Men can certainly function in important respects as mentors to women students. However, there is much to be learned about the subtle ways in which conscious or unconscious sexism may lead the male teacher to regard his female student as a little girl or a mascot or a sex object, rather than welcoming her into a truly compeer relationship.

Mentor relationships probably are also of crucial importance in initiating and working on the ego stage of *generativity versus stagnation* and its attendant virtue, *caring* (for adults). Erikson has identified this stage as beginning at around 40 and as involving one's relationship to future generations in general and to the next generation of adults in particular. This goes beyond caring about one's small children, which one ordinarily has to learn in the 20's. The issue now is caring about adults, being generative in relation to adults, taking responsibility in the adult world, and getting over being a boy in the adult world. We are saying that one can't get very far with this before age 40 and that the BOOM time of the late 30's is the beginning of work on it.

During BOOM a man wants desperately to be affirmed by society in the roles that he values most. He is trying for that crucial promotion or other recognition. At about age 40—we would now say within the range of about 39 to 42—most of our subjects fix on some key event in their careers as carrying the ultimate message of their affirmation or devaluation by society. This event may be a promotion or a new job—it's of crucial importance whether one gets to be vice-president of a company, a full professor in a department, or foreman or union steward. It may involve a particular form of symbolic success: writing a best seller or a prize-winning novel, being recognized as a scientist or executive or craftsman of the first rank, and so on. This event is given a magical quality. If the outcome is favorable, one imagines, then all is well and the future is assured. If it is unfavorable, the man feels that not only his work but he as a person has been found wanting and without value.

Since the course and outcome of this key event take several (perhaps three to six) years to unfold, many men at around 40 seem to be living, as one of our subjects put it, in a state of suspended animation. During the course of waiting, the next period gets under way.

The Mid-Life Transition (MLT)

The next period we call the Mid-Life Transition (MLT). A *developmental transition,* as we use the term, is a turning point or boundary region between two periods of greater stability. A transition may go relatively smoothly or may involve considerable turmoil. The Mid-Life Transition occurs whether the individual succeeds or fails in his search for affirmation by society. At 38 he thinks that if he gains the deserved success, he'll be all set. The answer is, he will not. He is going to have a transition whether he is affirmed or not; it is only the form that varies.

The central issue is not whether he succeeds or fails in achieving his goals. The issue, rather, is what to do with the *experience of disparity* between what he has gained in an inner sense from living within a particular structure and what he wants for himself. The sense of disparity between "what I've reached at this point" and "what it is I really want" instigates a soul-searching for "what it is I really want."

To put it differently, it is not a matter of how many rewards one has obtained; it is a matter of the *goodness of fit between the life structure and the self.* A man may do extremely well in achieving his goals and yet find his success hollow or bittersweet. If, after failing in an important respect, he comes primarily to castigate himself for not being able to "make it," then he is having a rough time but he is not having a mid-life crisis. He just regrets failure. He is having a crisis to the extent that he questions his life structure and feels the stirrings of powerful forces within himself that lead him to modify or drastically to change the structure.

In making the choices out of which the Settling Down structure was built, he drew upon and lived out certain aspects of himself: fantasies, values, identities, conflicts, internal "object relationships," character traits, and the like. At the same time, other essential aspects of the self were consciously rejected, repressed, or left dormant. These excluded components of the self—"other voices in other rooms," in Capote's vivid image—now seek expression and clamor to be heard.

We shall note briefly some of the major issues within the Mid-Life Transition: (a) The sense of *bodily decline* and the more vivid recognition of one's *mortality*. This brings the necessity to confront one's mortality and to deal in a new way with wounds to one's omnipotence fantasies, to overcome illusions and self-deceptions which relate to one's sense of omnipotence. It also brings greater freedom in experiencing and thinking about one's own and others' deaths, and greater compassion in responding to another's distress about decline, deformity, death, loss and bereavement. (b) The sense of *aging*, which means to be old rather than young. The Jungian concepts of puer and senex as archetypes that play a significant part in the mid-life individuation process are important here. (c) The polarity of *masculine and feminine*. Ordinarily in man's Settling Down structure masculinity is predominant; the emergence and integration of the more feminine aspects of the self are more possible at mid-life. During the mid-life period there is often a flowering of fantasies about various kinds of women, especially the maternal (nurturing and/or destructive) figures and the younger, erotic figures. These fantasies do not represent simply a belated adolescence, a final surge of lasciviousness, or self-indulgence or dependence (though they may have these qualities in part). The changing relationships to women may also involve the beginnings of a developmental effort. The aim of this effort is to free oneself more completely from the hold of the boy-mother relationship and to utilize one's internal relationships with the erotic transformative feminine as a means of healing old psychic wounds and of learning to love formerly devalued aspects of the self. It is the changing relation to the self that is the crucial issue at mid-life.

Restabilization and the Beginning of Middle Adulthood

For most men the Mid-Life Transition reaches its peak sometime in the early 40's and in the middle 40's there is a period of Restabilization. There seems to be a three to four year period at around age 45 in which the Mid-Life Transition comes to an end and a new life structure begins to take shape and to provide a basis for living in middle adulthood.

We are not presenting this as the last developmental change or the one in which everything will be resolved. For many men little is resolved, and the chickens come home to roost later. But it is a time both of possibility for developmental advance and of great threat to the self. Men such as Freud, Jung, Eugene O'Neill, Frank Lloyd Wright, Goya, and

Gandhi went through a profound crisis at around 40 and made tremendous creative gains through it. There are also men like Dylan Thomas and F. Scott Fitzgerald who could not manage this crisis and who destroyed themselves in it. Many men who don't have a crisis at 40 become terribly weighted down and lose the vitality that one needs to continue developing through adulthood. Arthur Miller's play *The Price* tells something of the crisis of a man of 50: The sense of stagnation he has because of what he didn't do earlier, especially at 40 when he considered changing his life structure and didn't; he is now sinking in it.

We regard the Restabilization, then, as an initial outcome of the Mid-Life Transition. We are examining various forms of Restabilization and considering their implications for an understanding of the possibilities and problems of middle adulthood.

REFERENCES

Brim, O.G., & Wheeler, S. *Socialization after childhood.* New York: Wiley, 1966.

Buhler, C. The curve of life as studied in biographies. *Journal of Applied Psychology,* 1955, *19,* 405-409.

Cain, L. Life course and social structure. In R.E.L. Faris (Ed.), *Handbook of modern sociology.* Chicago: Rand-McNally, 1964.

Campbell, J. (Ed.) *The portable Jung.* New York: Viking, 1971.

Epstein, C.F. Encountering the male establishment: Sex-status limits on women's careers in the professions. *American Journal of Sociology,* 1970, *75,* 965-982.

Erikson, E.H. Identity and the life cycle. *Psychological Issues,* 1959, *1*(1).

Erikson, E.H. *Gandhi's truth.* New York: Norton, 1969.

Jaques, E. Death and the mid-life crisis. *International Journal of Psychoanalysis,* 1965, *46,* 502-514.

Jung, C.G. *Memories, dreams, reflections.* New York: Pantheon, 1963.

Neugarten, B.L. (Ed.) *Middle age and aging: A reader in social psychology.* Chicago: University of Chicago Press, 1968.

Riley, M.W. et al. *Aging and society* (3 Volumes). New York: Russell Sage Foundation, 1968 ff.

Note: There are excellent biographies and autobiographies of persons such as Sigmund Freud, Eugene O'Neill, Bertrand Russell, Henry James, James Joyce, and F. Scott Fitzgerald. There are also novels and plays about men in the mid-life transition, often written by men during or just following their own mid-life transition—for example, *The Iceman Cometh* (O'Neill), *Who's Afraid of Virginia Woolf?* (Albee), *The Tempest* (Shakespeare), *The Man Who Cried I Am* (Williams), *Chimera* (Barth), and *Herzog* (Bellow). Works of this kind are of great value, both in forming a theory of adult development and in testing and extending our present theory.

Vicarious and Direct Achievement Patterns in Adulthood

JEAN LIPMAN-BLUMEN
National Institute of Education
Washington, D.C.

HAROLD J. LEAVITT
Stanford University

ABSTRACT

This paper presents a typology of direct and vicarious achievement orientations relevant to adult problems. Direct and vicarious achievement patterns are related to sex role socialization and sex-linked occupational choice. An achievement-sexuality scoring system is described for channeling adults into traditional sex-linked occupations. Recommendations are developed for reevaluating and redesigning adult occupational and interpersonal roles which would take into account vicarious and direct achievement orientations.*

VICARIOUS AND DIRECT ACHIEVEMENT PATTERNS IN ADULTHOOD

As current restrictive definitions of adult roles become more fluid, there is need to reconsider the validity of achievement patterns as they traditionally have been taught. Such a reconceptualization is a relevant task, because socialized achievement patterns are important precursors of adult occupational and sex roles.

Orientations toward achievement are one way in which adults differ markedly from one another. Some adults achieve their goals by confronting their environment directly. Others seek achievements through manipulation

---

*The authors are indebted to Denise Abrams, Jessie Bernard, Reuben Harris, Gail Parks, Susan Schaefer and Ann Tickamyer for helping them to clarify their ideas in numerous conversations.

of interpersonal relationships. Still others take a more indirect approach, experiencing pleasure through the accomplishments of others. This paper presents a typology of achievement orientations among adults, along with an effort to provide some theoretical linkages to early socialization and adult occupational and sex roles.

These orientations presumably are developed early in life; however, there is no reason to believe in their immutability. While one particular achievement orientation may assume salience for an individual, other less developed styles may remain accessible, ready to be evoked under changing circumstances.

It is not surprising, nonetheless, that individuals accustomed to using one primary achievement style may experience difficulty making these transitions. Counselors may begin to encounter such difficulty more commonly among their clients in response to accelerating shifts in occupational and sex role expectations.

Vicarious Achievement Patterns

The enigma of achievement patterns has captivated the imaginations of social scientists for many years (McClelland, Atkinson, & Lowell, 1953). Different correlates and different methodologies have been explored to plumb the depths of achievement motivation; however, systematic understanding of the problem remains elusive. Sex differences in achievement motivation have been particularly difficult to map because of the erratic and seemingly uninterpretable nature of the data on female subjects (Angelini, 1955; Baruch, R., 1967; French & Lesser, 1958; Lesser, Krawitz & Packard, 1963; McClelland et al., 1953; Veroff, Wilcox, & Atkinson, 1953).

More recent work by Horner (1968, 1969, 1972) has led to a plethora of studies focused upon one possible resolution of the inconsistent findings on female achievement patterns: fear of success (Alper, 1973, 1974; Baruch, G., Note 1; Curtis, Zanna, & Campbell, Note 2; Hoffman, 1972, 1974; Katz, 1972; Levine & Crumrine, 1975; Romer, Note 3; Tresemer, 1974). The methodological storm that has arisen regarding the burgeoning fear-of-success literature has obscured the importance of investigating other achievement patterns in both women and men. One such pattern which has won only scant attention (Blumen, 1970; Lipman-Blumen, 1972, Note 4; Papanek, 1973; Tresemer & Pleck, Note 5) is vicarious achievement.

In a general way, a vicarious achievement orientation involves finding personal fulfillment through a relationship with another, through the activities and qualities of another individual with whom the vicarious achiever, to some degree, identifies. Conceptually, we can consider a continuum of vicarious to direct achievement orientations. At least three points along the *vicarious* portion may be labelled: altruistic, contributory and instrumental.

By *altruistic vicariousness,* we mean the tendency to take satisfaction and pleasure from someone else's activities, qualities, and/or accomplishments as if they were one's own. This vicarious achiever basks in the reflected glory of the individual with whom s/he identifies. Being associated with the direct achiever is enough. The altruistically vicarious achiever can derive pleasure simply from having a relationship with a direct achiever. The relationship is primary. It is an end in itself. One example is the stereotypical self-effacing wife of the "great man," whose role is simply to be there to nurture him.

The *contributing vicarious achiever* is characterized by enabling or facilitating behavior and attitudes toward the direct achiever. The contributing individual, like the altruistic one, takes pleasure in the characteristics and successes of the other individual as if they were his/her own. But in the case of the contributing person, the pleasure is derived primarily from the belief that s/he has contributed in some measure to the success of the direct achiever, if only by maintaining the relationship.

Oftentimes, the contributing person can accept the other individual's success as his/her own, because s/he, indeed, has had a hand in it. The contributing vicarious achiever may make her/himself indispensable to the direct achiever, thereby meeting her/his own needs both to help and be helped.

To the contributing vicarious achiever, the relationship is important both intrinsically, for its own sake, and also extinsically, as the medium through which the contributing person achieves. A recent statement from a political wife summed up this orientation when she remarked that if she lost her husband, she also would be losing her best friend and her career (McCarthy, 1974).

Papanek's (1973) treatment of the two-person career, and Coser and Rokoff's (1971) and Coser & Coser's (1974) work on "greedy institutions" focus on contributing vicarious achievement roles for women. The political wife who campaigns for her husband and the graduate student's wife who types his papers are examples of contributing vicarious achievers.

Parents who encourage their children to attempt roles which they regret not having entered themselves may be considered within the camp of contributing vicarious achievers. Hollywood mothers who push their offspring to become child stars are examples of this form of vicarious achievement.

An *instrumental vicarious achiever* is more likely to perceive relationships as means to other things. It is the avenue to security, status, love, money, achievement and even other relationships. The instrumentally vicarious person may manipulate the relationship in order to achieve other ends, including success of various sorts which the vicarious individual may feel unsuited to attempt on his/her own. The relationship is used as the means to meet other needs. The man who marries the boss' daughter exemplifies this type.

For heuristic purposes, we can begin to imagine a continuum where altruistic vicariousness is one polar position, with contributory vicariousness placed somewhere beyond it, and instrumental vicariousness still somewhere farther along the continuum. The opposite pole of the continuum is the direct achievement end, with several forms of direct achievement (which we shall describe below) spanning the positions at this end. (See Figure 1.)

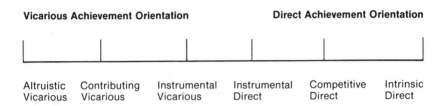

Figure 1. Achievement Orientation Continuum

Identification

Basic to this conceptualization of vicarious achievement is the concept of identification with another individual, usually a "significant other." By identification, we do not necessarily mean a perceived similarity of personality characteristics or character structure. Rather, identification here means accepting as one's own the interests, goals and sometimes values of another individual.

The degree of identification that the vicarious achiever experiences with another individual may vary from very intense to very attenuated. One possible result of intense identification, where the vicarious individual can barely distinguish him/herself from the other individual, is shared responsibility for the results of the direct achiever's actions or qualities. This responsibility sharing may involve both the negative and positive aspects of achievement. We expect that this type of identification is more likely to occur when the relationship between two individuals is direct, intimate, reciprocal, involved and significant, such as in relationships between family members.

This type of shared responsibility probably is always characteristic of altruistic vicariousness, typically true of contributory vicariousness, and sometimes true of instrumental vicariousness, where the identification process may be much more attenuated. For example, the altruistic parent whose child is a valedictorian may experience both strong identification and shared responsibility; conversely, the parent whose child suffers an emotional breakdown may suffer also through intense identification and sense of guilt.

The contributing father, who feels that his intense coaching has contributed to his son's athletic prowess, probably will feel responsible for the child's failure. But one also can imagine a more instrumentally vicarious parent who uses his son's performance as a surrogate for his own. Such a vicarious parent possibly may reject responsibility for his protege's inadequacy.

In the case of instrumental vicariousness, too, we should expect a range of degrees of identification. For example, the stage mother may identify very strongly, albeit selfishly, with her child's successes and failures. However, an instrumentally vicarious courtesan or campaign worker might be disappointed at the failure of the other individual, but then might readily abandon the relationship in favor of an attachment to a more promising individual.

Identification does not necessarily imply emotional symmetry between the individuals involved. Although this type of emotional symmetry may increase the level of identification on the part of the primary identifier, it is not a necessary component of identification. The sense of identification may be primarily unilateral or reciprocal. For example, film stars often are the objects of identification for their devoted followers, without reciprocal involvement with their fans.

The important point is simply that one individual takes as his or her own the goals, values and interests of another individual. Some degree of identification appears to be a necessary condition for the development of active or specific (versus latent or generalized) vicarious achievement orientation.

The tendency toward a vicarious achievement orientation can exist without a specific object of identification. We suggest that it is a generalized orientation that subsumes a readiness to identify with others, while the actual individual with whom the vicarious achiever identifies may vary over time (and for women, particularly, may covary with stages in the life cycle). In addition, the absence of a specific individual at any given point in time will not vitiate the vicarious achievement orientation, although it probably will convert it to its latent form. Thus, the vicarious achievement orientation develops as an abstract and latent mode in which to cast behavior, and may, in fact, be activated by the process of identification with a particular "significant other."

It is possible that the vicarious achievement orientation, once established, may drive its possessor to seek appropriate individuals with whom to identify for need fulfillment. And once the underlying pattern of vicarious achievement orientation is established, with its built-in predisposition to seek an object of identification, the actual identification of a specific individual may trigger the whole dynamic, casting it in its specific or active (rather than its generalized or latent) mode.

Direct Achievement

As suggested earlier, the other end of the continuum is the direct achievement pole. Again, it is possible to distinguish several "types" of direct achievers: intrinsic, competitive and instrumental. (See Figure 1.)

The *intrinsic direct achievement* orientation is characterized by the intrinsic pleasures of accomplishment. Individuals with this primary orientation are more attuned to individual accomplishment, the task at hand, than to other people or things (Deci, 1975). This type of individual is more involved with him/herself (as compared with the "other" orientation of altruistic vicarious types) and uses the self as a means to achieve goals. Confronting the environment, exercising one's autonomy, wresting accomplishments from the milieu by one's own efforts, experiencing the thrill of success are all trademarks of the intrinsic direct achiever.

The intrinsic direct achiever pits him/herself against a standard of excellence, an abstract expected level of performance, rather than against other individuals. The accomplishment is an end in itself; it is its own reward. This individual has some of the characteristics of McClelland et al.'s (1953) high N achievement person and Maslow's (1954) "self-actualizer." We would expect that this type of individual, more involved in her/his own self, is more comfortable working alone, rather than in the distracting context of a team—unless individual performance feedback is available within the team context.

The *competitive direct achievement* orientation is distinguished by the need to outdo a competitor. The excitement of achievement is specifically enhanced by the fact that the success is accomplished within a competitive setting, proving that the individual is not only succeeding, but succeeding more than anyone else in the competition.

Like the intrinsic direct achiever, the competitive individual uses the self to accomplish the goal. The competitive direct orientation, however, involves others. The self is used as a mechanism to prove the individual's superiority to other contenders. To the competitive achiever, relationships are secondary to the achievement. In fact, the often attenuated relationship to other competitors provides the means for the desired end: the demonstration of the competitive direct achiever's greater self-worth. The process of winning against competitors is the basic challenge. In some respects, the competitive direct person may be likened to Christie's high Machiavellian individual (Christie & Geis, 1970) who is motivated by the game itself, who delights in the bargaining process, and who often wins because s/he persists in the game long after the other players have wearied and lost their motivation to engage in the fray. The dedicated linebacker whose joy comes in the competition, as well as the individual whose pleasure is spoiled by comparable successes of others, are examples of the competitive direct achiever.

The third type of direct achiever is the *instrumental direct*. S/he uses his/her own achievements as a generalized means for achieving other goals, particularly relational goals, such as nurturance and affiliation, as well as more traditional goals, including power, status and more success. The instrumental direct achiever uses whatever talents and success s/he has to meet her/his other needs. In a sense, this individual uses her/his direct achievement skills as a medium through which s/he can acquire relationships to people.

Increased status, as well as control and power over other individuals, are not inconsequential concerns to the instrumental direct achiever. Concern with status, control and power in no way detracts from the seriousness and skill with which the instrumental direct achiever performs a task. Performing well is a necessary first order of business, first to satisfy the individual's own egoistic needs, and next to legitimate claims to other secondary gains of success. High standards of performance create the links that bind others to her/him in awe, in fear, in love, in greed, in ambition and in genuine respect. Not only sustained ability to perform, as in Weber's (1946) charismatic leader, but also exploitation of the vicarious needs of others, sustains the control that the instrumental direct achiever has over her/his following. The political figure who delights in the role of social lion, but must continually succeed politically to maintain both professional and social coteries, fits this mold. The successful businessperson whose campaign contributions lead to an ambassadorial appointment is another example of the instrumental direct achiever. The powerful male who uses (indeed seeks) his power to entice or coerce women into sexual relationships is still another.

It is perhaps unnecessary to caution that the described typology is meant primarily as an heuristic device.[1] It is clear that only rarely, outside the pages of a novel, are we likely to find clear cut "ideal typical" cases in the Weberian sense. For example, one individual could encompass both competitive and instrumental direct achievement characteristics. And we are more likely to find such "hybrid" individuals than either "pure" type.

We further would argue that any one of these orientations may have *primary* salience for an individual, while simultaneously being linked to a secondary achievement orientation. Thus, it is entirely conceivable to think of an individual whose primary achievement mode is one of the direct orientations, and whose secondary mode is a vicarious one, or vice versa. Other factors, such as context, specificity of relationship, time, centrality of the situation to one's value hierarchy, stage in the life and/or work cycle and even hormonal level, may mitigate the actual achievement response of a given individual in a specific instance. Thus, the same individual may be primarily a competitive direct achiever in the context of work life, but a contributing vicarious achiever within the parental role.

Underlying Factors[2]

There are important psychological and sociological dimensions to the achievement problem. The psychological model underlying this typology is a

[1]For a description of an empirical test of this model see Leavitt, H. L., Lipman-Blumen, J., Schaefer, S., & Harris, R. *Patterns of achievement behavior in men and women: Preliminary findings.* Unpublished manuscript, 1975. (Available from J. Lipman-Blumen, National Institute of Education, Washington, D.C. 20208.)

[2]For a more particular explication of the underlying model see Jean Lipman-Blumen & Harold J. Leavitt, *Toward a Theory of Direct and Vicarious Achievement,* submitted for publication.

now fairly conventional one (Freud, 1938; Maslow, 1954; Murray, 1938) of both the learning of needs and the learning of instrumental means for trying to satisfy those needs. We categorize needs into three major types: *physical* needs, assumed to be largely innate and largely operant from birth; and two classes of needs which we shall call *social* and *egoistic*. Our model assumes that social and egoistic needs are primarily learned. The key initial learning stems from differential degrees of reinforcement in the satisfaction of physical needs. The important learning mechanism is assumed to be the dependency of the infant on the behavior of parents and other forces in his/her environment.

The line of argument runs as follows: Infants are caught from the outset in dependency relationships. Different individuals experience different degrees of difficulty in satisfying their physical needs. Some children can satisfy most of their physical needs with relatively little effort most of the time in this dependent setting. Others, for various reasons, find that their available repertoire of behaviors yields only long delays, irregularities and frustration.

Infants whose early experiences are mostly satisfying are presumed, in this model, to generalize two related, but conceptually separable, perspectives. First, they will learn to value highly these satisfying relationships as ends in themselves. That is, they will develop relatively strong social orientations. Second, they also will learn a generalized achievement orientation—in this case vicarious (relational)—as the preferred means for need satisfaction of all kinds. That is, they will prefer tools they know how to use successfully—in this case, behavioral tools for manipulating relationships with others.

At the other extreme, children who, during this period of infantile dependency, encounter difficulty in satisfying their physical needs will learn quite different patterns of needs and will have to search for new behavioral means. They will develop stronger needs for independence, autonomy and achievement—the egoistic needs. They also will develop a generalized *independent* and *direct* orientation for achievements of all kinds. That is, they will prefer acting *directly* on the world to acting *indirectly* on it through relationships with other people.

The Socialization of the Sexes and Differential Achievement Orientations

We turn now to the issue of differential learning of achievement orientations of females and males. There is a general social science hypothesis that American male children characteristically have been more positively reinforced earlier in life for direct, independent behavior, and female children have been reinforced more for indirect (vicarious), dependent, relational behavior (Maccoby & Jacklin, 1974). Cross-cultural studies of sex role socialization (Block, Note 6) suggest that this belief extends far beyond the boundaries of American culture.

One important distinction between the socialization practices focused upon boys and girls appears to be consistent across many cultures. The distinction revolves around the contrasting qualities of directness, agency, initiation and activity for boys versus vicariousness, communion, implementation and passivity for girls (Bakan, 1966; Bandura & Walters, 1963; Gough, 1966). This basic discrimination between males and females is strongly developed by adolescence.

Individuals who adopt a vicarious achievement mode most likely, according to our model, also would have strong affiliation needs. Hoffman's (1974) review of the affiliation literature focuses on the relationship between females' affiliation needs and achievement motives. She concludes that girls' (compared to boys') less frequent engagement in independent exploration of their environments is related to early parental conditioning. Girls receive greater protection and support from parents (particularly mothers), less encouragement to establish a separate identity from mothers and less mother-child conflict associated with establishing an individual identity.

This pattern tends to support the formation of dependency in girls, to socialize girls to expect help from others, including help in the mastery of their environments. Thus, affiliation is a means of achieving mastery for girls. More often, they are socialized to seek help from others in mastering their environments, compared to boys who are more likely to be pressured into individualistic effectance and competence (White, 1963) through direct mastery of the environment. In this way, the link between affiliation and achievement may be strengthened in girls. Therefore, it should come as no great surprise if we find that women project the fulfillment of their own achievement needs onto the accomplishments of an individual with whom they have established strong affiliative bonds.

If women are not socialized to direct mastery of their environments (i.e., effectance) and are encouraged to seek help from others in accomplishing tasks, it would not be extraordinary to discover that some women may eschew direct confrontation with their adult environments beyond the confines of the home and are comfortable having someone else (husband or child) act for them. The vicarious achievement syndrome, when it exists among women, is a natural outgrowth of this set of conditions.

This has been the long and, until recently, the unremitting history of sex role socialization in the United States and many other countries. It has conditioned the expectations of females and males alike for their own and each other's behavior. Thus, despite the fact that the Women's Movement has wrought surprisingly swift and sharp changes in female behavior in some quarters, the stereotypes of the "dependent," vicarious achieving female and the direct, competitive male persist.

In an investigation of sex differences in achievement patterns (Leavitt, Lipman-Blumen, Schaefer & Harris, Note 7), some preliminary findings suggest that while female college students see women as direct achievers, unfettered by dependency longings, their male colleagues tend to perceive females in standard societal stereotypes—as vicarious achievers. Conversely, while male college students think that males can enjoy vicarious achievement patterns, their female colleagues persist in interpreting male behavior within the traditional sex stereotypes of direct, competitive patterns.

Generalized stereotypes about sex-linked behavior have their impact on every aspect of social life. They have a particularly negative effect on females' educational and occupational aspirations. In a recent study (Blumen, 1970; Lipman-Blumen, 1972) of correlates of educational aspiration of married women, the vicarious achievement ethic was linked directly both to traditional sex role stereotypes and low educational aspirations. In a subsample of married female college graduates, 40% of the women who held vicarious achievement orientations also reported no expectation of continuing their formal education. Among women who reported strong direct achievement orientations, only 12% gave this response. In addition, 60% of the women who described themselves as vicarious achievers also reported they subscribed to the standard sex stereotypes, compared to 24% of the direct achievers.

The vicarious achievement ethic, when applied to women, implies that marital and maternal roles—largely vicarious in nature—are *the* most desirable and appropriate roles for women. Within marriage, women vicariously may achieve family status, rank, power and money. Occupational roles for females often are treated as temporary waiting stations for the unmarried, until they can be rescued by marriage and maternity, or as emergency measures in times of family financial difficulty for the married. These notions persist despite the rapid increase of women (including married women and mothers of young children) in the labor force. Even when women do enter the labor force, they are channeled into roles that closely mirror their nurturant, enabling roles within the family: teacher, nurse, secretary, waitress, stewardess. Similarly, males are channeled into direct achievement roles, which are consonant with the male stereotype.

Sexuality-Achievement Scores

The remarkably persistent segregation of both women and men into sex-typed occupations is facilitated by a special mechanism: a sexuality-and-achievement score. It is a two-dimensional scoring system in which points are awarded or deducted for the sexuality (or glamour) and achievement potentials of various jobs when occupied by a female or a male. Underlying this system is the assumption that direct achievement roles are more highly valued by society than vicarious ones.

When vicarious jobs are filled by women, they receive a "plus" for sexuality or glamour and a "minus" for achievement potential. The aura of sexuality that surrounds traditional male and female jobs, when occupied by the "appropriate sex" person, is a social mechanism for attracting and retaining the "correct gender" worker. Oftentimes, this aura is more imagined than real and may serve to obscure the more menial aspects of the role. For example, the glamour and excitement that surround the image of the airline stewardess go far to minimize and conceal the drudgery of serving meals and responding to passengers' needs within very tight space and time constraints.

Conversely, sexuality decrements for entering the "wrong" role for one's sex steer individuals away from these roles. For example, the nursing role offers positive sexuality points for female entrants, but produces negative sexuality points for male nurses. The very old and the very young, perceived as devoid of sexuality in American culture, are reasonably protected from this occupational allocation mechanism. Thus, in the relatively small number of cases where the very old and the very young are employed, they are allowed to enter cross-sex roles without noticeable censure. The young (or very old) male babysitter provides such a case.

Sex of Role Occupant

**Achievement
Orientation of Role**

	Female			Male	
Direct Achievement Role	SCORING DIMENSIONS			SCORING DIMENSIONS	
	Sexuality	Achievement		Sexuality	Achievement
	–	+		+	+
Vicarious Achievement Role	+	–		–	–

Figure 2. Sexuality-Achievement Scoring Mechanism

Figure 2 indicates that males who enter "appropriate" (i.e., direct achievement) roles receive the highest scores: plus for sexuality and plus for achievement. Females who enter traditional feminine (i.e., vicarious) occupations receive a plus for sexuality and a minus for achievement. When women intrude on traditional male (i.e., direct achievement) occupational roles, they also receive a mixed rating, but this time the plus is for achievement and the minus is for sexuality. Males who trespass on traditional female roles receive the most damaging scores of all: minus for sexuality and minus for achievement.

It is clear that entering "sex-inappropriate" roles is dangerous for both women and men, but it is more dangerous for men who become "contaminated" by "women's work." For instance, the male secretary is maligned for the low level role he occupies and his lack of masculinity. Slightly better off is the female mathematician or surgeon who is seen as an accomplished, but unfeminine, creature. One structural way of diluting the double onus of the male in a vicarious role is to promote him as swiftly as possible to an administrative or managerial role, which is characterized by a greater degree of direct achievement. As a result, it is not surprising that, although most of the elementary school teachers are women, the majority of elementary school principals are men. Similar examples exist within the fields of library science, nursing and social work where males more often hold the higher status administrative roles.

In childhood, females with strong egoistic needs are allowed their expression. Boys, on the other hand, who express affiliative needs are more likely to encounter parental constraint (Maccoby & Jacklin, 1974). And from the few available studies (Maccoby & Jacklin, 1974), it appears that fathers, more than mothers, are the ones who reward daughters for traditionally feminine behavior and punish boys for stepping over the sex role boundaries. The sexuality-achievement scoring mechanism described above is the adult world continuation of this same phenomenon.

Flexibility in Adulthood

Dissatisfaction with sex roles, work roles, generational and racial roles has spawned considerable rethinking about traditional ways of allocating adult roles. Until recently, lower status individuals—women, the elderly, the very young, the poor and other minorities—have been channeled into vicarious roles and then criticized for their "choices." Higher status individuals in sex, age and cultural groups were tracked into direct achievement roles. But new research and new political demands have opened the door to a broader view of role choice.

As a result, we have begun to think about moving males into roles which can meet their stifled social needs and women into roles in which they can express more directly their egoistic needs. Perhaps it is not untenable to begin to talk in terms of different achievement orientations being suitable to males and females at different stages in the life cycle. This, in turn, leads us to consider different occupations or careers—perhaps a set of minicareers—for individuals, rather than one life-long choice in which changing levels of egoistic and social needs are only poorly handled. We also might consider the possibility of more role freedom, based upon looser role definitions.

Taking vicarious and direct achievement modes into account, perhaps it is time for us to begin designing mathematics and science courses to meet the special needs of vicarious achievers, and language and literature courses for direct achievers. Recent work on cognitive style and the hemispheres of the brain (Levine, 1966), as well as research on bicognition and cultural differences (Ramirez & Castaneda, 1975), offer important insights into ways of developing and meeting both social and egoistic needs, vicarious and direct orientations, emotional and analytic styles. The work of Baltes (1973) and Baltes and Labouvie (1973) suggests that learning is possible into late adulthood; and this should imply that retraining individuals to use both vicarious and direct modes, depending upon the situation, can be accomplished with mature adults.

Crisis is a condition under which all roles change with surprising ease (Lipman-Blumen, Note 4, Note 8, 1975a, 1975b). All social systems, from the two-person relationship, to families, to organizations, to large-scale societies witness role change in the face of crisis, when reallocation of resources becomes paramount. Further studies of defused crisis should permit us to develop strategies for introducing role change at different points throughout adulthood. Transitional points in the life cycle are obvious candidates—

almost natural experiments—for crisis-engendered treatment, times when individuals can learn most easily how to move across the barriers that separate vicarious and direct achievement modes.

Many occupational roles, which consume a great part of adult lives, would benefit from redesign. Various roles which are archetypes of direct achievement would gain from an infusion of vicarious attributes, and vice versa. If, for example, the surgeon's role called for more nurturant behavior, and the nurse's role allowed more direct decision-making and initiative, most likely both these professionals and their patients would reap a harvest of improved relations and better health (Lipman-Blumen, Note 9).

Increasingly, we see the questioning of the analytical role of the manager (Leavitt, 1975); and more intuitive, "feminine" qualities are being urged for this role. Indeed one can argue that the role of the manager is being steadily redefined from an entirely direct achievement role (in the tradition of the military commander) to a more mixed role involving morale building, counseling and other vicarious types of behavior. The very nature of contemporary models of problem-solving which emphasize analytic (i.e., masculine) skills to the exclusion of intuitive (i.e., feminine) strengths currently is being reconsidered (Leavitt, 1975).

New organizational structures which allow for the expression of both egoistic and social needs, as well as direct and vicarious achievement orientations, are being recommended. Such changes in structure should open new opportunities to both males and females, from different cultural traditions, to test the individual balance of vicarious and direct achievement styles most compatible with their needs.

Further research on the demands of institutions in terms of achievement orientations would provide valuable information regarding adult development and change. Institutions which reward intrinsic, asocial, apolitical and iconoclastic behavior are increasingly rare. Some institutions permit such behavior only as the reward for outstanding achievement. Most American work organizations reward primarily direct achievement behavior, preferably competitive or instrumental. Instrumental vicarious behavior and contributing vicarious behavior usually characterize lower level jobs within institutions; and it is not merely coincidental that these positions are most often occupied by women, other minorities and the youngest members of an organization. How achievement orientations change in adulthood to respond to the demands of the organization is an important area for additional investigation.

Adult interpersonal roles, particularly family roles, are equally likely candidates for reevaluation. The instrumental-expressive dichotomy (Parsons & Bales, 1955) has come under direct assault as a meaningful paradigm for family roles. The future of marriage has been described (Bernard, 1972a, 1972b, 1975) in ways that offer new insights and possibilities. And the emerging psychology and sociology of women are hopeful omens. But much remains to be done to loosen the constraints that hold males in the bonds of direct achievement and females in the grip of vicariousness.

Adult sexuality is another domain where traditional concerns of directness and vicariousness have played havoc. Medical technology and the Feminist Movement have made great inroads into stereotyped sexual behavior profiles of adult men and women. The new learning associated with sexual behavior—including searching behavior, experimentation, new awareness and new satisfaction—might serve as a model for delineating the changeovers that are necessary in other aspects of adult life.

Sex stereotypes, linked to achievement stereotypes, require more clinical investigation. Sex stereotypes seem more internally consistent than the actual behavior of females and males. If we considered individuals within the context of their own life space and age cohorts, we probably would discover a wide range of individual, rather than sex-related, patterns.

In any case, we propose that it may be time to try to change sex stereotyped achievement orientations to utilize the potential of vicarious and direct patterns, regardless of sex. It also may be time to redefine roles in organizations and other social institutions to take advantage of the full range of achievement orientations.

REFERENCE NOTES

1. Baruch, G. K. *The motive to avoid success and career aspirations of 5th and 10th grade girls.* Paper presented at the meeting of the American Psychological Association, Montreal, Canada, 1973.
2. Curtis, R., Zanna, M., & Campbell, W. *Fear of success, sex, and the perceptions and performance of law school students.* Paper presented at the meeting of the Eastern Psychological Association, Washington, D.C., 1973.
3. Romer, N. *Sex differences in the development of the motive to avoid success, sex role identity and performance in competitive and non-competitive conditions.* Paper presented at the meeting of the American Educational Research Association, Washington, D.C., 1975.
4. Lipman-Blumen, J. *The vicarious achievement ethic and nontraditional roles for women.* Paper presented at the meeting of the Eastern Sociological Society, New York, 1973.
5. Tresemer, D., & Pleck, J. H. Maintaining and changing sex-role boundaries in men (and women). Paper presented at the Radcliffe Institute Conference, *Women: Resources for a Changing World.* Cambridge, Mass., 1972.
6. Block, J. H. *Conceptions of sex role: Some cross-cultural and longitudinal perspectives.* (Mimeographed paper.) Bernard Moses Memorial Lecture, University of California, 1972.
7. Leavitt, H. J., Lipman-Blumen, J., Schaefer, S., & Harris, R. Patterns of achievement behavior in men and women: Preliminary findings. Unpublished manuscript, 1975. (Available from J. Lipman-Blumen, National Institute of Education, Washington, D.C. 20208.)
8. Lipman-Blumen, J. *The relationship between social structure, ideology and crisis.* Paper presented at the meeting of the American Sociological Association, Montreal, Canada, 1974.
9. Lipman-Blumen, J. *A sociological perspective on emerging health care roles: A paradigm for new social roles.* Paper presented at the annual meeting of the American Association for the Advancement of Science, New York, January, 1975.

REFERENCES

Alper, T. G. The relationship between role-orientation and achievement motivation in college women. *Journal of Personality,* 1973, 11, 9-31.

Alper, T. G. Achievement motivation in college women: A now-you-see-it-now-you-don't phenomenon. *American Psychologist,* 1974, *29,* 194-203.

Angelini, A. L. (A new method for evaluating human motivation.) *Boletin Faculdade de Filoşefia Ciences, Sao Paulo,* 1955, No. 207.

Bakan, D. *The duality of human existence.* Chicago, Ill.: Rand McNally, 1966.

Baltes, P. B. Prototypical paradigms and questions in life-span research on development and aging. *Gerontologist,* Winter 1973, pp. 458-467.

Baltes, P. B., & Labouvie, G. V. Adult development of intellectual preference: Description, explanation, and modification. In C. Eisdorfer & M. P. Lauton (Eds.), *Psychology of adult development and aging.* Washington, D.C.: American Psychological Association, 1973.

Bandura, A., & Walters, R. H. *Social learning and personality development.* New York: Holt, Rinehart & Winston, 1963.

Baruch, R. The achievement-motive in women: Implications for career development. *Journal of Personality and Social Psychology,* 1967, *5*(3), 260-267.

Bernard, J. *The sex game.* New York: Atheneum, 1972a. (Originally published, 1968).

Bernard, J. *The future of marriage.* New York: Bantam, 1972b.

Bernard, J. Sex role transcendence and sex role transcenders. In *Women, wives, mothers: Values and options.* Chicago, Ill.: Aldine, 1975.

Blumen, J. L. *Selected dimensions of self-concept and educational aspirations of married women college graduates.* Unpublished doctoral dissertation, Harvard University, 1970.

Christie, R., & Geis, F. R. *Studies in machiavellianism.* New York: Academic Press, 1970.

Coser, R. L., & Coser, L. A. The housewife and the greedy family. In L. A. Coser, *Greedy institutions.* (Chap. 6). New York: The Free Press, 1974.

Coser, R. L., & Rokoff, G. Women in the occupational world: Social disruption and conflict. *Social Problems,* Spring 1971, pp. 535-554.

Deci, E. L. *Intrinsic motivation.* New York: Plenum, 1975.

French, E., & Lesser, G. S. Some characteristics of the achievement motive in women. *Journal of Abnormal and Social Psychology,* 1958, *68,* 45-48.

Freud, S. *(The basic writings of Sigmund Freud.)* (A. A. Brill, Ed. and trans.). New York: Random House (Modern Library), 1938.

Gough, H. G. A cross-cultural analysis of the cpi femininity scale. *Journal of Consulting Psychology,* 1966, *30,* 136-41.

Hoffman, L. W. Early childhood experiences and women's achievement motives. *Journal of Social Issues,* 1972, *28*(2), 129-155.

Hoffman, L. W. Fear of success in males and females: 1965 and 1972. *Journal of Consulting and Clinical Psychology,* 1974, *42*(3), 353-358.

Horner, M. S. *Sex differences in achievement motivation and performance in competitive and noncompetitive situations.* Unpublished doctoral dissertation, University of Michigan, 1968.

Horner, M. S. Fail: Bright woman. *Psychology Today,* November, 1969, pp. 36-38; 62.

Horner, M. S. Femininity and successful achievement: A basic inconsistency. In J. M. Bardwick, E. Douvan, M. S. Horner, & D. Gutman (Eds.), *Feminine personality and conflict.* Belmont, Calif.: Brooks/Cole, 1970.

Horner, M. S. The motive to avoid success and changing aspirations of women. In J. M. Bardwick (Ed.), *Readings on the psychology of women*. New York: Harper & Row, 1972.

Katz, M. L. *Female motive to avoid success: A psychological barrier or a response to deviancy?* (Unpublished manuscript, Stanford University, School of Education, 1972). Published under Lockheed, M. E., *Sex Roles*, March 1975, pp. 41-50.

Leavitt, H. J. *Managerial psychology* (3rd ed.). Chicago: The University of Chicago Press, 1972.

Leavitt, H. J. Beyond the analytic manager. *California Management Review*, Spring 1975, pp. 5-12; Summer 1975, pp. 11-21.

Lesser, G. S. Achievement motivation in women. In D. C. McClelland & R. S. Steele (Eds.), *Human motivation*. Morristown, N.J.: General Learning Press, 1973.

Lesser, G. S., Krawitz, R. N., & Packard, R. Experimental arousal of achievement motive in adolescent girls. *Journal of Abnormal and Social Psychology*, 1963, *66*, 59-66.

Levine, A., & Crumrine, J. Women and the fear of success: A problem in replication. *American Journal of Sociology*, 1975, *80*, 964-974.

Levine, S. Sex differences in the brain. *Scientific American*, 1966. *214*(4), 84-90.

Lipman-Blumen, J. How ideology shapes women's lives. *Scientific American*, 1972, *226*(1), 34-42.

Lipman-Blumen, J. Role de-differentiation as a system response to crisis: Occupational and political roles of women. *Sociological Inquiry*, 1973, *43*(2), 105-129.

Lipman-Blumen, J. A crisis framework applied to macrosociological family changes: Marriage, divorce and occupational trends associated with World War II. *Journal of Marriage and the Family*, November, 1975a.

Lipman-Blumen, J. Vicarious achievement roles for women: A serious challenge for women. *Personnel and Guidance Journal*, 1975b, *56*(9), 650.

Maccoby, E. M., & Jacklin, C. N. *The psychology of sex differences*. Stanford, Calif.: Stanford University Press, 1974.

Maslow, A. *Motivation and personality*. New York: Harper, 1954.

McCarthy, A. Political wives. *The Potomac/Washington Post*, March 17, 1974, pp. 10-12; 21-26; 32.

McClelland, D. C., Atkinson, R. A., & Lowell, E. L. *The achievement motive*. New York: Appleton-Century Crofts, 1953.

McClelland, D. C., & Steele, R. S. (Eds.) *Human motivation*. Morristown, N.J.: General Learning Press, 1973.

Murray, R. A. *Explorations in personality*. New York & London: Oxford University Press, 1938.

Papanek, H. Men, women and work: Reflections on the two-person career. *American Journal of Sociology*, 1973, *78*, 852-70.

Parsons, T., & Bales, R. F. *Family socialization and interaction process*. Glencoe, Ill.: The Free Press, 1955.

Ramirez III, M., & Castaneda, A. *Cultural democracy, bicognitive development, and education*. New York: Academic Press, 1975.

Tresemer. D. Fear of success: Popular but unproven. *Psychology Today*, 1974, *7*(10), 82-85.

Veroff, J., Wilcox, S., & Atkinson, J. The achievement motive in high school and college-age women. *Journal of Abnormal and Social Psychology*, 1953, *48*, 103-119.

Weber, M. (The sociology of charismatic authority). From *(Max Weber: Essays in*

Sociology). (H. H. Gerth & C. W. Mills, Eds. and trans.). New York: Oxford University, 1946.

White, R. W. Ego and reality in psychoanalytic theory. *Psychological Issues,* 1963, *3*(3). (Monograph II).

FRAMEWORK FOR COUNSELING 2

The Case for Counseling Adults

NANCY K. SCHLOSSBERG
University of Maryland

ABSTRACT

The inevitability of role transformations in adulthood—transformations that often involve crises, conflict, and confusion—frame the case for adult guidance. To facilitate these changes and help clients regain a sense of control over their lives, counselors need to understand the dynamics of the decision-making process; they need to be aware of the salient issues of adulthood; and they need to confront their own age bias.

THE NEED FOR COUNSELING

Our society is set up so that most women lose their identities when their husbands die. . . . We draw our identities from our husbands. We add ourselves to our men, pour ourselves into their lives. We exist in their reflection. And then. . . ? If they die. . . ? What is left? It's wrenching enough to lose the man who is your lover, your companion, your best friend, the father of your children, without losing yourself as well [Lynn Caine, *Widow*, p. 11].*

And here I am. . . sturdy, youthful, prospering, virile. . . saddled already with the grinding responsibility of making them, and others, happy . . . .

---

*From *Widow*, by L. Caine. Copyright © 1974 by Lynn Caine. This and all other quotations from this source are reprinted by permission of the publisher, William Morrow and Company, Inc.

77

Who put me here? How will I ever get out? What the fuck makes anyone
think I am in control? [Joseph Heller, *Something Happened,* p. 209.]

These two passages—the first from an autobiographical account of what
it means to be a widow, the second from a novel about a fortyish man whose
life is going to pieces—epitomize the crises of adulthood and summarize the
essential differences between the lives of men and women. Most women are
governed by what sociologist Jean Lipman-Blumen (1972) calls the "vicarious
achievement ethic." That is, they define their identities not through their own
activities and accomplishments but through those of the dominant people
around them: at first, their fathers, then their husbands, still later their
children. Even women who work usually occupy a low-status position, play a
supportive role, and derive their identities from their bosses. The events of
middle age—possible divorce or widowhood, children leaving home—are
critical for a woman. Now that her props are gone, what does she do? After
spending half her life living vicariously, she is told—and she tells herself—that
now she must act on her own to build a new life. The urgency with which she
searches for ways to express herself is understandable; the obstacles she faces
are often overwhelming. Not only are her personal resources inadequate to
cope with the situation, but also social institutions impose crushing
restrictions on her.

Men, on the other hand, are dominated by a direct achievement
syndrome. They are "success objects," as Warren Farrell (1974) puts it, whose
value as human beings is measured by their ability to provide for their
families. They work, like it or not; they do not have the option of remaining at
home. If they try to change careers in mid-life they are labeled "immature" or
"neurotic." Typically, however, the 40-year-old man begins to reexamine his
motivations, to question his drive for achievement, to become increasingly
self-aware and preoccupied with emotions.

In short, as Neugarten and Gutmann (1958) have pointed out, a
paradoxical shift occurs: Though middle-class adults of both sexes change
their views of themselves and of the world during middle age, they go in
opposite directions, women becoming more achievement-oriented and men
more affiliative. Lowenthal found that sex differences were greater than life-
stage differences among the adults she studied. She writes: "Indeed, the life
course trajectories—and in turn the needs, goals, and problems—of men and
women not only do not parallel each other but at points seem to threaten a
potential collision course" (Note 1, p. 8).

Despite these differences in the nature of the crises experienced by adult
men and women, what should be emphasized is that both sexes go through
crises and may need help in coping with them.

THE INEVITABILITY OF ROLE TRANSFORMATIONS

In the common view, adulthood—in contrast to childhood, adolescence,
and youth—represents stability and certainty. It is assumed that people in the
30-to-60 age group have made their important decisions and settled into a

steady and secure pattern of living, untroubled by the doubts, conflicts, and upheavals that mark the earlier years. But this view is patently false. Adulthood is a time of change. These changes take place in five main areas: vocation, intimacy, family life, community, and the inner life (Schlossberg & Troll, 1976).

In the vocational area, the individual is expected to consider and narrow down career choices during adolescence, making a specific choice in the early 20's, and subsequently enter a particular career. Actually, a variety of job changes—some minor, others major—take place in the middle years. People get promoted or stay in the same position. They change jobs; they get fired and either find new employment or become unemployed. Eventually, they retire. The career pattern of some women is marked by disruptions as they leave a job to bear and rear children and then reenter the labor force. Each worker's vocational history is unique, but all workers experience some kind of change. Even the person who remains for 40 years in the same job at the same level experiences changes, in that his or her self-concept and self-evaluation alter as time goes by and other, younger people move past on the career ladder.

To take the dimension of intimacy: Every adult follows his/her own path in achieving a relatively long-lasting, mutually satisfying relationship. For some, this takes the form of heterosexual or homosexual marriage; for others, serial marriages. In a few cases, the need for intimacy is satisfied by living in a commune with a number of other people. But as the statistics on separation, divorce, and widowhood show, however the question of intimacy is resolved, it is not forever. Moreover, even a single, durable relationship alters subtly over time.

The area of family life is somewhat broader and includes one's relationships with parents, other older relatives, siblings, and—perhaps most important—one's children. Children are born, they grow up, they leave home; and these events inevitably affect the parents.

The area of community is still broader, encompassing a wider network of relationships: friends, acquaintances, co-workers, and so forth. Throughout life, an individual meets new people, forms new friendships, joins organizations that lead to new interpersonal bonds. Contemporary American society is characterized by considerable geographic mobility: Few of us do not at some time in our lives make major moves from one locale to another.

The kinds of changes discussed so far involve definite external events: getting married, changing jobs, moving from one city to another, and so forth. The changes in one's inner life are more subtle, perhaps indiscernible except to the person undergoing them. They may or may not be connected with external events. One of the most dramatic turning points in adult life is a change in time perspective when one begins to think in terms of time until death rather than time since birth (Neugarten & Gutmann, 1958). This change in time perspective can be triggered by anticipated retirement, by the last child's leaving home or by dissatisfaction with one's current life.

To some degree, the five areas defined overlap; moreover, a change in one may lead to changes in others. Some of the changes that occur in the lives of adults are the result of deliberate decisions: to get married, to quit work and go back to school, to move to a warmer climate. Some are in the hands of other people: the employer who fails to give a promotion, the grown-up daughter who decides to get married, the spouse who packs up and moves out. Still other changes are beyond human control: the death of a parent or a spouse. Some changes involve what Lowenthal, Thurnher, and Chiriboga (1975) call *role increments:* marriage, the birth of a child, a job promotion involving greater responsibilities. Others involve *role deficits:* divorce, retirement, widowhood. In some cases, the changes engender feelings of excitement, expectation, eagerness; in others, they breed frustration, depression, and loneliness. But whether deliberate or not, whether connected with an expansion or diminution of the self, whether positive or negative in affect, all these changes are periods of crisis and stress, often fraught with ambivalence. Moreover, any change results in some disruption and requires new adjustments, new assessments, new sets of relationships. Thus, they can be regarded as *role transformations.*

As adults move through these role transformations, certain common themes emerge. The most consuming theme is that of stock-taking. Periodically throughout their lives, people reassess themselves, their options, their potentialities. Often this reassessment leads to the difficult realization that one has not lived up to earlier expectations. The dream—of becoming a great writer, a college president, a noted politician—bumps up against the hard reality that one has gone as far as possible and falls short of the mark set in younger days. The individual suddenly realizes that he or she is not the ideal parent or spouse. Most devastating of all, one realizes that personal and interpersonal harmony are elusive. Even someone who is relatively successful in a particular area may reach a negative assessment: options are narrowed, certain potentialities must go unfulfilled, the desire for completeness is thwarted. When the bubble bursts, apathy and depression may set in. The feeling abounds: "I can't do anything to change my life now. I'm trapped. It's all over." Orville Brim (1976) talks about the sense of sadness that many men experience when they face their unfulfilled dreams. But that sadness is not confined to men. As one woman wistfully remarked: "There are no more surprises. I miss that."

Other people may react to the stock taking not with despair but with desperation. Their interior monologue goes like this: "Here I am, but who am I? What do I want out of life? If I want to be a lawyer, an ecologist, a gem collector, a minister, I'd better do it NOW! If I'm going to learn to read Greek, to visit the cathedrals of Europe, to climb Everest, I've got to act NOW! If I want to achieve happiness in sex, friendship, marriage, I'd better grab for it NOW!" The longing for excitement and self-fulfillment leads some people to make abrupt changes which result in exciting newspaper articles. Others are so afraid of any change that, though longing for it, they become immobilized and depressed. Whatever form the overt behavior assumes, the underlying theme is stock-taking.

Other themes may accompany role transformations: a growing preoccupation with the death of others and the painful recognition of one's own mortality (Brim, 1976), the fear that one is losing control over one's life. Indeed, the feeling of helplessness is a dominant theme of adulthood.

Recently, social scientists have begun scaling life events and relating them to physical and psychiatric illness. Zill discusses the Social Readjustment Rating Scale developed by Holmes and Rahe, in which changes are assigned numerical weights, with "death of a spouse" at the top of the list as a major stress point and "minor violations of the law" near the bottom. The person who has a high total score at the end of a given year is more likely to evidence illness than a person with a low score (Zill, Note 2, pp. 11-12). Other studies report qualitative differences between the way people respond to exit crises (e.g. death, divorce) and the way they respond to entrance crises (e.g. marriage, birth).

The changes that characterize infancy, childhood, and adolescence occur in relatively discrete and well-defined stages. But this does not hold true of the changes that occur in adulthood. Though certain events are linked by probability to certain ages (e.g., getting married in the 20s, retiring in the 60s), there is no absolute time nor exact sequential order. As Neugarten (1968) points out, adults are governed by a social rather than a biological clock. These internal and external transformations may recur and may develop at different times for different people.

The salient issues of adulthood and the inevitability of role transformations frame the case for the counselor's intervention. Adults need guidance and support in coping with crisis, in expanding their repertoire of responses, and simply in coming to accept that certain changes are unavoidable and near-universal. Counselors can help their clients to feel increasingly competent, autonomous, and unafraid. To be effective, however, the counselor must have a clear understanding of the needs of adults and a firm knowledge of techniques for effective delivery of services.

SPECIAL DIMENSIONS OF COUNSELING ADULTS

That adult counseling requires distinct and special training was forcefully brought home several years ago at a workshop. During one of the demonstration sessions, a graduate student whose experience was limited to counseling elementary school students and to a few courses in adolescent psychology modeled an interview with a 45-year-old man who was trying to decide whether to apply to graduate school. The graduate student conducted the session as if the client were a 17-year-old trying to decide whether to enter college; for instance, he seemed unaware that a 45-year-old man might feel some discomfort over age deviancy. His counseling skills and his knowledge-ability about childhood and adolescence were not enough to make him an effective counselor of adults. If this counselor had possessed a knowledge of the decision-making process, an understanding of adult development and an awareness of his own age bias, he would have been able to help his client. These three requisites for counseling adults are briefly discussed.

The Decision-Making Process: Basis for Diagnosis and Intervention

As we move through life, all of us are constantly making decisions. Sometimes, these decisions precede a role transformation, as when a person decides to change jobs or to get a divorce or to move to another city. Sometimes, the decision comes after a role transformation, as when the newly widowed woman decides to return to college or the retired man decides to get involved in volunteer work. Sometimes the decision is simply whether to give up and accept one's fate or to search for and exercise new options.

As was mentioned previously, many adults increasingly come to feel that they no longer have control over their own lives. Rotter (1966) has introduced the construct *locus of control* and developed an instrument to measure an individual's position on a continuum ranging from feelings of complete self-direction to feelings of helplessness. One way in which the counselor can intervene to help adults regain the feeling of being in control is by helping them to understand the components of the decision-making process. The model described here (Tiedeman & O'Hara, 1963) serves as both a diagnostic and an intervention tool.

Obviously, some decisions are more salient than others. But whatever the decision, it has two stages: anticipation and implementation. To take an example from the vocational area: During the anticipatory stage, one fantasizes, role-plays, dreams—in short, explores various occupational choices. Such exploration is as typical of the mature woman reentering the labor market as of the little girl playing house, hospital, or school. As the anticipatory stage unfolds, one begins to consider and evaluate numerous alternatives, to reject some, to pursue others. Finally, the decision crystallizes, and the choice is made. The second stage—implementation—begins when one enters the new system: enrolls in graduate school, starts a new job, sees a divorce lawyer, moves to a new town, has a baby. After induction into the system, one gains a sense of oneself in the new role, and this identification leads to integration.

After introducing adults to the two components of decision making, the counselor's next task is to stimulate them to expand their dreams, widen their horizons, explore their potentialities. Only after they have been encouraged to brainstorm wildly, ridiculously, romantically should the counselor help them to take their dreams and analyze them in detail. Eventually, the choices will be narrowed, but this winnowing out will be far different for the adult who has first been encouraged to fantasize freely about a wide variety of options than for the one who has from the beginning viewed his/her future as a given. The more options one entertains, the closer the final choice will be to one's real desires.

But anticipation is just half the battle; the other half—implementation—remains to be fought. Unfortunately, society often erects unnecessary and artificial barriers to implementation, most obviously in the vocational area. For instance, the 36-year-old man who decides that he wants to become a dentist can do little to implement that decision if schools of dentistry decree that age 35 is the cut-off point for admission. The adult woman who wants to become a carpenter but realizes that the union discourages female membership may hesitate to act upon her choice.

What can the counselor do to facilitate decision making in cases such as these? To answer this question, it is necessary to define the three major functions of counselors: one is working with individual clients, another is developing programs that will reach a wider constituency, and the third is initiating change through social actions. An excellent example of effective program development is the recent proliferation of women's centers on college campuses across the nation. These centers give adult women a place to turn when they want to consider new options and careers or get specific information on job and educational opportunities. The kinds of programs that can be developed for adults are almost infinite, limited only by the imagination and energy of the counselor. They include courses to introduce new life styles, skill training workshops, presentations over local television stations, displays at the public library. Such programs can be particularly helpful during the anticipatory stage, when people need to explore a wide variety of choices.

Examples of social activism may take many forms: organizing groups to lobby for various policies, bringing political pressure to bear, even initiating court action. Not all counselors have the time or energy to become social activists, but those who do may go a long way toward helping adults to implement the decisions they have made.

Many adults have questions about who they are and where they want to go; others have questions about how to get where they want to go. Exploration and implementation occur cyclically throughout life and in all developmental areas. Whether the counselor functions as a personal advisor, program developer, or social activist will depend on the needs of particular clients, the stage of the decision, and the kinds of difficulties involved in implementing particular decisions.

Knowledge of Adult Development: Listening with the Third Ear

The second requisite for the counselor of adults is an understanding of adult development. The counselor must be aware of what Neugarten calls "the salient issues of adulthood" (1968) and what Brim refers to as "the causes and content of the mid-life period" (1976). The counselor who has such an awareness can listen to adult clients from a different perspective than the counselor whose knowledge is limited to child and adolescent psychology.

An illustration from the area of intimacy may indicate the usefulness of such knowledge: A 35-year-old woman, married 12 years, complains to the counselor that the love has gone out of her marriage, that the joy of the first few years is dead, that she and her husband can no longer communicate. The unsophisticated counselor could easily conclude that this marriage is in trouble (as indeed it may be). But the counselor who knows something about the pattern of the typical marriage may come to a different conclusion. Couples at different stages experience satisfactions and define marriage in dramatically different ways (Lowenthal et al., 1975). Newlyweds describe the unique qualities of their partners, their close communication and special relationships. When children are born, traditional marriages become defined by roles, with the mother parenting and the father providing; it is at this period that the greatest dissatisfaction occurs. Then, after the children leave home, there is often a resurgence of happiness (Bernard, 1972). As couples move into the preretirement stage, they evidence a "renewed interest in the personalities of their spouses" (Lowenthal et al., 1975, p. 25). A knowledge of this typical developmental pattern does not mean that the counselor will interpret all marital difficulties as part of the evolving relationship, but it does provide a backdrop for both counselor and client, a framework for understanding a particular marriage.

Often, adults undergoing a crisis in role transformation can be helped merely by realizing that their feelings are not unique, that other people share them, and that they have a pattern. Lynn Caine makes this point about widowhood when she writes: "I am convinced that if I had known the facts of grief before I had to experience them, it would not have made my grief less intense . . . [but it] would have allowed me hope" (1974, pp. 91-92).

A knowledge of adult development also enables the counselor to go beneath what the client says to the "subtext." In making judgments about where the client is in the decision-making process, the counselor must "listen with the third ear," in Theodore Reik's phrase (1948). For example, a counselor received an urgent phone call from a middle-aged man who said that he wanted her help in framing his argument to be accepted at a nearby law school. He was in a panic that he might be rejected on the grounds that he was too old. But it soon became clear to the counselor that, although the man was asking "implementation" questions—"How do I get accepted into this law school?"—he was really still in the anticipatory stage. What he was saying was: "I am discontent. I want a change. I want to think through who I am." The man was uncertain that he even wanted to attend law school; that merely gave him a reason for calling the counselor. Realizing this, the counselor focused on the client's explorations by reflecting on his panic that time was running out. This response seemed to help the client immeasurably. This illustration shows how important it is to look beyond the obvious and to focus on the underlying problem.

Knowledge of adult development allows the counselor to listen with a third ear. This can provide the necessary framework so that the client can begin to look at the many available options and can make an informed decision about his or her future.

Awareness of Age Bias

Finally, counselors must become aware of age bias: both their own and that of others. Whenever it is suggested to counselors that they may be guilty of such bias, their first reaction is usually to deny the charge. Yet few of us are free from age bias. Neugarten and her associates (Neugarten, Moore, & Lower, 1965) tested the degree to which middleclass Americans concurred in their "expectations regarding age-appropriate behaviors." Building on these findings, Troll and Schlossberg examined the degree to which counselors hold these expectations and concluded: "There are some counselors who show no bias, others who show bias throughout, but most of the counselors show bias in some of the items some of the time" (1971).

The extent to which counselors are age-biased is directly and inversely related to the amount of support and encouragement they can give the clients to make free choices. All human beings are influenced by considerations of what is expected of them—by themselves and others—because of their age. Should they "make do" with an undesirable or unsatisfactory way of life because at their age they can expect nothing better or because at their age uncertainty and discontent are signs of neurosis? All too frequently, the injunction to "act your age!" can be translated to mean that the individual should remain passive, meekly surrendering control of his or her own life. Since one of the aims of counseling is to return the locus of control to the individual, it follows that the counselor should be as liberated as possible from age bias. Even the covert attitude of the counselor may be coercive.

Moreover, it is important that counselors deal with their feelings about their own advancing age. Many counselors are themselves fearful of growing old and see middle age as a time of narrowed horizons and diminished potency; unless they can acknowledge these anxieties, they may simply pass them on to the client. Thus, self-confrontation about one's own fears of aging, stagnating, being surpassed by younger colleagues, retiring, dying is essential if the counselor is to function effectively.

A RESTATEMENT

The goal of guidance is intervention that will enable people to take control—and to feel in control—of their lives. Adults in their middle years, who typically experience role transformations requiring extensive readjustments and reevaluations, are often in need of such intervention because they have lost the sense of control.

To be effective, the counselor of adults must first have a knowledge of the decision-making process that can be used in diagnosing the problems of the individual client—and in particular determining whether the client is at the anticipatory or the implementation stage and in devising appropriate interventions. Occasionally, the counselor may have to go beyond the function of counseling the individual into program development and social activism. The second requisite is an awareness of adult development and an ability to penetrate beyond what the client says to what is left unsaid. Finally, the counselor must be aware of any tendency to define options and possibilities solely in terms of the client's age. Only when counselors are able to free themselves from (or at least control) age bias can they help the client make free and informed choices.

REFERENCE NOTES

1. Lowenthal, M.F. Psychological variations across the adult life course: Frontiers for research and policy. Condensed version of a paper given on receipt of the Robert W. Kleemeler Award of the Gerontological Society, Portland, Oregon, 31 October 1974. San Francisco: University of California at San Francisco, 1974. (Dittoed)
2. Zill, N. Developing indicators of effective life management. Paper presented at the meeting of the Urban Regional Information Systems Association, Atlantic City, New Jersey, August, 1973.

REFERENCES

Bernard, J. *The future of marriage.* New York: World Publishing Co., 1972.

Brim, O. Theories of the male mid-life crisis. *Counseling Psychologist,* 1976, *6*(1), 2-9.

Caine, L. *Widow.* New York: William Morrow, 1974.

Farrell, W. *The liberated man: Beyond masculinity: Freeing men and their relationships with women.* New York: Random House, 1974.

Heller, J. *Something happened.* New York: Alfred Knopf, 1974.

Lipman-Blumen, J. How ideology shapes women's lives. *Scientific American,* January 1972, *226,* 34-42.

Lowenthal, M.F., Thurnher, M., & Chiriboga, D. *Four stages of life.* San Francisco: Jossey-Bass, 1975.

Neugarten, B.L., Ed. *Middle age and aging.* Chicago: Univ. of Chicago Press, 1968.

Neugarten, B.L., & Gutmann, D.L. Age-sex roles and personality in middle life: A thematic apperception study. *Psychological Monographs,* 1958, *72,* No. 17 (Whole No. 470).

Neugarten, B.L., Moore, J.V., & Lower, J.C. Age norms, age constraints, and adult socialization. *American Journal of Sociology,* 1965, *70,* 710-17.

Reik, T. *Listening with the third ear: The inner experiences of a psychoanalyst.* New York: Farrar, Straus, 1948.

Rotter, J.B. Centralized expectancies for internal vs. external control of reinforcement. *Psychological Monographs,* 1966, *80,* No. 1 (Whole No. 609).

Schlossberg, N.K., & Troll, L. *Perspectives on counseling adults.* College Park, Maryland: University of Maryland, Umporium Bookstore, 1976.

Tiedeman, D.V., & O'Hara, R.P. *Career development: Choice and adjustment.* New York: College Entrance Examination Board, 1963.

Troll, L., & Schlossberg, N.K. How age-biased are college counselors? *Industrial Gerontology,* Summer 1971, pp. 14-20.

A Developmental Approach to Counseling Adults

GENE BOCKNEK
Boston University

ABSTRACT

The author enunciates basic tenets of developmental theory and shows their application to work with adults. Counseling intervention is conceptualized as mobilizing resources to facilitate growth. Implications for the future of counseling psychology are considered.

Counseling psychologists working with adults have usually traced their origins to two sets of ancestors. One, the medical psychiatric tradition, is oriented to a treatment model. Correction of abnormalities, adjustment to disabilities, restoration of function are talismen of this approach. Educational guidance, the other ancestral tradition, takes as its hallmarks providing information and recommending courses of action.

These historic influences have in recent years been effectively challenged, by phenomenology and by behaviorism. Even as controversy between these seemingly incompatible parents rages on, a new generation of advocates has arisen, growing its own branch on the family tree. This latest influence, the developmental approach, languished for as long as it remained a psychology of childhood. Now that developmental psychology is expanding in scope to cover the entire life span (Pressey & Kuhlen, 1957), its relevance for counseling psychology is becoming more explicit. To explore the relevance of developmental theory in working with adults it is necessary to review some basic tenets inherent in the developmental perspective.

THE DEVELOPMENTAL PERSPECTIVE

1. Development represents a thrust. Undergirding all developmental theory is some concept of movement and change. The inevitability of and inexorable pressure to change are indigenous to all human experience, including the entire adult span. The extension of this basic principle from childhood to the adult years permits us to discard anachronistic notions of adulthood as a stable period of five decades, with rapid deterioration and decline at the end as the only variation. From another perspective, it is clear that fixation (i.e., arrested development) is more accurately described as decelerated development.

The discovery of growth characteristics throughout the adult years requires that counselors and allied professionals reexamine and redesign their theories and strategies of intervention.

2. Growth is the law of life. People change as a function of time and place, but mainly by virtue of their nature as living organisms in a finite evolutionary span from birth to death.

Although the rate of growth is most rapid in earliest years, significant changes occur over the 50 year adult period of life. Levinson (1974) suggests that a new stage of development emerges every 7 years. Buhler (1935) indicates three major adult stages. My own research has identified four periods: young adult, established adult, middle adult, senescent adult. However conceived, as milestones (Loevinger, 1966) or stages, qualitative changes have been noted in time sense (Kimmel, 1974; Neugarten, 1968), cognitive function (Perry, 1970), personal orientation (Gould, 1972; Levinson, 1974) and ego development (Loevinger, 1966; Bocknek, Note 1).

3. Development is directional. The onward thrust of life is neither random nor haphazard. The natural history of psychological evolution is sometimes continuous, often cumulative, frequently sequential, and always productive of new qualities or combinations. It is in the adult years that social skills, rudimentarily developed during the first two decades of life, achieve refinement in the ability to make subtle distinctions (e.g., between friend and partner) and integrate more complex social relationships into one's self-image (e.g., parent-breadwinner-mate).

The direction of developmental thrust is often quite predictable: simple to complex; differentiated to integrated; egocentric to allocentric. However, one does well to heed Loevinger's (1966) caution that growth does not always imply improvement. The discernible shift toward conservatism with age is inherently neither good nor bad.

4. Growth unleashes new potential. Each new period, each subtle restructuring of personal qualities, brings with it resources not previously available to the person. The reverse side of the imperative to change is the discovery of new capability or potential. This may emerge through a change in self-image: "I really am responsible!", "I'm not only older, I'm better!" It may occur from an awareness of the changing reactions of others: "She called me 'sir'!" "They really respect my opinion!" It may evolve as an aggregate effect after years of experience: "I am truly my own person." "My methods do get results."

An important corollary of finding new potential with adult development is that with continued growth the person may acquire resources to attack problems that were not previously available. An important change in the transition from adolescent to young adult, for example, is the acquisition of the capacity for personal perspective or insight (Bocknek, Note 1). This has obvious importance in the way one approaches counseling strategy, inasmuch as personal perspective is necessary for insight to occur.

5. *The adult life span contains its own challenges and resources.* Each period brings changes in the person's intrapsychic organization: a new level of self-awareness; a refined interpersonal sensitivity; a different sense of one's relatedness to the world. In turn these changes evoke needs, strengths, vulnerabilities previously suppressed, unnoticed or non-existent. One's sense of mortality, and all that death implies, is obviously affected by one's own place in the life span. The vague future becomes the imminent present, depending on whether one is 25 or 45. The historical perspective at 65 is noticeably absent at 20. But the innovative, activist capacities of young adulthood are never again repeated *as a stage characteristic* in the adult life span.

6. *Development is irreversible.* This principle acknowledges the necessary sequencing of the growth experience. The capacity for certain kinds of psychological growth (e.g., intimacy) is predicated upon the prior acquisition of other psychological properties (e.g., identity formation). Even in regression the person cannot reverse his/her developmental experience. The adult acting like a child, or reverting to earlier modes of gratification, does so with the experience and behavior patterns of an adult life incorporated into those actions. Grandpa can neither crawl nor experience crawling the way his year old grandchild does. Nor can one leapfrog over developmental steps without suffering significant decrement in the process.

7. *There is a developmental imperative.* As personal qualities evolve and change, the person *of necessity* is confronted with an urgency to respond to this internal demand for change. The urgency may be experienced as challenge, opportunity, threat, or vague unease. Whether it is clearly recognized or only dimly perceived, the imperative to respond is like a demand from within oneself. Many a client requests counseling precisely because of the inability to cope with this felt need to change or because a mode of function that was previously acceptable has been rendered obsolete by the person's growth.

In addition, cultural expectations and demands upon the individual undergo parallel changes. Society's tasks and attitudes vary according to one's perceived status in the adult age structure. The bearded young adult is asked, "When are you going to settle down?" The white-haired old man is asked, "When are you going to retire?"

Social definitions of developmental maturity may be quite different from psychological ones. Indeed, as we learn more about psychological development in adulthood we discover that sometimes cultural demands to adapt are at variance with the felt imperatives of personal development. Some young adults may need to "retire" for awhile. Some senescent adults are far from ready to retire.

Indeed, environmental pressures toward foreclosure (Marcia, 1966) of one's identity development are so powerful that most adults "adapt" to the roles expected of them (Trent & Medsker, 1969) rather than opt for autonomous growth. We will return to this topic in more detail later in this article.

SPECIFIC ISSUES IN DEVELOPMENTAL COUNSELING WITH ADULTS

From the perspective described above, the applications to developmental counseling are twofold. First, it provides an orientation to defining and understanding human problems. Second, it has implications for methodology and focus relative to intervention.

Counseling Older Adults

It has long been asserted that counseling is of dubious value with people of middle age and older. Consistent with the notion that adulthood brings only stability and decline, many therapeutic schools have tacitly assumed that only medication and support are useful intervention modalities in the latter half of the adult span. The compelling evidence that development is part of the entire life process opens the door to growth-enhancing work with people of all ages. It is not only the "youthful" older adult who can be counselled beneficially. Educators such as Knowles (1973) have long insisted that adults learn more effectively when teaching methods are designed for adult learning styles. Possible reasons for the poor results in counseling with older adults include not only antipathetic counselor attitudes of various kinds. Counseling techniques developed with younger adults (e.g., reflection of feelings) and practiced largely *by* younger adults, may not take account of the developmental needs of older adults (e.g., historic perspective). The problems of adults change over the life span, as does mode of thought and locus of concern. Sexual attractiveness has a different priority at 20, 32, 47 and 70. But the developmental perspective allows one to assert that resources and growth potential exist at *all* these ages. As one adapts counseling procedures to the varying needs of these different periods, one discovers that age is of itself no barrier to counseling.

Developmental Crises

In adult counseling many problems are of long standing, with a history of antecedents extending well back into childhood. Others seem to be of much more recent origin. In either case, the client requests assistance *now* because somehow his/her *presentday* life circumstances are unacceptable. Thus, irrespective of the apparent chronicity or early etiology of the problem, its most painful manifestations are contemporary, in the here-and-now.

It has been found useful to consider many of these problems as *developmental crises.* Whatever other origins or issues may be identified, a significant number of adult problems can be usefully conceptualized as results of the person's (usually) adverse encounter with one or more aspects of the developmental imperative. It is possible to classify several kinds of developmental crisis:

a. fear of an impending life stage. The person sees forthcoming changes as threatening, frightening, damaging. Examples include fear of death as one enters senescent adulthood or fear of the demands of parenting as one concludes the young adult stage.

b. reluctance to leave a gratifying stage. It is not uncommon for anxiety, depression or loss feelings to be precipitated by an awareness that one can no longer continue as one has, that one has outgrown a period that brought satisfaction or security. Birthdays, anniversaries, and some holidays put people in touch with the passage of time. Forsaking the familiar satisfactions of college for an uncertain future (and, incidentally, having to acknowledge one's adulthood) provides a common example of this issue.

c. trauma of unexpected developmental demands. For some people the advent of an awaited developmental phenomenon brings with it unexpected and unpleasant side effects. The homemaker's anticipated liberation from the demands of parenting are deadened by loneliness and the sound of an empty house. As a general feature of development, any increase in freedom and autonomy is usually accompanied by a dystonic sense of personal isolation and responsibility.

d. unresolved earlier issues. To the extent that one meets cultural expectations of appropriate role behavior it is possible to obscure, even to oneself, the psychological challenge of development. Having attained sexual competence may present the appearance but lack the substance of being capable of intimacy, love, sharing. One's evolution into a committed relationship such as marriage may provide the person his/her first real confrontation with vital developmental issues heretofore skirted or avoided.

e. cumulative erosion of energies. Sometimes the sheer energy investment necessary to meet a developmental demand may cause a breakdown of function. Usually this occurs in people who have encountered difficulty in previous periods, or who otherwise find their psychic resources depleted at the time of a new demand. One more bill to be paid, another pregnancy, additional work responsibility—any further strain on a psychic system already extended to its limit can precipitate one of the more serious developmental crises.

f. positive growth experience. Some adults come to experience a satisfaction in living that calls to their attention characteristics or conditions that inhibit further self-actualization. It may be an exogenous condition (e.g., a stultifying job or marriage) or an endogenous characteristic (inhibition of emotional expression). Either way, their general level of satisfaction serves to highlight by contrast areas of relative dissatisfaction.

The Challenge to Counseling Psychology

The role of psychotherapist is neither new nor unique to counseling psychology. Career counseling has not attained the status in our profession which it merits. What then serves to identify the distinctiveness of the counseling psychologist? One role which seems to emerge from contemporary literature is that of developmental facilitator. Such a notion has its origin in the counselor's work with children and in schools. The growing body of knowledge about adult development indicates that the same role has cogency for working with the adult span of life.

Traditionally, counselors and other psychologists have focussed on the ways growth is inhibited: conflict, debilitating anxiety, repression, fixation, regression. Other workers have been concerned with distortions in development, the more severe and distinctive psychopathological syndromes of psychosis, perversion, depression, character disorder, neurosis, psychosomatic disorder. By emphasizing facilitation, counseling psychologists can bring a new set of tools to their traditional workbench. Alternatively, some of us may want to take the new ideas and design new tools as we modify the way we work.

As a developmental facilitator the counseling psychologist working with adults has a major task as change agent. Rather than accept the tacit goals many of our clients are wont to present—restoration of "normalcy," or social adjustment—how to live with the bomb and like it, can we offer them the alternative of becoming what they might be? Can we expose our clients to the rewards of growth as counterleverage to its risks? Clearly this approach is already being offered in growth groups and psychological education courses. Within the more conventional counseling interview, however, the issues are more complex. The counselor cannot give priority to the goals and values he/she brings to counseling. A developmental "diagnosis" may ignore or minimize limits and vulnerability due to underlying psychopathology. It is obvious that the client's expressed needs and goals, and an assessment of his/her at-risk status, must be given first consideration. Once having accomplished that, however, one can go on to assess the extent to which the client's issues are developmental issues. Does this young adult woman's conflict with parents reflect chronic unresolved dependency needs? Or can the client utilize her own adult capacity for personal perspective, understand parental demands as reflections of their fear of aging, and help them feel more secure? Either assessment may be correct in the specific case. Either strategy may be appropriate in the specific case. But the second assessment may only be available to the psychologist who is sensitive to both dynamic *and* developmental issues.

The developmental perspective thus provides an *alternative assessment schema.* In terms of intervention it opens the possibility of *recruiting client resources not previously available to help clients resolve their problems.*

A 55 year old male physician, assailed by doubts about his medical competence, is differently situated than a 21 year old pre-medical student with the same concerns. Combining assessment and intervention, one might make explicit use of the older man's experience and carefully inquire with him into the specifics of his practice: details of his treatment approach, evidence of outcome, patient's feedback.

This approach allows the counselor to set a common purpose with client and establish a working relationship as usual steps in counseling. In addition it identifies client as an experienced adult; it exploits the expanded time perspective of middle adulthood; provides exploration of presenting problem as a possible displacement defense and/or manifestation of depression; opens possibility for clients utilizing their own judgment to confront themselves with evidence they can best marshall. One inevitable consequence is that clients will have a reality-based contact with their own competence, an experience that can only augment their sense of self in a solid way.

Space does not permit further elaboration of this approach. These anecdotes are only suggestive of an orientation to working developmentally with adults.

Foreclosure: A Unique Challenge?

A final point deserves attention: the significance of identity foreclosure for the work of the counseling psychologist. As elucidated by Marcia (1966) foreclosure occurs when the developing person accedes to the demands—or rewards!—in his/her environment to meet certain role expectations rather than press toward continued growth of self. In return for adapting to the cultural (or sub-cultural) mold one receives praise, acceptance, a secure place. Marcia (1966, 1967) describes the identity foreclosure person as an obedient, approval-oriented individual. He/she accepts the role laid out by others (commonly parents) as his/her identity. The person thus avoids the identity crisis and gains a sense of security and confidence. Foreclosure protects the person from doubt and anxiety at the cost of personal growth. Some convenient examples include a young adult who reluctantly accepts a secure job in the family business rather than pursue a longstanding interest in marine biology; a married woman who adopts the stereotypic full-time housewife role urged by her family rather than resist and start a small retail business. Such choices are everyday occurrences and can hardly be said to indicate psychopathology. But in subtly significant ways such actions may well impede personal development, leading to blunting of personality, and often eventuates in the apathy, discontent and vague dissatisfactions so frequently observed in later adult years.

We are accustomed to thinking of immaturity, alcoholism, rigidity, apathy, depression as evidence of psychopathology and, more recently, of oppression. It may be that the single greatest etiological factor behind these symptoms is "normalcy!" The apparent ubiquity of foreclosure in a majority of post high school Americans (Trent & Medsker, 1969) is discouragingly supplemented by the research of Golden et al. (1967), who studied fifty "normal" white males. Using unusually dependable, long-term criteria of freedom from psychopathology, these well adapted people were

> found to have little imagination and generally limited interests and social activities. They indicate limited educational and vocational aspirations for themselves, and also for their children [p. 34].

What does this say about the cost to personal development of successful social adjustment?

Many disciplines already offer therapeutic counseling to people with emotional problems. Can counseling psychology serve best by committing its resources to meeting vital developmental needs in "normal" people? More precisely stated, does counseling psychology have a role in mitigating the adverse effects of socialization on human potentiation?

From what has thus far been considered, it is apparent that the application of a developmental perspective to counseling adults has many other points of impact as well. Clearly there is need for more active research in adult development.

What kinds of properties are distinctive of the several adult periods? What is the nature of the interaction between aging and actualizing? Which specific procedures or techniques are most suitable for counseling at different adult life stages?

What is the natural history of male and female adult development? Which observed differences are culture-specific? Are present changes in sexual awareness having any impact on male or female development in adulthood? It exceeds the scope of this article to do more than sample the range of areas of study available to those interested in adult development.

The counselor applying the developmental approach to adult clients offers primarily a focus, a way of conceptualizing the human condition. The developmental perspective almost certainly commits the counselor to a growth rather than deficit (Maslow, 1962) model of counseling. As Blanck and Blanck (1974) observe, the developmental approach of ego psychology transformed psychoanalytic theory from a science of psycho-therapy into a psychology of "normal development."

Corollary to this commitment is an affirmation of actualization-oriented counseling rather than adjustment or adaptation-oriented counseling. The counselor acknowledges a value structure placing priority on helping clients to "become" rather than "restoring" them to some prior status, or helping them "adjust" to a role others (e.g., family, society) have allocated to them. It would be the counselor's responsibility here to make explicit to the client the opportunity to choose between restorative and growth goals.

To summarize this approach, the developmental adult counselor does not deny the existence of psychopathology. In many instances, psychotherapy may be the intervention of choice. Whether as catalyst, active interventionist, group leader or consultant the counselor's focus is on enhancing growth potential and mobilizing those resources which will augment optimal development.

The developmental perspective is just that: a way of thinking about people and their concerns. It can encompass many theories and diverse methods. Wittenberg (1968), for example, has modified classical psychoanalysis to the particular problems and needs of young adults. Actualization counseling (Brammer & Schostrom, 1968) attempts to gear counseling objectives to hypothesized developmental crises. A more radical, and highly promising role for the developmental counselor is that of psychological educator (e.g., Mosher & Sprinthall, 1972). In general, any counselor whose explicit goal is enhancing the self-potentiating capabilities of clients— whether through behavioral or client-centered techniques—can be arguably described as an applied developmental counselor. The present author finds his own grounding in ego psychology more than compatible with developmental precepts. As used here, ego psychology is defined eclectically to include any work dealing with ego structure, function, and development. Included are the writings of Hartmann (1958), Erikson (1964), White (e.g., 1963) as well as Maslow (1962), Super (1963), Kohler (1947), Murphy (1947), and many others.

The common ground of such disparate viewpoints is a focussing on the positive growth aspects of the person and the counselor's explicit alliance with those strengths. The counselor of necessity becomes concerned with *identifying* and *recruiting* the client's psycho/bio/social resources. In this generic sense one finds kinship in activities as diverse as leading a women's consciousness-raising group; helping a 27 year old resolve his rivalry with an older brother; teaching policemen interpersonal skills; life management counseling with a 43 year old mother of grown children. In each of these instances the developmental counselor would be asking "what psychological assets are available or potential for the client(s)?" and "how can I assist in their mobilization and utilization?"

Increasingly such concerns find their emphasis on the present, and aimed at future consequences or outcomes. The past is not necessarily prologue. The counselor may be interested in what was, but the commitment is to what can be. This forward thrust is characteristic of the developmental orientation.

Perhaps more so than at any time in this century, product and outcome are receiving priority attention. Popularization of human services has favorably affected *quantity*. A remarkable variety of therapeutic, religious, rehabilitative, and educative structures have emerged offering as their common project the amelioration/improvement of human experience through their unique methods, insights or gifts. What remains unclear is the ultimate *quality* of these offerings. What outcomes or results accrue to those who avail themselves of the services?

To its credit, psychology in general (e.g., McMillan, 1974) and developmental counseling in particular has moved to establishing formal criteria for accountability. In this context it is of interest to note that outcome focus is inherent in the very process of many developmental counseling interventions. Developmental counseling is rooted in goals, expressed intentions, and an actual or implied contract to work toward their implementation. This is particularly true in the counseling of adults, who can much more dependably give voice to their expectations, make explicit their objectives, and take responsibility for participating in a goal-oriented working relationship.

REFERENCE NOTE

1. Bocknek, G. *Psychology of the young adult.* Book in preparation, 1976.

REFERENCES

Blanck, G., & Blanck, R. *Ego psychology: Theory and practice.* New York: Columbia University Press, 1974.

Brammer, L., & Shostrom, E. *Therapeutic psychology.* (2nd Ed.), Englewood Cliffs, NJ: Prentice-Hall, 1968.

Buhler, C. The curve of life as studied in biographies. *Journal of Applied Psychology,* 1935, *19,* 405-409.

Erikson, E.H. *Childhood and society.* (Rev. Ed.), New York: W.W. Norton, 1964.

Golden, G. et al. A summary description of fifty "normal" white males. In L.Y. Rabkin & J.E. Carr (Eds.) *Sourcebook in abnormal psychology.* Boston: Houghton Mifflin Co., 1967.

Gould, R. The phases of adult life: A study in developmental psychology. *American Journal of Psychiatry,* 1972, *129,* 521-531.

Hartmann, H. *Ego psychology and the problem of adaptation.* New York: International Univ. Press, 1958.

Kimmel, D. *Adulthood and aging.* New York: John Wiley & Sons, Inc., 1974.

Knowles, M. *The adult learner: A neglected species.* Houston: Gulf Publishing Co., 1973.

Kohler, W. *Gestalt psychology, an introduction to new concepts in modern psychology.* New York: Liveright Publishing Corp., 1947.

Levinson, D. et al. The psychosocial development of men. In D. Ricks, A. Thomas, & M. Roff (Eds), *Life history research in psychopathology.* Minneapolis: Univ. of Minnesota Press, 1974.

Loevinger, J. The meaning and measurement of ego development. *American Psychologist,* 1966, *21,* 195-206.

Marcia, J. Development and validation of ego-identity status. *Journal of Personal and Social Psychology,* 1966, *3,* 551-559.

Marcia, J. Ego-identity status: relationship to change in self-esteem, "general maladjustment", and authoritarianism. *Journal of Personality,* 1967, *35,* 118-133.

Maslow, A. *Toward a psychology of being.* Princeton, NJ: Van Nostrand, 1962.

McMillan, J. Peer review and professional standards for psychologists rendering personal health services. *Professional Psychology,* 1974, *5,* 51-58.

Mosher, R. & Sprinthall, N. Deliberate psychological education. *The Counseling Psychologist,* 1972, *2*(4), 3-82.

Murphy, G. *Personality: A biosocial approach.* New York: Harper and Brothers, 1947.

Neugarten, B. (Ed.) *Middle age and aging.* Chicago: University of Chicago Press, 1968.

Perry, W.G. *Forms of intellectual and ethical development in the college years.* New York: Holt, Rinehart and Winston, Inc., 1970.

Pressey, S.L. & Kuhlen, R.G. *Psychological development through the life span.* New York: Harper and Row, 1957.

Super, D.E. et al. *Career development: self-concept theory.* New York: CEEB Research Monographs, 1963.

Trent, J. & Medsker, L. *Beyond high school.* San Francisco: Jossey-Bass, 1969.

White, R. Ego and reality in psychoanalytic theory. *Psychological Issues,* 1963, *111,* 3.

Wittenberg, R. *Postadolescence.* New York: Grune and Stratton, 1968.

"How Old Are You?" — The Question of Age Bias in the Counseling of Adults

LILLIAN E. TROLL
Rutgers University

CAROL NOWAK
Wayne State University

ABSTRACT

Attention is called to the probability that counselors and psychotherapists share the age stereotypes of other Americans. These definitions of appropriate behavior vary somewhat by age and sex of people under consideration and perhaps by age, sex, and other characteristics of those who are stereotyping. Three kinds of age bias are noted: age restrictiveness, age distortion, and negative attitudes associated with particular ages.

KINDS OF AGE BIAS

When several hundred counselors were surveyed by Troll and Schlossberg (1971), over half could be considered "age biased." They indicated that particular behaviors should be restricted to particular age groups. Only a few wrote that age as such should never be a significant variable for adults, though these few were shocked that it would ever be considered relevant. Yet if counselors or others in the helping professions can be said to have a creed, it would be that all who come to them for help should be regarded as unique individuals—that they should not be prejudged on the basis of age or any other ascribed category: skin color, social class, ethnic background, or sex. If the goal is to approach each client with an open mind and a clear eye, "raising consciousness" about age stereotypes may be as critical as "raising consciousness" about ethnic and sex stereotypes.

On first meeting people, counselors and therapists, as well as their clients, start with a primary question, "How old are you?" They may ask this question directly and overtly or they may estimate age so automatically that they are not aware they are doing so. Whether the question is asked explicitly or implicitly, however, its answer is sure to determine subsequent assumptions about attitudes towards each other and the world, about probable life experiences, and about what they want out of life (cf. Neugarten, 1968). These assumptions are embodied in stereotypes common to all. Essentially such stereotypes are group expectations of how people should be and act. They are usually products of early socialization, and prove remarkably resistant to change in the face of contradictory evidence. Social theorists like Rubin (1973) suggest that this persistence is due to a "primacy effect"—that first impressions set the framework for future encounters. When such stereotypes obscure the individualized characteristics shown by people in actual experience, they could be called biases or prejudices. They can distort judgments and decisions and can make counseling more dangerous than helpful.

In general, three kinds of age bias can be noted:

1. Age restrictiveness: setting of arbitrary or inappropriate age limits for any behavior;
2. Age distortion: misperception of the behavior or characteristics of any age group;
3. "Age-ism" or negative attitudes towards any age group (cf. Butler, 1969).

All three kinds can be applied to people of all ages. The norm of dignity can be as restrictive for middle adults as the norm of disengagement from social roles is for old people. Misperceptions about children and adolescents are perhaps as common as misperceptions about older generations. And many people have more negative attitudes toward adolescents than they do toward the old. However, a review of studies to date—sketchy and awkward as most of them are—points to different kinds of bias for different times of life—restrictiveness as the primary mode for youth and negative attitudes for the older years.

Age restrictiveness. Restrictions can be expressed in a variety of ways. Limits can be set for entry into or exit from particular roles or activities. One can be considered either too young or too old to go to school, hold certain jobs, get married, make political decisions, or engage in specific kinds of recreation. Limits can be set on what is appropriate behavior for a given age group, and what is inappropriate for that age. It may be proper to be impulsive or romantic at one age but not later on. It may be desirable to be sober and restrained at one age but not earlier. Neugarten, Moore, and Lowe (1965) found remarkable consistency among Americans—young and old, middle class and working class—with regard to their ideas about age-appropriate behavior. Their findings have been replicated in a number of other studies. These generalized expectations are summarized below.

Primarily, men and women in the twenties are supposed to be entering into adult roles. They are supposed to be establishing themselves in life, in job and family, and turning to each other and away from their parents and other kin. This is supposed to be a time of goal orientation, of job establishment, of life adjustment, and of movement and activity. Sex differentiation is expected. Age limits are usually earlier for women than for men. For example, women are expected to marry between 19 and 24, men between 20 and 25. While a salient issue for men should be getting started in the job world, for women it should be having children. For women, also, youth is the prime time for "good looks."

In general, competence, maturity, responsibility, and stability are the normative personality characteristics for middle adults, though there are foreshadowings of unpleasant things to come. This is a time of socialized control and mature restraint. Neugarten (1968), Bengtson and Kuypers (1971), and Wood (1971) all report that this time of life is seen as a time of arrival—a time to reap the harvest of earlier labors in the form of vicarious enjoyment of the successes of children and grandchildren, accrued status due to job success, and an active social life with many friends and acquaintances. For both sexes, it is supposed to be the time to stop parenting and to begin grandparenting. Wood's respondents saw middle-aged people as "too old to adopt a baby," but right for grandparenting.

Sex differences persist into the stereotypes for middle age. Middle-aged men are supposed to be at the "prime of life," to accomplish most, hold their top job, and have the most responsibilities. Middle-aged women, however, are considered to be at the "tail end" of responsibilities and accomplishments, since their principal duties are seen as child rearing and then child launching. They are supposed to "let go" of their children and remove themselves from this central role that has so far regulated their lives. While men are supposed to reap the harvest of their own labors, women are supposed to get their status from the job success of their husband, or, to some extent, their sons.

Two major areas of stereotyping about middle age for women are the menopause and the "empty nest." The menopause is supposed to be accompanied not only by distressing physical symptoms but by a wide variety of psychological discomforts as well. The departure of children is supposed to leave women desolate and deserted. Finally, middle-aged women are expected to show dramatic declines in physical attractiveness, particularly from "the neck up." In some cases, it is as though a quick "hag-like" transformation into old age is expected to take place, a move from youthful beauty to a wrinkled, gray, and pallid decline.

The overall expectation for old age is gloomy. Typically, old people are portrayed as socially, psychologically, and physically isolated, restricted, and deteriorated. According to a recent Harris poll, the image of old people in America is that of "senile, lonely, used-up bodies, rotting away and waiting to die."

Old people should be exiting from former roles and not thinking about entering new, age-inappropriate, ones. It is time to leave the work role and assume the role of retiree. It is not the time to run for public office. Neugarten, Moore & Lowe's (1965) respondents thought people should be ready to retire between the ages of 60 and 65. In fact, 65 is seen as a cut-off age for almost all activities. Subjects in Whittington, Wilkie & Eisdorfer's study (Note 1) did not differentiate between 65 and 75-year-old men—when you're old you're old!

Some specific behaviors not approved for old people (Wood & O'Brien, Note 2) are: 1) a widower of 70 remarrying against the objection of his children; 2) a retired couple wearing shorts to go shopping downtown; 3) a recently widowed woman of 65 buying a red convertible; 4) a retired couple attending night clubs frequently; or 5) a 68-year-old widow inviting a widower to her home for dinner.

Sex differences in stereotyping appear for old age as well as for younger ages, but here they tend to move toward less differentiated rather than more differentiated roles. Neugarten and Gutmann (1968) report that the old man in the Thematic Apperception Test picture they used was seen as losing his familial authority and becoming a passive figure while the old woman was perceived as relatively demanding and aggressive.

There is another aspect to age restrictiveness. Not only are limits set, for particular expectations, but there is greater pressure to act one's age during the entry phase than during the exit phase. Another way to look at this is that it is worse to be an "age deviant" (see discussion below) in youth than in the later years of life. Pincus, Wood, and Kondrat (Note 3) state:

> In comparing the entry and exit scores within each sample group, both the young and old respondents have higher restrictiveness for entry items than for exit items . . .. This also confirms our earlier finding that there is a greater acceptance of age as a criterion for entry into roles and for engaging in behavior than as a criterion for relinquishing roles and behaviors [p. 3].

Similarly, Troll and Schlossberg (Note 4) found less leeway allowed for the timing of the onset of adult activities: beginning career and marriage, than for the timing of the events of later life, like job success or retirement. This aspect of age restrictiveness may be seen as a paradox because youth is also allowed greater experimentation and vacillation in roles (Wood, 1971).

Distortion. Stereotypes or biases are frequently accompanied by distortion. Strong expectations of certain kinds of behavior do not so much cloud our vision as warp it. We tend to fit the perception to the expectation. If we expect adolescents to be extravagant and reckless, irresponsible and radical we interpret their actions as extravagant and reckless, irresponsible and radical. If we expect old people to be rigid and conservative and short on intelligence, we interpret the behavior of old people as rigid and conservative and short on intelligence. Two separate investigations, Ahammer and Baltes (1972) and Bengtson (1971) compared the values and personality characteristics expressed by people of particular age groups with the values and personality characteristics attributed to them by people of other age groups. In general, the greatest distortions tended to be for the two extreme age groups: adolescence and old age. Judgments of the beliefs and reactions of young and middle adults tended to agree more with the beliefs and attitudes they reported for themselves.

Negative attitudes. Robert Butler (1969) has written about the "ageism" prevalent in our society. Old age has a decidedly negative valence. People classified as "old"—and this may encompass anybody over 35, or even 20—are seen as intellectually unfit, narrow-minded, ineffective, and ready to die at any moment. In a communication task, college students "talked down" to presumed children and old people but gave more complex instructions to those targets they believed were adults of their own age or older (Rubin & Brown, 1975). They demonstrated their expectations that "older people" would have a deficient cognitive and personality structure and would need to be treated like children instead of like adults. The older one gets, the less exciting, full, and worthwhile one expects life to be. It is no wonder, then, that people tend to call themselves relatively younger as they get chronologically older (Streib, 1968, for example). In fact, "felt" age or subjective age is more closely related to psychological adjustment than is actual chronological age (Peters, 1971). Those who think of themselves as younger tend to be better adjusted, to have higher morale, and to react more favorably to role changes than their age mates who have older age identifications.

SOCIAL CLOCKS AND AGE DEVIANCY

Because people are expected to behave in particular ways, they feel they have failed in some important dimension if they don't. Even if Western culture does not have elaborate initiation ceremonies to mark the moment of leaving one age period and entering another, we do have what Neugarten (1968) calls built in social clocks by which to judge whether we are on time in particular behaviors. There is a time to go to school and a time to marry, a time to have one's first child and a time to start a career. To be "off time" is to be an "age deviant." It feels good to be on time and it feels bad to be off time, either early or late. A woman who is not married by 25 used to (and maybe still does) feel shame. It is as "bad" to have a baby at 15 as at 45. A man who is still in school at 30 feels shame. Huyck (Note 5) found, for instance, that with advancing age, Army officers who were age deviants in their career—either early or late—were more and more influenced in their attitudes about career competence.

WHO STEREOTYPES MOST?

While Americans as a whole show remarkable agreement about what people of different ages are supposed to be like, there is some variation by age, social class, and education. It is interesting to note that neither sex nor occupation has been found to make a difference.

Age. Age concepts seem to be learned early in life and modified only partially thereafter. Even before they start school, children assign ages to figures in drawings (Britton & Britton, 1969a). By five and six they associate "old" with physical decline and death (Treybig, Note 6). However, they do not attribute particular personality characteristics to particular ages until the school years. This differentiation seems to be a part of general cognitive development. (See, for example, Britton & Britton, 1969b; Hickey & Kalish, 1968; Hickey, Hickey & Kalish, 1968; and Kahana, 1970). While adolescents on the whole tend to be lowest of all age groups in restrictiveness (Sabatini & Nowak, Note 7), and their descriptions of adult characteristics are more valid than adults' descriptions of them (Ahammer & Baltes, 1972), they still tend to exaggerate older peoples' needs for dependency and nurturance.

Among adults, there is an essentially linear relationship between age and restrictiveness. The middle aged are more age-restrictive than young adults, and the old are the most age-restrictive of all (e.g., Kogan & Wallach, 1961; Wood & O'Brien, Note 2). Age distortion seems to follow a different pattern. Ahammer and Baltes (1972) report, for instance, that their middle-aged subjects were the most likely to misperceive the characteristics of other age groups, and to see old age in a negative light. On the other hand, middle-aged mothers surveyed by Traxler (Note 8) were slightly more tolerant of "old people" than their college-student daughters.

Elderly subjects are not exempt from age bias. While they see middle age more positively than do college students (Whittington, Wilkie, & Eisdorfer, Note 1), and probably old age less negatively than any younger respondents (Nardi, 1971), they are notably age-restrictive, and particularly intolerant of disabled persons (Gozali, Note 9).

Social class. Middle-class Americans tend to assign older ages to life events and labels like "middle-age" than do working-class Americans (Neugarten & Moore, 1968). For example, working-class respondents are likely to set the beginning of middle-age around 35 and middle-class respondents around 55, even though their description of what middle age is like are essentially similar. Middle class people may also have fewer negative attitudes and be less age restrictive (Hickey, Hickey & Kalish, 1968; Rosencrantz & McNevin, 1969).

Education. So far as amount of education is concerned, more schooling is associated with more positive feelings towards the aged (e.g., Campbell, 1971; Thorson, Hancock & Whatley, 1974). As for special courses, Troll and Schlossberg (1971) found that counselors who had taken counseling courses were more likely to be age restrictive than those who had not. The effect of such courses seems to have been to lead them to believe that they knew the "facts" about age decrements in abilities and interests which would justify restrictive counseling.

What is more, all studies to date show that professional people who work with older clients or patients view them as rigid and slow to respond to treatment. Thus, their treatment prescriptions for anyone they defined as "old" would be limited to custodial, impersonal care. This is as true of physicians and dentists as of physical therapists, nurses, and social workers (e.g., Coe, 1967).

STATE OF THE FIELD

Unfortunately, almost all the studies reviewed here are cross-sectional. People of different ages were examined at the same point in time. What we are guessing to be age changes may in fact only be age differences, and we may be seeing historical rather than developmental effects. The finding that older adults are more age restrictive or more age-biased than younger adults or adolescents, for example, may be due to a general societal shift away from age-restrictiveness. The present group of adolescents and young adults may continue to be more flexible and less biased than their parents throughout their lives.

In addition, most of the studies in the field are preliminary. They tend to be deficient—or at least casual—in sampling, in methodology, and in interpretation. Most samples are small in size and seem to be obtained on a "catch as catch can" basis. Age categories are particularly arbitrary. Definitions of "youth" range from 10 to 30, and of "old" from 40 to 90. It is often difficult to judge whether a behavior is characteristic of "old" or of "older" individuals. This can be awkward if "older" is just older than college students.

IMPLICATIONS FOR COUNSELING ADULTS

Neither the accuracy nor the appropriateness of adult age stereotypes is the concern of this paper. To check stereotypes against present research findings on adult development, the reader is referred to textbooks in that area (e.g., Troll, 1975; Kimmel, 1974). It is the prevalence and content of age stereotypes rather than their validity that have concerned us here.

Since counselors have shared the socialization of other Americans, it should not be surprising that they also have built-in assumptions about age and sex-appropriateness. This becomes important when we consider that the decisions confronting many clients are related directly to what is expected of them, by themselves and by others, because of their sex and age. Should they "make do" with an undesirable or unsatisfactory way of life because at their age they can't expect any better? Is it all right for young men to explore the world for ten years before they settle into a job or career, or for young men and women to delay both marriage and child rearing into their thirties? If 30, 40, or 60-year-olds try something new like going back to college, or branching off into a new career, or terminating a crippling marriage, will they "make fools of themselves?" If middle-aged (or old) people are neurotic or disabled, can they—at their age—expect to profit from counseling or psychotherapy enough to justify their own and their counselor's expenditure of time and effort? If middle-aged and older parents remain highly involved with their children will they cripple them? If people over 60 want to continue in central roles in life's affairs are they to be criticized and discouraged?

Students of adult development like Neugarten (1968) and Brim (1966) feel that adults are controlled by social clocks more than by biological clocks. It may not be the onset of puberty that shakes the adolescent so much as the shift in expectations by others around them. They can no longer act like children. They must "all of a sudden" act "grown up." Similarly, it could be more the ambiguity or negative character of social expectations in middle-age rather than the menopause or loss of physical attractiveness or the empty nest which shakes women in their forties and fifties.

These implications are central to the functioning of therapists. Presumably, social conditions can be changed more easily than can biological. We do not need to be tied to a rigid adherence to socially prescribed ordering of life events. What may have been appropriate for earlier medical, social, and economic conditions may not necessarily be appropriate today. We can begin to take a freer look at the adult years, to question our "built-in" assumptions about what people should rightly do according to their age. As we move away from an assumption of the inevitability of certain events occurring at certain ages, we can move towards the possibility of trying new options at every age. We may even forget to ask, "How old are you?" and inquire instead about more relevant characteristics.

REFERENCE NOTES

1. Whittington, S., Wilkie, F., & Eisdorfer, C. *Attitudes of young adults and older people toward concepts related to old age.* Paper presented at Gerontological Society, Puerto Rico, 1972.
2. Wood, V., & O'Brien, J. Normative expectations for age roles: The views of three age groups. Unpublished paper, School of Social Work, University of Wisconsin, Madison. Cited in Wood, V. Age-appropriate behavior for older people. *Gerontologist,* Winter 1971, *2*(4, Part 2), 74-78.
3. Pincus, A., Wood, V., & Kondrat, R. *Perceptions of age-appropriate activities and roles.* Paper presented at the Gerontological Society, Portland, Oregon, 1974.
4. Troll, L., & Schlossberg, N. *Explorations in age-bias: A preliminary investigation of age-bias in the helping professions.* Paper presented at the Gerontological Society, Toronto, 1970.
5. Huyck, M. *Career timing, age, and career attitudes among Army officers.* Paper presented at Gerontological Society, Toronto, 1970.
6. Treybig, D. *Language, children, and attitudes toward the aged: A longitudinal study.* Paper presented at the Gerontological Society, Portland, Oregon, 1974.
7. Sabatini, P., & Nowak, C. *Bias for the ages: Perceptions of age-appropriate behavior from adolescent, middle adult and late adult samples.* Paper presented at the Gerontological Society, Louisville, Ky., 1975.
8. Traxler, A. *Intergenerational differences in attitudes toward old people.* Paper presented at Gerontological Society, Miami Beach, Fla., 1973.
9. Gozali, J. *The relationship between age and attitude toward disabled persons.* Paper presented at Gerontological Society meeting, Toronto, 1970.

REFERENCES

Ahammer, I., & Baltes, P. Objective vs. perceived age differences in personality: How do adolescents, adults, and older people view themselves and each other? *Journal of Gerontology,* 1972, *27,* 1, 46-51.
Bengtson, V. L. Inter-age perceptions and the generation gap. *Gerontologist,* Winter 1971, Part II, 85-89.

Bengtson, V. L., & Kuypers, J. A. Generational differences and the developmental stake. *Aging and Human Development,* 1971, *2,* 249-259.

Brim, O. Socialization through the life cycle. In O. Brim & S. Wheeler, *Socialization after childhood.* New York: John Wiley & Sons, 1966.

Britton, J. O., & Britton, J. H. Discrimination of age by preschool children. *Journal of Gerontology,* 1969a, *24,* 457-460.

Britton, J. O., & Britton, J. H. Discrimination and perception of age and aging by elementary school children. *Proceedings, 77th Annual APA Convention,* 1969b.

Butler, R. N. Age-ism: Another form of bigotry. *Gerontologist,* 1969, *9,* 243.

Campbell, M. E. Study of the attitudes of nursing personnel toward the geriatric patients. *Nursing Research,* 1971, *20,* 147-251.

Coe, R. Professional perspectives on the aged. *Gerontologist,* 1967, *7,* 114-119.

Hickey, T., Hickey, L., & Kalish, R. Children's perceptions of the elderly. *Journal of Genetic Psychology,* 1968, *112,* 227-235.

Hickey, T., & Kalish, R. Young people's perceptions of adults. *Journal of Gerontology,* 1968, *23,* 215-219.

Kahana, B. Old age seen negatively by old as well as young. *Geriatric Focus,* 1970, *9,* 10.

Kimmel, D. *Adulthood and aging.* New York: John Wiley and Sons, 1974.

Kogan, N., & Wallach, M. Age changes in values and attitudes. *Journal of Gerontology,* 1961, *16,* 272-280.

Nardi, A. H. Apperception and heteroperception of personality traits in adolescents, adults, and the aged. Unpublished doctoral dissertation, West Virginia University, 1971. Cited in Nardi, A. Person-perception research and the perception of life-span development. In P. Baltes & W. Schaie (Eds.) *Life-span developmental psychology: Personality and socialization,* New York: Academic Press, 1973, pp. 285-301.

Neugarten, B. (Ed.) *Middle age and aging.* Chicago: University of Chicago Press, 1968.

Neugarten, B., & Guttman, D. Age-sex roles and personality in middle age: A thematic apperception study. In B. Neugarten (Ed.) *Middle age and aging.* Chicago: University of Chicago Press, 1968, pp. 58-74.

Neugarten, B., & Moore, J. The changing age-status system. In B. Neugarten (Ed.), *Middle age and aging.* Chicago: University of Chicago Press, 1968, pp. 5-21.

Neugarten, B., Moore, J., & Lowe, J. Age norms, age constraints and adult socialization. *American Journal of Sociology,* 1965, *70,* 710-717.

Peters, G. Self-conceptions of the aged, age identification, and aging. *Gerontologist,* Winter, 1971, *2*(4, Part 2) 69-73.

Rosencrantz, H., & McNevin, T. A factor analysis of attitudes towards the aged. *Gerontologist,* 1969, *9,* 55-59.

Rubin, K. H., & Brown, I.D.R. Life-span look at person perception and its relationship to communicative interaction. *Journal of Gerontology,* 1975, *30,* 4, 461-468.

Rubin, Z. *Liking and loving: An invitation to social psychology.* New York: Holt, Rinehart and Winston, 1973.

Streib, G. Are the aged a minority group? In B. Neugarten (Ed.) *Middle age and aging.* Chicago: University of Chicago Press, 1968, pp. 35-46.

Thorson, J., Hancock, K., & Whatley, L. Attitudes toward the aged as a function of age and education. *Gerontologist,* 1974, *14*(4), 316-318.

Troll, L. *Development in early and middle adulthood.* Monterey, California: Brooks/Cole, 1975.

Troll, L., & Schlossberg, N. How "age-biased" are college counselors? *Industrial Gerontology,* Summer 1971, 14-20.

Wood, V. Age-appropriate behavior for older people. *Gerontologist,* 1971, *2*(4, Part 2), 74-78.

EMERGING PROGRAMS AND ISSUES **3**

Existing Programs and Emerging Strategies

LAURIE R. HARRISON
American Institutes for Research
Palo Alto, California

ALAN D. ENTINE
State University of New York
at Stony Brook

ABSTRACT

An examination of the scope and dimensions of adult counseling programs in the United States. Emphasis is placed upon a 1974 national survey of adult career planning and development programs conducted by the American Institutes for Research. Counseling programs for women, ethnic minorities, and mid-career change are highlighted. Prospective strategies to improve the future effectiveness of adult counseling efforts are discussed.

Laurie R. Harrison is Associate Research Scientist at the American Institutes for Research, Palo Alto, California. Alan D. Entine is Assistant Academic Vice President at the State University of New York at Stony Brook.

EXISTING PROGRAMS AND EMERGING STRATEGIES

In recent years counseling programs for adults have come to reflect many of the societal, demographic, and economic changes which are taking place in the United States. The feminist movement, the trend toward early retirement, the lengthened life span, and current high unemployment rates have caused many individuals to re-examine personal futures in the middle and older years.

Rapid technological change and the energy crisis have also altered the planned career paths of many adults who find themselves in need of making vocational shifts to match changes in the American economy. Moreover, the literature discussing the "mid-life" crisis and work alienation has added new dimensions to adult counseling perspectives (Brim, Note 1; Sheppard & Herrick, 1972).

This paper will examine the scope and dimensions of adult counseling programs in the United States. A primary source for this information is the 1974 American Institutes for Research national survey of adult career planning and development programs. The paper will also examine counseling programs for women, ethnic minorities, and mid-career changers. It will also discuss prospective strategies which may improve the future effectiveness of adult counseling efforts.

The AIR Survey

The American Institutes for Research conducted a national survey of adult career counseling programs in 1974.[1] A total of 752 programs was identified and contacted. Four hundred and sixty or 61% responded. Of the 460, 93 felt that they did not qualify as an adult career counseling program. The remaining 367 completed the survey and their responses form the basis of this section.

The identified programs were primarily sponsored by five types of agencies or groups. These five are: four-year colleges and universities (34%), community and junior colleges (20%), private groups and agencies, such as the YWCA, YMCA, and B'nai B'rith Career and Counseling Services (18%), government agencies (16%), and public adult schools which are usually an adjunct to a unified or high school district (12%).

Adult career counseling centers undertake a variety of functions and utilize a range of methods and techniques to reach their clients. They gather information about adult vocational and educational options and disseminate this material to clients and the community; they offer vocational aptitude and achievement testing and utilize the results of these tests in counseling sessions.

---

[1]The survey was conducted pursuant to OEG 0-74-1722, "Assessing and Field Testing Career Planning and Development Approaches for Adults: Focus on Ethnic Minorities and Women" (Note 2)

They may offer assistance with personal and family problems. They may also attempt to develop work opportunities for clients through job placement and job development activities.

Career counseling techniques vary greatly. The most common format in which career planning and development assistance is provided to adults is the class. Some are held in the evening, some during the day; they may last from 4 weeks to a full year. The second most popular format is the workshop, seminar, or small group meeting. While these formats may seem fairly standard, many programs are using workshops and classes in innovative ways. As a part of an outreach function of many programs, classes in career planning and development are being offered in unique settings such as prisons, hospitals, and local libraries. Several programs offer seminars at unique times to accommodate working adults. For example, "Brown Bag" sessions have been held at lunch time. Other programs have arranged for release time for workers in order to conduct workshops in business and industry settings.

A portion of the programs is attempting to provide services and information to the adults in their homes. Four methods for doing this are the use of telephones, mobile vans, cassette tapes, and home-study "correspondence" courses. The method of telephone counseling has been most widely utilized by the Education Development Center (EDC) of Providence, Rhode Island. In the EDC program counselors help callers map out a career and keep in touch as long as they are needed. The service does not find jobs for people nor is it a "hotline." Appointments are made for phone call career counseling sessions. Follow-up calls are made to assist participants with their career plans.

Another strategy which eliminates the need for participants to travel to the program is to take the program to them via mobile vans. Mobile units have been used by many programs in an effort to reach home-bound adults in their neighborhoods or to make information more easily accessible by taking the van to suburban locations such as shopping centers. Mobile units have also been used to introduce program participants to local businesses, industries, and community agencies. Foothill College in Los Altos Hills, California, sponsored a Career Exploration by Bus, a day-long tour for local women. The purpose was to investigate and identify employment opportunities. In Dallas, Texas, the Home and Family Life Program of the Dallas Independent School District uses mobile vans to reach home-bound inner city adults. Most of the participants are women, and the program brings them information on child rearing, comparative shopping, and budgeting. The "English on Wheels" program sponsored by the Salinas Adult School in Salinas, California, uses the community as a classroom with the aid of a mobile van. The Mexican-American participants of this program are helped to learn English as well as function in the community. For example, the van takes participants to a hospital where they learn emergency room and admittance procedures.

A unique method for providing career planning and development assistance to home-bound adults has been used by the Bergen County, New Jersey, "Women Returning to Work" program. This program has offered a home-study course in an effort to reach adults in a wider area. This course consists of printed learning packets which are sent to the home covering such topics as "Why do you want to return to work?" "Saving Money," and "Food Buying and Convenience Foods." The participant goes through the materials and completes an assignment at the end. When the material and assignment are returned to the program headquarters, the next learning packet in the series is sent to the participant.

An alternative to taking the program to the participant is to take the participant to the program. The Mountain Plains residential career education program for families does this in a major way. Participants who are selected for this program and their families are relocated to the Glasgow, Montana, Air Force Base which now serves as the site for the program. At the center, skill training as well as planning and development assistance are provided to the entire family.

Self-instructional, information cassette tapes are being employed in a few programs. The Curricular-Career Information Service of Florida State University at Tallahassee uses self-instructional tape-slide presentations, augmented with written material to provide students with information on campus and community resources, sources of information, self-assessment, and guidelines for career decision-making. As part of a myriad of other functions, the Center for Continuing Education of Women at Miami-Dade Community College in Miami, Florida, offers a self-directed learning cassette tape membership program. This provides a self-enrichment opportunity for participants. Topics discussed on the tapes include self-discovery, changing values, psychology, and philosophy.

Programs for Women

The feminist movement of the past decade has been a key force contributing to the recent growth of adult vocational and educational counseling programs. As women have sought a more equal economic role in American society, women's counseling centers have been established to provide information and guidance to those who are seeking new educational and career trajectories.

Counseling centers for women are now found in nearly every major city in the country. In smaller communities they are also in evidence and are usually associated with educational institutions. Whether free-standing or associated with host institutions, they have usually operated on a not-for-profit basis and charge modest fees. They are staffed by women, many of whom are part-time paraprofessionals. In the more established centers where personal counseling is provided, there is a professional staff who generally have graduate degrees in psychology, guidance, counseling, or social work.

It is difficult to learn the precise number of these centers. Many are operating from a precarious financial base and have unpredictable life-spans. The Catalyst Organization, a national non-profit network of counseling centers which were established to serve the vocational and personal needs of college trained women, lists 127 resource centers in 30 states as of May 1975. Of these, 82 centers are affiliated with institutions of higher education while the remainder are primarily independent non-profit agencies.

Thirty-two (32) percent of all the AIR surveyed programs were designed specifically for women. There appears to be no dearth of programs for women, although not all groups of women are assisted in equal proportion. There are many more programs for middle-class, educated women who have never worked or who have been out of the labor market for a considerable time, than there are for low-income women and female heads of households who are frequently working full time but in low level, dead end jobs. Many programs designed for the former group are of a "consciousness raising" type consisting of workshops and seminars designed to awaken women's full potential and serve as a forum for discussing problems and concerns. These programs are usually offered through women's centers which offer workshops on many topics as well as support services (for example, child care), information sources, referral services and/or job banks, etc. The specific content or precedures used in these programs are often vague, and evaluation usually consists solely of participant reactions to the programs.

For middle-income women, two particularly well-defined programs were identified. The University of Kansas Continuing Education Division has developed procedures and materials for a Career Exploration for Women Workshop. This counseling plan for women is presented in leaders' and participants' manuals. The focus of the workshop is on helping women choose careers, overcome internal, cultural, and familial obstacles to their growth, and succeed in their chosen fields. The content includes self-assessment, family problem assessment, assertiveness training, career information, and job seeking advice. The materials encourage realistic evaluations of self, job, family, and opportunities.

Everywoman's Center at the University of Massachusetts has developed a Modular Life Planning/Career Development Program for Women. This program takes a woman through a series of stages where she first defines her concerns, fears, and problems, then moves into a phase devoted to current information on the world of work, non-traditional opportunities available to women, and changing roles of women. Following these phases, an individualized program is set up for each woman to work on modules which meet her specific needs.

While programs for middle-income women often focus on expanding personal awareness, programs for low-income women are more apt to focus on coping or survival skills. For women of limited educational backgrounds, the Women's Reentry Program (WREP) sponsored by DeAnza Community

College in Cupertino, California, is a particularly fine example. The program introduces women to the college environment and provides a host of supportive services including an integral child care program. Women bring their children to the child development center at 8:30 a.m. and then attend classes from 9 a.m. to 1 p.m. During their first academic quarter, emphasis is on home economics, sociology, and English skills; during subsequent quarters, more flexibility is allowed, and women take classes ranging from typing to biology. Two hours a week, the woman devotes to participation with the children in the child development center.

Many low-income women with limited educational backgrounds hold full-time jobs and do not have the flexibility to enter a program such as the WREP. Yet many of the jobs they hold are very low level, and the women in them could benefit greatly from further skill development. It was for this type of women that the National Council of Negro Women, Inc. developed their Center for Career Advancement. Their program is designed to reach employed clerical workers and help them increase their confidence and skills. The academic content of the program deals with language arts skills, and there are small group sessions which reinforce the academic content and relate it to actual job challenges. Monthly workshops relating to such topics as how to apply for jobs, to work effectively with staff, and to organize one's work are also held.

The AIR survey sought to identify programs which were attempting to expand career options for women and break down some of the sex stereotyping which occurs in the labor market. The survey identified several management training programs for women. The Women's Leadership Project in Adult Education sponsored by the Boston University School of Education, the Leadership and Management Course for Women sponsored by the Office of Women's Programs at the University of Tennessee, and Middlesex Community College's Women's Opportunity Research Center are all examples of programs which focus on developing managerial skills in women.

Getting women into the more male-dominated trade and union jobs is something few programs tackle. The Women in Apprenticeship Program sponsored by Advocates for Women in San Francisco, California, was the only program in the survey with this as its primary purpose. This program works with women to make them eligible for the apprenticeship employment lists as well as offers them support in seeking and maintaining jobs. The program also works with the Joint Apprenticeship Councils and Training Committees to make them cognizant of the availability of skilled women workers and receptive to hiring them.

Another way in which career options for women can be expanded is to provide actual work experience for women who have none (although they may have much volunteer experience). Correspondingly, efforts can be made to make the labor market more flexible and responsive to the needs of many women workers by having more part-time jobs available. The Oregon

Division of Continuing Education is one of a handful of agencies which is responding to this concern. They have developed a work experience internship program for women which involves a 3-month, half-time on-the-job exploration. This provides women with valuable experience which makes them more employable, and the employer cooperation in the project may open up the possibility for more future part-time jobs.

Women's counseling centers are now opening their career and educational services to men. As indicated by Anderson (Note 3):

> Most of our clients are women returning to the world after years in the house but 10% to 20% are men and now we are getting more and more school dropouts. The men are now often retiring from a job as a policeman or fireman . . . or even from the public schools. Some are still employed at a job they loathe and looking for a different direction.

Counseling centers which serve both men and women report very heavy interest in their educational and career guidance services. Two of the most active are described by Comly (Note 4):

> With virtually no advertising campaign, the New York City Regional Center for Lifelong Learning received over 5,000 phone inquiries in its first year of operation. In two years the Providence (Rhode Island) Career Education Project (CEP), which does advertise, has had 5,000 call-ins; 4,000 of these became clients each of whom received six or seven phone-counseling sessions lasting thirty to forty-five minutes apiece.

The Program Advisory Service of the University of California at Los Angeles reports that since its inception in 1971, it has "served over 20,000 men and women, many of whom are struggling with career change in their 30's right up to planning for retirement challenges. In this latter group some individuals are concerned with generating income while others are focusing more on self-actualization during retirement" (Hummel, Note 5). While it is likely that counseling efforts in less populated areas would draw smaller responses than the centers mentioned, these reports indicate that there appears to be genuine demand for adult vocational and educational counseling services.

Programs for Ethnic Minorities

Sixteen (16) percent of the programs responding to the AIR survey had a minority enrollment of 30% or greater.[2] Within this group, the percentage of programs with particular ethnic group representation is as follows:

---

[2] A particular focus of the AIR survey was to look at programs designed for women and ethnic minorities. There is obviously overlap in these two categories, and within each, there are numerous subcategories, many of which are also parallel.

Table. 1 Ethnic Minorities Served

Ethnic Group	Percentage
Black	59%
Spanish-speaking	23%
Both Black and Spanish-speaking over 30%	3%
Asian	5%
American Indian, Eskimo, Aluet	5%
Mixed (No one group greater than 30% but combined minority enrollment of 30% or more)	5%
	100%

In addition to choosing, obtaining, and keeping a job, programs with heavy minority enrollments also focused on teaching survival or coping skills, and better English. A unique aspect of programs for ethnic minorities is leadership training. Almost all programs which have a high ethnic minority enrollment have a component of their program which addresses learning how to function in or deal with society—often called coping or survival skills. These skills include money management and budgeting, income tax filing, health care and facilities, nutrition, legal rights, dealing and cooperating with agencies and resources in the community, etc.

Programs with a large Spanish speaking enrollment often have an English as a Second Language class available. Three programs in California with 100% Chicano enrollment taught English in a career context. The "English on Wheels" program in Salinas, California, teaches English through job interviews, job application forms, and resume building. A program entitled "English and the Dollar" is sponsored by the Glendale, California, Community College. Its purpose is to help make Chicanos more employable by giving them competence in using English and in transacting business. In San Diego, California, the Padre Hidalgo Center of the Catholic Community Services sponsors a program for Spanish speaking women. The program teaches the women English as well as clerical and job seeking skills.

Two programs were identified which address the need for minority leadership training. The ALPHA program (Adult Leadership Program in Housing and Agencies) in the Bronx, New York City, New York, has a 90% Black and a 5% Spanish speaking population. Its purpose is to confront the problem of the lack of leadership in the community by developing a nucleus of knowledgeable adults who will progressively exert leadership for the social, economic, and political betterment of the community. The Leadership Training in Advocacy Program in San Jose, California, has the mission of training low-income Puerto Ricans to assume leadership in their community, to develop advocacy skills, and to become agents of their own socio-economic development. Training is provided to individuals who in turn train and activate members of their communities.

Programs for Mid-Career Changers

Rapid technological change and increased life span have brought about the need for career planning and development programs for people in their middle and late years. A mid-career change is being faced or sought by increasing numbers of men and women who have worked for the majority of their life in a single profession. This is the issue being addressed by many women's programs, and it is also the focus of several programs for men and women. The Mid-Career Counseling and Information Program at the State University of New York, Stony Brook, is actively addressing the needs of individuals who must face or choose to make a mid-career change (Entine, Note 6).

The profile of the first group of Stony Brook participants (autumn, 1975) provides a pattern of backgrounds and interests which may be representative of largely middle-class adults who are seeking counseling services. Table 2 shows the breakdown of age and sex among the program participants.

Table 2. Sex and Age Distribution

	Total	*Under 35*	*35-39*	*40-49*	*50-59*	*60 and over*
Men	31	1	5	19	4	2
Women	44	4	5	24	11	0

The 75 individuals were engaged in a variety of occupations when they entered the program. Twenty-three were employed in the private or business sector; seven were in professional occupations; eight were in education; four were in government occupations; three were unemployed; and one was retired. The largest single category—30 women—were homemakers who were pursuing a variety of part-time jobs and volunteer activities. Twenty-two of these women were married. The remainder were either separated, divorced, or widowed.

Individuals were asked to express their reasons for entering the program. The homemakers—the largest single category—generally expressed the desire to re-enter the world of work on a full-time basis. They were anticipating the time when their children would no longer need them at home. They wanted to plan an educational and career path which would bring them satisfying and productive work some time in the future. Some women viewed this stage beginning when their youngest child entered first grade; others would wait until the youngest family member finished high school before entering full-time employment.

Those who were in the labor market came to the counseling program primarily to learn about other career options which would either bring a less pressured and/or more satisfying work experience (14 responses) or more job security (11 responses). Others gave no reasons for desiring a change other than to explore what might be available (eight persons). The three individuals who were unemployed desired immediate information on job openings; they were the most difficult to help and were among those least satisfied with the counseling program.

The individuals also were asked to express their preference for a new occupation or career path. The largest single response focused on mid-life careers which emphasized the helping or service professions (39 responses). Counseling, social work, health care delivery, special education, and physical therapy were sub-specialties in this area.

The primary theme of these responses was the desire to enter a field where one could work with and help people. This appears to be a theme running through the desired mid-life career changes of many persons; similar patterns were apparent in the responses given by those interested in Columbia University's New Careers Program nearly a decade ago.

To be sure, there were other career changes desired. Four persons wanted to explore communications and writing; seven wanted to enter a business field (including setting up individual proprietorships). Included in the last group were two employed county social workers who wanted to enter fields where they could work with their hands instead of dealing with people. Finally, a large group—25—had no fixed new occupational or educational goals in mind and wanted to explore various options and opportunities with the counseling staff.

The program provided an opportunity for these individuals to attend a series of non-credit classes which were led by persons from a variety of vocational and professional fields where work options existed for persons in mid-life. These included the allied health professions, accounting, computer programming, small business, government service, and other areas. Program participants also attended individual counseling sessions with paraprofessionals who helped to identify and match personal goals with the manpower requirements of the economy.

The counseling staff has indicated that they felt successful in identifying positive and viable educational and career options for approximately 35% of the program's initial participants. An additional 50% may have benefited from increased awareness of the range of possible options which may be pursued at a later date. For these individuals a change in attitude about what is in the realm of the possible may be an important program accomplishment. Finally, 15% were unable to identify solutions to career or educational dilemmas through the resources of the program. Some would benefit from additional personal counseling while others must face such options as moving to metropolitan areas where particular employment options are brighter than they are in suburban or exurban settings. (It must be remembered that the onset of the 1974 recession made it particularly difficult to find swift solutions for the unemployed individuals.)

PROGRAM STRUCTURE: STAFFING, COSTS, PLANNING, AND EVALUATION

While staffing patterns varied greatly among the surveyed programs, the one clear trend was that the paraprofessional plays a visible and vital role in the majority of programs. Peer counseling and assistance from adults who do not hold formal counseling degrees, but who have backgrounds similar to the clients' backgrounds, take place in many programs. These paraprofessionals have generally received some training for their roles. The skills most frequently mentioned as prerequisite for all staff of the surveyed programs were "empathy, understanding, and an ability to relate to adults" and "knowledge of career development."

The cost data which were received were very difficult to use on a comparative basis. Some programs included overhead and facility costs, while others reported costs for materials and staff only. Furthermore, since staff salaries vary from urban to rural settings and in various sections of the country, and since many of the programs' paraprofessional staff members were also volunteers, cost figures alone do not provide particularly valuable information. In order to replicate a program, consideration should be given to the facility or space requirements; the number, level, and proportion of time of staff members involved; and whether materials must be purchased or developed.

The status of planning and evaluation efforts in these programs was weak. Only a small percentage of programs were keyed to measurable client objectives; however, most did have fairly clearly stated goals, which are much broader than objectives. Unfortunately, if the objectives of a program are not clearly stated, evaluation of that program is also more difficult. Twenty percent of the programs did provide evaluation data related to specific changes in program participants' lives as a result of the program, or data keyed to measurable objectives. However, the most prevalent form of evaluation data provided was the anecdotal report of success or participant reactions. Thirty-three percent of the AIR surveyed programs were evaluated in this manner. An equal percentage (33%) had done no evaluation whatsoever, and an additional 12% provided such sketchy evaluation data ("An evaluation was done and the results were positive.") that they are difficult to categorize. Two percent of the programs indicated that an evaluation was in progress for the first time. The programs which were most likely to have conducted an evaluation keyed to measurable objectives were those receiving federal or state funds where evaluation was probably a requirement for the funding. Because of a lack in sophistication in the majority of evaluations and the variability of the cost data which were provided, it unfortunately is not possible to draw cost/benefit conclusions for the surveyed programs.

THE FUTURE

The long-term outlook for adult counseling efforts depends, in an era of ever tightening resources, upon the identification of a counseling model with a favorable cost/benefit ratio. The New York State workshop on counseling recognized that an adult career and educational informational dispersal system should exist in locations which were easily accessible to the public and non-threatening. The workshop report suggested that the New York State Library System be designated as the key agency to support and coordinate a state-wide adult career information service (Comly & Kurland, Note 7).

The role of state library systems might well be expanded at relatively low cost to provide adult counseling as well as information. Public libraries are found in nearly every community in the nation, and all of them undoubtedly have some materials which relate to adult educational and vocational opportunities. It might well be far less costly to add a mid-life vocational and educational counselor to existing library staff than to support a free-standing community-based adult counseling service. The library-based counselor would also be responsible for maintaining adequate counseling materials and resources in the library and could participate very easily in a computer assisted network such as the one being developed at the University of Illinois (Farmer, Note 8). The University of Illinois computer assisted network will also identify appropriate referral linkages in each community when these are an appropriate part of the counseling process. Designed for use by adult clients, the system focuses upon providing information to meet non-traditional needs: part-time educational options, mid-life vocational options, credit for life-experience, child-care facilities, etc.

Additional help for adult counseling programs is beginning to appear. Manuals, workbooks, and computer based information systems have been developed to provide assistance to counseling programs. Perhaps the most extensive set of materials developed to assist adult counseling centers are those which have been recently published by the Career Education Project in Providence, Rhode Island (Note 9), which has operated in Rhode Island since 1972 under a contract with the National Institute of Education. The project has provided information, guidance, and referrals to several thousand home-based adults. As described above, the telephone is the primary means of providing counseling assistance for the Providence project.

The five manuals issued by the center provide much information to prospective counseling programs in the following areas: (a) designing and operating a career counseling service for adults; (b) attracting clients to service oriented programs; (c) establishing and operating a career resource center for adults; (d) developing career-related materials for use with and by adults; and (e) integrating research and evaluation into the operation of service oriented programs.

The publications emphasize step-by-step procedures which are likely to be especially helpful to centers which are collecting extensive educational and vocational resource materials. The manuals leave out one important dimension: the cost of establishing and maintaining the services and resources for such a program. It is highly probable that the Providence project costs are too prohibitive for most adult counseling centers unless they receive ongoing institutional or grant support or charge prohibitive fees. It would have been helpful if the manuals indicated the number of person hours required, for example, to build a career resource library or to train a paraprofessional staff. Counseling centers would then have the option to develop those portions of the Providence project which would have the most favorable cost/benefit results for their own programs.

The long-term financial base for adult counseling programs must become more secure. Major independent counseling programs, such as the Syracuse Regional Learning Service and the Providence Career Education Project, have relied heavily on short-term grants from government and private sources. Counseling centers associated with colleges and universities have received direct or indirect support from their host institutions. Few programs are able to sustain their efforts from the revenues derived from fees alone.

State legislatures have begun to consider providing ongoing support to adult counseling centers. For example, a bill has been introduced in the Washington State Legislature to "establish a set of career change centers which would enable those who are unemployed to make career changes for economic, technological or health reasons. The centers would provide diagnostic services, family, resource and situational counseling, supporting services, job training and placement." The State Department of Employment Security would be responsible for management of the program (Slee, Note 10). A bill has been introduced in the Florida State Legislature to establish area councils which would determine the most appropriate method of delivering educational and community services in each of 28 regions of the state. Appropriate adult counseling services would be provided in each area and would be funded under provisions of the bill.[3]

States might become more receptive toward funding adult career programs if the cost-effectiveness of such efforts was known. As the AIR survey indicated, this requires additional research into counseling programs now underway with greater emphasis on follow-up studies of client activity. Increased attention must be placed on program evaluation before state fiscal authorities can be expected to underwrite adult career counseling programs on an ongoing basis.

REFERENCE NOTES

1. Brim, O. *Theories of the male mid-life crisis.* Invited address to Division 20, 82nd Annual Convention, American Psychological Association, New Orleans, September, 1974.

[3]Florida State Senate Bill 1003, introduced in the 1975 Regular Session.

2. Harrison, L. *Survey of career planning and development approaches for adults: Focus on ethnic minorities and women.* American Institutes of Research, Palo Alto, California, 1975. OEG 0-74-1722.
3. Anderson, M. T. Personal communication, March 28, 1975.
4. Comly, L. *Community-based educational and career information and counseling services for the adult public*—Draft report. State Educational Department, Albany, New York, January 20, 1975.
5. Hummel, L. Personal communication, June 27, 1975.
6. Entine, A. *The first four months.* A report of the Mid-Career Counseling and Information Program at Stony Brook, New York. Mimeograph, December 15, 1975.
7. Comly, L., & Kurland, N. *Workshop summary report: Recommendations and Plans.* State Education Department, Albany, New York, May 16, 1975.
8. Farmer, H. *Inquiry project: Computer-assisted counseling centers for adults.* Presented at AAHE, Drake University, Iowa, May 20, 1975.
9. *Career Education Project:* Providence, Rhode Island, Education Development Center, Newton, Massachusetts.
10. Slee, J. Personal communication, June 16, 1975.

REFERENCE

Sheppard, H. L., & Herrick, N. O. *Where have all the robots gone? Worker dissatisfaction in the seventies.* New York: Free Press, 1972.

INQUIRY Project:*
Computer-Assisted Counseling
Centers for Adults

HELEN FARMER
University of Illinois
at Urbana-Champaign

ABSTRACT

INQUIRY centers for adults offer counseling for persons who seek to make career changes, to continue their education, or to re-enter the world of work (i.e., women) but who are unaware of most of the available opportunities. Computers are used to assist in the counseling by providing a comprehensive data bank of information on educational, leisure time, and occupational opportunities and by teaching problem-solving processes and awareness of self as decision-maker. Educational and career development tasks provide a diagnostic and prescriptive framework for services. Centers are being developed at the University of Illinois at Urbana-Champaign, a leader in advanced computer technology. An integrative computer-assisted counseling service, such as INQUIRY centers are designed to be, could make needed counseling and information services available to many more adults than are currently being served.

> It is possible that a computerized society may have effects that are quite opposite from those suggested ... the creation of a mass society of automatons [Bell, 1967, p. 983].

PURPOSE OF INQUIRY COUNSELING CENTERS

Many adults need specific information about educational and career opportunities at convenient locations (Carp, Peterson, & Roelfs, 1973; Knox, 1968). Some adults who seek to continue their education, make career changes, or re-enter the world of work (i.e., women) are *unaware* of most of the available opportunities. Research studies have found that about 25% said

*A project funded in part by the U.S. D.H.E.W., Fund for the Improvement of Post Secondary Education (FIPSE). With appreciation to the staff of the INQUIRY project for many of the ideas expressed herein.

they would have participated if they had known where to sign up for specific courses and training opportunities (Carp, et al., 1973). Another 33% of those adults studied said they did not know about the existence of continuing education programs for adults. This is especially true for adults with lower levels of formal education or occupational prestige who have not been traditionally represented in higher education.

The purpose of INQUIRY centers is to design and field test adult counseling centers capable of providing a full range of information and counseling services relevant to the educational, career, and leisure time planning needs of adults (who are not currently full-time students), in an efficient cost-effective manner.

In other states in the U.S. recent efforts to serve the educational, leisure time and career planning needs of adults (Bailey & Macy, 1974; Career Education Project, 1975) have been successful in some important respects, particularly in providing counseling support services. However, all report a critical need for efficient storage and retrieval of educational and career information, both of a traditional and a non-traditional nature. There is an urgent need at the community and regional level for a central clearinghouse for information about educational and career opportunities. With this type of information, the adult will be better able to make decisions about increased competence and/or career development, and proceed to contact the appropriate institutions, agencies and employers.

The University of Illinois at Urbana-Champaign, because of its leadership in computer systems (Lyman, 1975) and the vision of some of its faculty (especially Alan Knox), was selected as an ideal site for the design and field testing of an adult counseling system which would be able to deliver both the necessary counseling support and an efficient system for storage and retrieval of relevant educational and career information.

Site visits by INQUIRY project staff to existing computer-assisted counseling systems (reviewed elsewhere by Harris, 1974) indicated that these systems, without exception, were designed for full-time students. Unlike full-time students, adults often need information about part-time educational opportunities, obtaining academic credit for experience gained outside the traditional classroom, entry and training requirements for occupations open to the older adult, non-traditional forms of financial aid, and child care.

It was concluded that an essentially new system design was needed for the counseling and information needs of adults, a design that integrated counseling and information services into a computer program in a cost-effective manner. Technology may be used to depersonalize human development and growth or harnessed to the cause of greater individualization of learning and enhancement of a personal sense of self as a free agent. The philosophy underlying INQUIRY design is not new and was well articulated previously by Ellis and Tiedeman (1970) and Super (1970). Computer technology, however, has advanced rapidly in the past decade, making cost-effective today what was prohibitively expensive then.

INQUIRY centers will be located in the community where a broad cross-section of adults are likely to be at least once each week.

CAREER DEVELOPMENT TASKS: A DIAGNOSTIC AND PRESCRIPTIVE FRAMEWORK

The design of the INQUIRY centers was based on the rationale of Tiedeman and O'Hara (1963). Center services are responsive to the educational and career development needs of the adult in four broad areas presented in Figure 1 as exploration, crystallization, planning, and implementation.

Adults who are dissatisfied with their work, planning for career change,

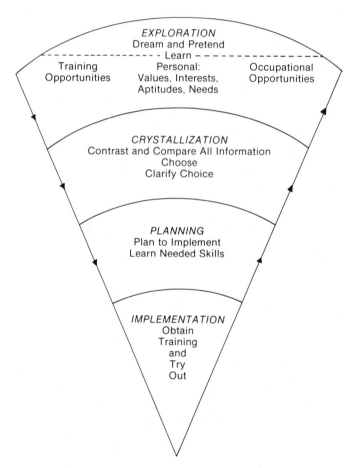

Figure 1. Career Counseling and Career Development Tasks

or planning for lifelong educational development benefit most by beginning with their dreams. Later they move from fantasy goals to exploration of various possibilities. It is important that they explore their own interests, values and potentials, along with available educational and career opportunities. Then they are ready to narrow down the choices. The crystallization task includes evaluation of each possibility in relation to what is known about both self and the environment. This task involves convergent thinking (Guilford, 1959) and reality testing, in contrast to the earlier exploration tasks which involve divergent thinking and are less concerned with choosing. Some other adults come to counseling centers seeking to upgrade their present skill or training. These persons might begin with planning and implementation tasks, skipping exploration and crystallization tasks entirely.

The INQUIRY computer program is designed to identify which educational or career development need each client represents, based either on information provided directly by the client (e.g., about goals and satisfaction or dissatisfaction with life) or on information obtained from the client's scores on Super's *Career Development Inventory* (Note 1), developed especially for adults. INQUIRY computer information files and counseling components are designed to encourage clients to complete the career development task identified as appropriate for them. There is no pressure to choose when clients are exploring. When clients are ready to narrow down their choices the system encourages crystallization. In a similar way the system encourages client activity appropriate to planning and implementation tasks as these become relevant.

The application of this approach is not new. Schlossberg (1972) adapted the Tiedeman/O'Hara paradigm to the career development needs of women.

GUIDED INQUIRY: STRUCTURE FOR LEARNING PROBLEM-SOLVING

Using educational and career information wisely requires some structure for planning and decision-making. Guided Inquiry counseling (Farmer, 1974; Healy, 1974; Sorenson, 1967) is one procedure for providing this structure. Figure 2 presents the six Guided Inquiry phases in summary form.

The description of Guided Inquiry which follows assumes a client-counselor interaction. In computer-assisted INQUIRY centers the counselor's role is more often taken by the computer, which is programmed to teach problem-solving processes and to facilitate client awareness of self as decision-maker.

Guided Inquiry is basically a method adapted from the problem-solving research of Gagne (1970), the learning theory research of Bruner (1966), and the counseling theory of Sorenson (1967) and Rogers (1961, 1975). The result is an approach in which the counselor allows the client to get in touch with the self, teaches the client problem-solving processes, and encourages the client to accept responsibility for decisions. The procedure is reflective at times,

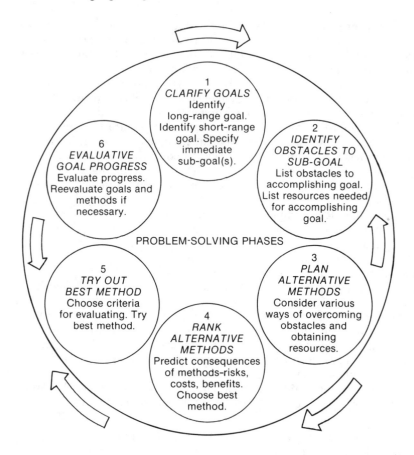

Figure 2. Guided Inquiry Problem-Solving Phases

didactic at others. It is useful for personal problems as well as educational and career planning.

The phases of Guided Inquiry counseling are logically ordered and represent a typical problem-solving path. However, the procedure is dynamic and flexible as the arrows in Figure 2 attempt to indicate. Many clients will find it beneficial to recycle back to an early phase after working on some later phase (e.g., reformulate goals after considering methods of overcoming obstacles). When clients neither need to nor want to work on some phase, they can skip it. A brief description of the 6 phases of Guided Inquiry follows.

Clarify goals. Phase 1 entails the identification of long and short goals related to educational and/or career development. Although long range goals may be as general as "Choose a satisfying career," intermediate goals should be specific to enable the client to begin working toward goal achievement.

Identify obstacles to subgoal. In phase 2 the client thinks about what might prevent accomplishment of the subgoal (e.g., need for daycare services) and lists needed resources such as finances, time, references and prerequisite skills.

Plan alternative methods. In phase 3 the client considers as many methods as possible for overcoming obstacles and obtaining needed resources. The client is encouraged to draw on his/her own experience in thinking of methods to use.

Rank alternative methods. The client tries to predict the consequences of using each method identified in phase 3. Guided Inquiry provides the client with a cost/benefit inventory to assist him/her in weighing the pluses and minuses of each method in phase 4.

Try out best method. In phase 5 the client tries out the method determined best in phase 4. In order to get feedback on how well (s)he is doing, it is helpful for the client to set realistic standards of success for himself/herself.

Evaluate goal progress. Finally the client reviews progress toward goal achievement and revises the methods currently being used if necessary. At this point the client may continue to work through phases 5 and 6, recycle to some earlier phase, or terminate counseling. INQUIRY centers use a computer to assist with the counseling role of teaching problem-solving.

WILL ADULT CLIENTS USE THE COMPUTER?

Many adult clients feel uncomfortable with the idea of using a computer (Costar, 1975). INQUIRY centers are designed to counter these fears in several ways. First, if a client has never used a computer or typewriter keyboard the counselor helps the client learn how to use and become comfortable with it. In extreme cases the counselor operates the computer for the client. Second, computer terminals are optionally equipped with a touch panel permitting the user to merely touch the desired response on the screen. This eliminates the use of the keyboard for many types of interaction. Third, orientation to the use of the computer takes the form of a humorous game. The graphic capability of PLATO (the computer based instructional system at the University of Illinois) allows for more interesting presentations during the orientation. Fourth, the client has the option to remain anonymous and (s)he may use the system with a pseudonym to protect against any possible invasion of privacy. Once the client is comfortable using the computer he/she is ready to benefit from its services.

THE ROLE OF THE COMPUTER IN INQUIRY CENTERS

The INQUIRY computer makes available thousands of facts on educational and career opportunities to the adult client. It also provides the means for converting these facts into personally meaningful and useful information. The speed with which information is retrieved reduces greatly the time and frustration expended by the client and the counselor. The educational and career development counselor cannot keep at his/her fingertips all the information clients need to make choices wisely, but the computer can.

Research and evaluation of client use and system effectiveness is facilitated by computer storage of summary data on client characteristics. Analysis of this data is easily performed at timely intervals for reporting to sponsor agencies and for internal evaluation and redirection of center services.

The computer performs the counselor role of inventory and test administrator and interpreter. Inventories and tests may be rapidly scored and the results provided clients without waiting. Summary scores are stored in the computer for future reference and possible interrelating with other information about the client. For example, if a client's inventory scores indicate a high interest in working with people and the client selects a career to consider which is oriented more to working with data and things (i.e., lab technician), the computer points this out. Interpretation of inventory results is designed to be nonprescriptive (Goldman, 1971) and consistent with the recent guidelines for eliminating sex-bias (Diamond, 1975).

The computer performs the counselor role of teacher. The PLATO instructional design provides a means of individualizing client instruction. The counselor, the computer and the adult client are all members of an interactive team. The computer presents concepts such as decision-making to the client while at the same time monitoring the client's performance as decision-maker. Each client works at his/her own pace with access to special information and help when problems arise.

The PLATO computer system's capability for carrying on a conversation with the client makes it possible for the computer in INQUIRY centers to take on the role of guide, as described in Guided Inquiry counseling. The computer is information giver, teacher, and guide. Details on these computer services are provided next.

The computer system in INQUIRY centers is organized into five component systems—Query (the counseling function), Educational Information System (EIS), Occupational Information System (OIS), Self Information System (SIS), and Guidance System (GS). These systems and the subsystems which comprise them are summarized in Figure 3. One important feature of the entire system is that the several subsystems all are cross-referenced to each other (e.g., educational requirements for a particular career are cross-referenced to descriptions of educational opportunities). Broken lines in Figure 3 represent this potential for interaction among subsystems.

The counseling function is performed by the computer component named Query, depicted on the screen as a neutral comic character. Query reviews with the client what (s)he has done at timely intervals, prompts the client to

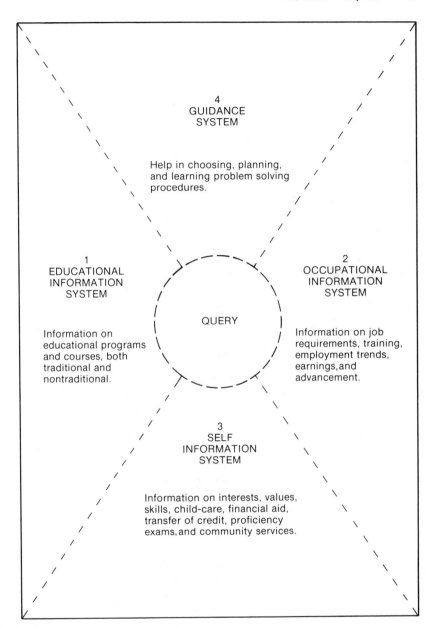

Figure 3. Inquiry Computer System Components

finish any of the career development tasks (i.e., exploration; crystallization; etc.), and describes the process the client is using to make decisions in order to facilitate the client's awareness of self as decision-maker. Query also routes the client to the various information and guidance services in INQUIRY. Query is programmed to note the client's acceptance or rejection of information such as that yielded by inventories and tests. When rejection occurs Query makes a note which the counselor picks up later. Direct messages given by the computer to the counselor link these functions.

EIS is designed to contain three subsystems of information about traditional (i.e., college) and non-traditional (i.e., manpower, WIN, military, etc.) educational programs. One subsystem contains program descriptions, including prerequisites, licensing, apprenticeships, and credentialing requirements. A second file contains information on individual courses (credit and noncredit). A third contains information on the characteristics of training institutions and agencies offering educational courses and programs.

OIS is composed of two subsystems. One contains local, regional, state, and national information on at least 800 of the most common occupations. This information indicates employment trends, work requirements, expected salary ranges, and where to obtain further information. A second subsystem in OIS provides the user with a means for selecting a small subset of occupational descriptions matching the user's interests or specifications.

SIS is designed to provide the user with information about his/her interests and competencies, work related values, general intelligence and self estimates of personal strengths and weaknesses. An aids subsystem provides information on childcare, financial aid, CLEP exams, legal aid, and other community services. SIS also contains a vita subsystem for storing information about the user, obtained either by SIS or other parts of the system.

GS has four subsystems designed to provide a variety of functions and services. One of these orients the client to the use of computer equipment, collects biographical data about the client, summarizes the services available at INQUIRY, and describes the philosophy of the center. A second subsystem assists the client in comparing and contrasting alternative educational and career choices. A third assists the client in working through the six Guided Inquiry phases of problem-solving. A fourth provides help when the user is having trouble with the computer itself.

INQUIRY counseling centers for adults are unique in their integration of computer and counseling services. The career development tasks provide a focus for services. Guided Inquiry problem-solving procedures are taught as the mechanism for using information wisely in educational and career planning. INQUIRY centers supply "the format for experience with facts, and for their conversion into personally meaningful and useful information while teaching the processes of problem-solving" (Super, 1970, p. 379).

The case of one adult is given next as an example of how INQUIRY centers might work. Although INQUIRY centers are still in the development stage it is possible to extrapolate the path of a client through the system from our experience with persons who have helped with the field testing. The case presented is composite and hypothetical. Other adult clients might require more or less time and services than the one described.

An Illustration

Marcia was a 29 year old divorced woman who came to the INQUIRY center asking for help in finding a better job. The counselor invited her to talk about herself and her situation. Marcia was bored with her job which was responding to customer complaints and unhappy with her pay which barely covered living costs for herself and her two year old daughter.

Marcia thought of work as a means of economic support and had never viewed work as a potential source of personal satisfaction. She did get satisfaction from hobbies such as music, writing poetry for close friends, and decorating her apartment.

The counselor told Marcia that services at the INQUIRY center could probably help her. With the counselor's assistance, Marcia learned to use the computer and recorded information about her background and interests on the computer. Query suggested that Marcia explore other work roles and consider possible relationships between work roles and her own interests and skills. Query described the kinds of information available and invited Marcia to choose among them.

Marcia chose to take the *Self-Directed Search* (Holland, 1973) in order to learn more about herself. Her scores on this inventory indicated high art interest and low interest in helping people. Some careers related to her interests were interior decorator, newswoman, artist, musical performer, and entertainer. Query gave Marcia a printed copy of the inventory's results and also stored summary scores with earlier information about her.

Marcia obtained from the computer printed descriptions of several careers which interested her. When she decided to leave, Marcia made an appointment to return to the center. Query summarized what she had done and reminded her that she was still exploring options for career planning. Teaching awareness of self as decision-maker is an important aspect of INQUIRY center design.

When Marcia returned to the center she had narrowed down her career choices to interior decorator and newswoman. She chose these careers on the basis of their favorable employment outlooks. Marcia had now begun to crystallize her career choice.

Query reviewed Marcia's previous visit to the center and asked what she would like to do today. Marcia indicated her current career choices and the reasons for them. She requested more detailed information on training requirements for interior decorator and newswoman. Query indicated to Marcia that she was moving fluidly back and forth between exploration tasks and crystallization tasks, and between Guided Inquiry problem-solving phases of clarifying goals and identifying obstacles and resources needed to achieve her goals. The information on training for the careers of interior decorator and newswoman indicated that Marcia could attend a professional school, obtain on-the-job training, or attend a two or four year college. Each option had a different price tag, class schedule, and length of training. Financial aid and salary range were about equal for either career. But since the minimum training time required for becoming a newswoman was twice that for an interior decorator, Marcia decided that interior decorator was the most attractive career.

Marcia discussed her choice with the counselor and said that she was somewhat frightened about going back to school after nine years of employment. Because Marcia viewed herself as intelligent the counselor suggested that she might wish to take a current measure of her intelligence. Marcia liked this suggestion and took a mulitple choice adaptation of the Wechsler Adult Intelligence Scale (Costar, 1975) which was on the computer. She was surprised and pleased when she obtained a superior rating on general intelligence. Marcia also chose to obtain information on her art judgement skill. Her above average rating on the Maier Art Judgement test gave her the confidence she needed to choose interior decorator as the career to pursue. Crystallization and exploration were complete for the time being for Marcia and she was ready to begin planning to implement her choice.

Marcia indicated that a formal degree program was superior to an on-the-job training program if sufficient financial aid could be arranged. Guided Inquiry problem-solving phases two, three and four were used to help Marcia find a solution to her financial needs. From the computer Marcia obtained information on costs and on financial aid available at colleges and professional art schools in the Chicago area. She discussed the comparative advantages of various schools with the counselor. Together they worked out a plan for her to interview with the most desirable schools to determine whether she met their requirements and whether they could help her financially.

Marcia's plan to interview at several training schools and colleges in the Chicago area worked well. She was accepted in both a professional school and a two year college. Because the two year college's offer was generous enough to take care of both Marcia's financial needs and those of her daughter, she accepted it. Marcia's tryout was a successful illustration of Guided Inquiry problem-solving phases five and six. She was ready to begin implementing her career choice in earnest.

The case of Marcia was presented to illustrate the integration of the counseling and computer function in INQUIRY centers and the related time savings for the client and the counselor. The exact roles of the counselor and Query will vary somewhat from client to client. Many clients will come for specific kinds of information and leave within fifteen minutes. Other clients will stay several hours and return on repeated occasions. All services at INQUIRY have as their goal increasing the number of educational and career options open to adults. Clearly, not all counseling works out as well as this illustration. Marcia's superior abilities and the availability of financial help were crucial in her success.

IN CONCLUSION

INQUIRY centers being developed in Illinois are intended to be an answer to the information and counseling needs of adults who seek to extend their educational or career development. Lack of a central clearinghouse for information about educational, career, and leisure time opportunities prevents many adults from taking advantage of available resources. INQUIRY centers are computer-assisted so that vast amounts of educational, occupational, and leisure time information can be stored for quick accurate retrieval. Other advantages of computer-assisted counseling are noted, such as the computer's ability to sort information on client variables and to interrelate divergent types of client information faster and more reliably than a human counselor. The computer teaches decision-making procedures to clients, in the context of the career development tasks. The integration of the counseling function into the computer is the main contribution of INQUIRY centers.

The success of INQUIRY centers in demonstrating that they represent a cost-effective way for delivering needed services to adults will determine to some extent the future of this model. A truly interactive computer-assisted counseling service, such as INQUIRY is designed to be, can make needed information and counseling services available to many more adults than those served by existing services. The challenge to technology is to expose all adults to learning experiences more conducive to developing their creative capacities.

REFERENCE NOTE

1. Super, D. *Career development inventory*. Unpublished inventory. Available from the author at Columbia University, Teachers College, New York City, N.Y., 1974.

REFERENCES

Bailey, D., & Macy, F. *Regional learning services*. Syracuse, N.Y.: Syracuse University Research Corporation, 1974.

Bell, D. The working parties. *Daedalus*, 1967, *96*, 979-983.

Bruner, J. *Toward a theory of instruction*. New York: W.W. Norton & Co., 1966.

Career Education Project. *Career development series*. Newton, Mass.: Education Development Center, 1975.

Carp, A., Peterson, R., & Roelfs, P. *Learning interests and experiences of adult Americans*. Berkeley, Ca.: Educational Testing Service, 1973.

Costar, E. *Estimation of intelligence and motivation as a screening procedure for programs on PLATO IV.* Unpublished doctoral dissertation, University of Illinois, Champaign-Urbana, 1975.

Diamond, E. (Ed.) *Issues of sex bias in interest measurement.* Washington, D.C.: U.S. Government Printing Office, 1975.

Ellis, A., & Tiedeman, D. Can a machine counsel. In W. Hultzman (Ed.) *Computer-assisted instruction, testing and guidance.* New York: Harper & Row, 1970.

Farmer, H. *Guided inquiry group career counseling.* Champaign, Illinois: University of Illinois, Illini Bookstore, 1974.

Gagne, R. *The conditions of learning.* New York: Holt, Rinehart and Winston, 1970.

Goldman, L. *Using tests in counseling.* New Jersey: Prentice-Hall, 1971.

Guilford, J. *Personality.* New York: McGraw Hill, 1959.

Harris, J. The computer: Guidance tool of the future. *Journal of Counseling Psychology,* 1974, *21,* 331-339.

Healy, C. *Career counseling in the community college.* Springfield, Illinois: Charles C. Thomas, 1974.

Holland, J. *Making vocational choice: A theory of careers.* Englewood Cliffs, N.J.: Prentice-Hall, 1973.

Knox, A. Interest and adult education. *Journal of Learning Disabilities,* 1968, *1,* 8-10.

Lyman, E. *PLATO highlights.* Urbana, Illinois: Computer-based Education Research Laboratory, University of Illinois, 1975.

Rogers, C. *On becoming a person.* Boston: Houghton Mifflin, 1961.

Rogers, C. Empathic: An unappreciated way of being. *The Counseling Psychologist,* 1975, *5,* 2-10.

Schlossberg, N. A framework for counseling women. *Personnel and Guidance Journal,* 1972, *51,* 137-143.

Sorenson, A. Toward an instructional model of counseling. *Occasional Report No. 6.* Center for the Study of Evaluation of Instructional Programs, University of California, Los Angeles, 1967.

Super, D. Of Tiedeman, Ellis, and machines that become media when given the right messages. In W. Hultzman (Ed.) *Computer-assisted instruction, testing and guidance.* New York: Harper and Row, 1970.

Tiedeman, D., & O'Hara, R. *Career development: Choice and adjustment.* Princeton, N.J.: College Entrance Examination Board, 1963.

Continuing Education and the Development of Adult Women

HELEN STAVRIDOU ASTIN
University of California
Los Angeles

In the late 1960's and early 1970's interest in nontraditional education, with its diverse students and new goals and programs, emerged in higher education. Today, nontraditional study is growing: College and university espousal of innovative approaches is reflected in external degrees, flexible curricula and requirements, and open universities.

As institutions have opened their doors to new populations—veterans, housewives, second-careerists—they have been challenged to provide appropriate and flexible curricula. However, little information exists about the specific needs and interests of these populations or about their personal characteristics and modes of learning.

About one-and-a-half years ago, the National Coalition for Research on Women's Education and Development sponsored a study to address some of the issues concerning the characteristics, interests, and needs of one of these populations: adult women returning to higher education. Colleges and universities have responded to this group with continuing education programs for women (CEW).

This paper focuses on the women in this study, describing their needs, interests, aspirations, goals, and views about education, work, and social action. It also shares perceptions of how families view the wife and mother who is returning to school. What have been some of the changes in the family and in the women themselves which permit them to assume new responsibilities and to combine new roles with old? In what ways have the educational development and aspirations, occupational status and plans, and personal growth of these women been directly affected by their experiences in programs of continuing education?

Fifteen diverse CEWs were selected for this study: they represent rural

Presidential Address, Div. 35 (Division of the Psychology of Women). APA meetings, Chicago, August, 1975. Some data in this article are from *Some Action of Her Own*, edited by H. S. Astin, Lexington Books, D. C. Heath and Co., 1976. Reprinted by permission.

versus urban settings, two- versus four-year institutions, coed versus primarily single-sex institutions, sectarian versus non-sectarian status, mixed versus homogeneous populations, state versus institutional bases, and large multi-faceted versus small, single-focus programs.

In the spring and summer of 1974, case studies of the 15 programs were conducted through site visits and in-depth interviews with administrators in the parent institutions, program directors, and members of the staff. In addition, about 300 women who had participated or were participating in various programs, such as group counseling, credit or noncredit courses, and certificate or degree programs, were randomly selected and interviewed. We also conducted interviews with spouses and children.

In the fall and winter of 1974, a mail survey of about 1,000 participants, 300 of their spouses, and 1,000 alumnae (women who had participated 3-to-5 years earlier) of the 15 programs was conducted. The discussion here is based primarily on responses from 649 women (68%) participating in the programs during the survey period and from 153 spouses (54%). Some data from the interviews are also presented.

ADULT DEVELOPMENT AND EDUCATION

Scholars in the field of adult development (Flavell, 1970; Neugarten, 1973; Simon, 1968) have generally agreed that adults passively accommodate experiences, whereas children and youth actively assimilate them. While children's cognitive development is based on physical and maturational aspects, adults, cognitive style is based on unprogrammed experiences, such as psychotherapy and adult education.

While youth is described as a search for identity, adulthood is depicted as a search for "integrity" and a denial of despair. However, adult women in continuing education are searching not only for integrity but also for identity, in that they are asking themselves who they are other than wife and mother.

Differences have been observed in the coping styles of men and women in later life. Although men become more affiliative as they mature, women show a great need for independence, become more outward and assertive, and remove themselves somewhat from the role of nurturer (Brim, Note 1; Lowenthal & Chiriboga, 1973). Baruch (1967) found that a temporal cycle in the achievement motive is associated with the age and family situation of college-educated women. The high achievement need that a woman experiences before she begins a family appears to be followed by a decline in achievement need. However, once the children are grown, the need for achievement returns to the previous high level. Changes in the life cycle of women suggest a need for redirection, accomplishment, and new work orientation.

Although they are defining self in terms of new roles and experiences, adult reentry women also typify the adult learner in that they are conscious of their reason for learning and understand the benefits of education (Tough, 1968).

Even though the literature on adult development has described the developmental differences between youth and adulthood and between adult men and women, it has not differentiated adult women by past roles and experiences. Adult women described in the literature have primary roles of wife and mother. There is no information on the similarities and differences between women with career commitments and those primarily with family commitments. Also, do women who had careers, who were involved in scholarly, scientific, and artistic endeavors, have adult crises similar to those of men? Do adult women who have always been outwardly oriented show needs for affiliation in adulthood similar to those of adult men?

The largest proportion of the population in this study was adult women who are searching for identity and integrity, who have new outwardly defined goals, and who are actively assimilating new experiences. However, the study includes a small proportion of women who have always had careers, and who have returned to college to update or to develop skills for a second career.

The study also addressed the complex interactions between familial variables and educational and occupational outcomes. Questions central to the study were: How do the internalized sex roles and the support—or lack of it—from significant others (spouses and children) affect women's self-concept, achievements, and aspirations? What kinds of attitudes and behaviors, exhibited by the immediate family, elicit differential perceptions and behaviors by women about their self-concept, sense of personal worth, emotional well-being and mental health, need achievement, motivation, and educational-occupational accomplishment?

Since adult women in continuing education programs are a unique population (age span, diverse education, career continuity and discontinuity), we could examine the complexities in the educational and career development of women. For example, because of the age range, we were able to analyze the interest, aspirations, and concerns of women between 20 and 65 or over. Thus, we could examine interests and status as they appear for women 30 and under, between 31 and 40, between 41 and 50, and 51 or older.

In the literature on adult education, four basic terms, which are often used interchangeably but which communicate specific ideas and concepts, frequently occur. They are adult education, continuing education, recurrent education, and lifelong learning. Adult education, offered primarily by secondary institutions and community agencies, refers to vocational and avocational courses and experiences specifically for adults. Continuing education, offered in postsecondary institutions, refers to programs that enable adults to upgrade their education and occupational skills. Recurrent education and lifelong learning refer to learning for learning's sake or to training for better jobs.

Recurrent education is a European idea largely pioneered by the Centre for Educational Research and Innovation of the Organization for Economic Cooperation and Development. It provides for "new relationships between individuals, educational opportunities, and working careers that would lead to more equity between social classes, ethnic and age groups, men and women" (Gass, 1973). Recurrent education implies the distribution of education over a life span, permitting leisure, work, and education to alternate throughout life.

The important premises of recurrent education are:

1. Learning can take place at any time.
2. Learning should be equitable; the goal of recurrent education is to achieve educational and social equality.
3. The need for recurrent education results from rapid change and growth in knowledge and information.
4. Work and social experiences should be important considerations in admissions and curricular designs.
5. Recurrent education expands the concept of educational opportunity to include all of one's life.

Since the primary purpose of recurrent education is to reduce inequality and offer a second chance, women's interest in recurrent education is closely allied to their concern for equal opportunity in the form of equal rights, chances, and achievement. Moreover, since recurrent education provides opportunities for career development, it is a way to update skills obsolete because of long-term interruptions for family.

Recurrent education epitomizes the public concern for equal educational opportunity which began in the 1960s and paralleled the efforts of women leaders of CEW. Even though it was only recently that a national conference took place (the 1973 National Institute of Education conference on recurrent education) and a publication was issued (*Lifelong Learners—A New Clientele for Higher Education* in 1974), the efforts of CEW directors were evident in the early 1960s.

However, women in continuing education programs constitute only one part of the adult population seeking education. In 1962, a national study (Johnstone & Rivera, 1965) sponsored by the Carnegie Corporation inquired into adult education in America. Specifically, the study examined educational activities, reactions to continuing education, and facilities.

About 25 million adults were active in some form of learning during the year of the study. About one-half had enrolled in courses part time. Their activities ranged from vocational to recreational to academic. Their median age was 36.5. They were about equally divided between men and women. They were somewhat better educated than the typical adult and more likely to hold white-collar than blue-collar jobs.

When rates of study were examined among men and women at different age levels, a substantially higher proportion of men than women under 35 were engaged in learning activities. In general, more adults were taking courses because of interest than because of specific occupational objectives. However, more men than women were participating in educational activities directly related to occupational goals.

The more facilities available in a given community, the more likely were the adults to pursue educational activities. Johnstone and Rivera concluded in 1962 that the audience for adult education would increase more rapidly than the population as a whole and that learning-for-work and learning-for-leisure together would dominate the adult education scene in the future.

A close examination of studies of the educational needs of adult women and the programs designed to serve them reveals parallels to the findings of this study. Johnstone's and Rivera's 1962 predictions have been realized and one can now forecast that the growth will continue.

CONTINUING EDUCATION PROGRAMS FOR WOMEN

Continuing education programs for women were originally developed to facilitate the entry or reentry of women past the traditional age of 18 into the academic world. A recent publication by the Women's Bureau, *Continuing Education for Women: Current Developments* (1974), highlights the historical development of women and continuing education. The first CEWs emerged in the early 1960s. Although by 1963 there were only about 20 such efforts, the Women's Bureau identified about 100 programs in 1966. In 1971, 376 institutions with special programs or services for adult women were listed with a brief description in *Continuing Education Programs and Services for Women.* However, research efforts by both Mattfeld (Note 2) and Mulligan (Note 3) have indicated that these programs vary considerably in quality and services. Mulligan received 190 responses to her survey of the 376 programs; 61 indicated no special services for mature women. She surmised the programs were included in the publication either because they offered courses of interest to women or courses at times convenient for women.

Continuing education programs for women have expanded rapidly. To a large extent, this expansion has resulted from the increasing numbers of women seeking employment, technological changes that have reduced housework, declining birth rates, longer life spans, rising living costs, and encouragement and support by the women's movement.

The literature highlights some of the characteristics of those in continuing education. Women who continue their education can be roughly divided into two groups: Those whose goal is a career or work and those whose goal is further education or a degree but not employment.

Women who need to work come to continuing education programs to gain or to update marketable skills. Some women have jobs but have discovered that without a college degree they have no opportunity for advancement. Also in continuing education are men and women who have been employed for a number of years and who are now preparing for midlife career changes. For the largest proportion of women in continuing education, family demands have decreased and work is an appealing prospect.

Non-career-oriented women are attracted to continuing education for various reasons. Generally, they wish to keep abreast of the advances in so many fields; rapid proliferation of knowledge has made an education a life-long endeavor. Precisely what motivates them to enter these programs?

Avocational interests often lead individuals to enroll in courses. Some women find they are bored; their children are in school or gone, their husbands have an active social life, and philanthropic activities no longer seem satisfying. For a few women, enrolling may serve as an excuse to refuse the community agencies trying to enlist their services or as a refuge from marital and family problems. Some women in degree programs left college to work or marry and now find that they can complete their degrees.

As women reenter the academic world, they are confronted with both personal problems and institutional barriers. The first problem a woman faces is how to go about returning to school or beginning a career. Another problem is the lack of confidence which a woman invariably feels after being out of school for some time, particularly if she has been a homemaker in the interim. She is apprehensive about taking notes, remembering material, using the library, and writing papers and exams. Afraid she will not be able to keep up with the 18-to-22 year-olds, she hesitates to enter competitive academic situations. Arranging a schedule to include both academic and household responsibilities is a problem for many women, particularly those with families. A return to college involves not only classes, but also library work and study, which all require a major time investment.

Guilt is another problem with which these women must cope. Because of an internalized concept of their primary role as wife and mother, they feel guilty about leaving their homes and families to undertake a time-consuming venture so personally fulfilling. Sometimes they feel selfish for neglecting their families or spending money that could have gone toward a family trip or the children's college educations.

CEWs were established by individuals who recognized that these problems were major impediments to women contemplating a return to college or work. The programs were developed to help women make the transition with a minimum of extraneous complications, as well as determine the direction they wished to take.

THE WOMEN AND THEIR FAMILIES

The women in continuing education programs vary a great deal in age, socioeconomic and marital status, religious background, and so forth. To view them only as adult middle-class women whose family responsibilities have been reduced so they can return to education for personal development would be shortsighted and quite erroneous. Unfortunately, colleges have often viewed these women as dilettantes who have come back to take a course here and there. They have not been considered persons who need to develop their talents so they can have greater access to occupations and support themselves or their families. The study included women who were young and single. Some were very poor, some had high educational attainment, and some had not completed high school. For example, among women enrolled during the past academic year, one-third were under age 30, with one in seven under 25. One in seven were also over 51 years of age. The women's educational level prior to entry varied: one in seven had never been to college while one in 10 had graduate degrees.

The women also differed in family status. Seventeen percent had never married while 15% were separated or divorced. About one-third were childless.

Education and Job Aspirations

What are the educational and occupational aspirations and plans of women in continuing education programs?

When asked why they sought continuing education, the women most often mentioned becoming more educated, achieving independence and a sense of identity, and preparing for a job. Job preparation was a much more important objective for single, separated, divorced, or widowed women than for married women.

A little less than half of the women were involved in some kind of academic or training program. Financial barriers seem to prohibit access to education. Women who indicated that their ability to finance their education was a major concern were less likely to be in a degree or certificate program.

Women in degree or certificate programs had come to continuing education because of job dissatisfaction. These women may have been in dead-end and low-paying jobs; thus, dissatisfaction with their status motivated them to seek further education and training to improve their occupational status. Certificate programs are usually intensive courses of short duration which provide training for paraprofessional jobs: e.g., legal assistant, assistant landscape architect, and counseling aide. Such programs permit women to get jobs without spending a lot of time in training. This preparation also provides for interim work experience before a woman makes a long term commitment. In an interview, one woman said, "I'll try the legal work. If I like it and feel competent in it, then I can consider the longer and more expensive training to become a lawyer."

In general, women in academic programs have a great sense of direction, feel independent, and have mapped out a plan of action. The continuing education program provides the means for them to reenter college and to work toward their goals without the usual obstacles of a regular program, i.e., admissions requirements, inflexible programming as to time and place, and restrictions on part-time study.

Occupational Status

At the time of the survey, over half of the women in the programs were also working. Of them, two-thirds were working full time. The majority of these were again in clerical, secretarial, and teaching jobs. Nearly half of all working women were making less than $10,000. Working women often utilized the program primarily to get information about career possibilities.

Whether a woman worked or not related to several independent factors;

being single, and for married women, being childless and having a husband with a relatively low income, were factors in her being employed.

Working women reported that their mothers worked while they were growing up, that their husbands approved of their working, and that they perceived themselves as independent. They held liberal views about the appropriate age for children before the mother returns to college or work, i.e., a mother's decision does not depend on a child's age.

For a married woman to work, unless she has an economic need, the conditions must be right. She must have had early experiences that socialized her to value independence. A working mother could have provided a model, as well as contributed to personal development and a sense of independence. The married woman also needs to feel that her husband supports her in her activities outside the home. Other important conditions are a childless marriage or children who have grown up.

Further analyses identified the characteristics of women who had a strong career orientation and of those who aspired to nontraditional fields. Career orientation was identified by an item in which women indicated the importance of a career to their personal fulfillment. The career-oriented women were more likely to aspire to careers in nontraditional areas for women, were more liberal in their views about age of children and mother's involvement outside the home, were more positive toward the women's movement, rated themselves high on intellectual self-confidence, and were more likely to be working and to have worked in the past. Career-oriented women were also more likely to have been discontent at home. However, their husbands approved of their working.

Benefits to Women and Families

How have the woman and the family been affected by the woman's return to college? What changes have taken place in these women, or their families, work, and interpersonal experiences and relationships? Have their lives changed and, if so, in what ways?

Overall, women see great benefits to themselves. Invariably, they feel increased self-awareness and self-esteem. They are more confident and open to new ideas and to a variety of new people. In open-ended interviews with more than 200 women, a question asked was, "In what way have you changed?" Here are some typical comments:

"The Program was a turning point for me. It showed me what was available. I had been vegetating while married. The program made a significant change in the direction of my life."

"I am not stupid. I lived with that image for 28 years. In the last 3 years that image has changed."

"It gave me my whole future. It kept me from a nervous breakdown. I thought after marriage had failed me I had nothing and I was very unsure of myself. The program has made me realize that there was more to the world than just my little bit of trouble."

The women also value the newly acquired knowledge and skills.

"I don't feel inadequate anymore. I can approach issues critically and evaluate things, situations properly."

"I really look forward to the mornings of school and to thinking about *just me.*"

"I like me better. I am more worthwhile, more realistic, honest."

Not only has their own self-respect increased, but their respect for other women has also grown. Of course, these two go hand-in-hand: A woman cannot like and respect herself as a woman unless she has positive feelings toward other women and vice versa.

Fewer than 3% of the women reported negative effects from continuing education: such as greater confusion or decreased self-confidence.

As to consequences for the family, the overall effects of continuing education were positive. Family members became more organized and self-reliant:

"The family has become closer."

"We interact to a greater extent."

"Marriage has improved."

"The children's respect for me has increased."

Of course, some women and their families experience some negative consequences, such as more tensions in the marital relationship or disapproval by neighbors.

Women's Self-Perceptions

What views do these women hold about themselves and their roles as wives, mothers, and workers?

In addition to motivation, self-concept is an important variable in a woman's decision to pursue higher education or to go to work. For some women who have been away from school for a long time and who were skilled in other than educational or occupational areas, the sense and acceptance of self are important determinants in whether they will venture outside the home.

Unfortunately, this study could not examine changes in the self-concept prior to the decision and entry into continuing education. Also, it could not compare these women with a group similar in other respects which opted to remain at home.

In responding to the question, "Where do you rate yourself on various traits compared to the typical woman of your age?", the women emerge with a positive self-image: at least one-fifth rated themselves in the highest 10% of their peers on effectiveness on the job, independence, academic ability, and drive to achieve. They rated themselves similarly on success as a mother and as a wife. Only four ability traits were consistently rated low: mathematical, athletic, artistic, and public speaking. Comparing the women's self-ratings with those of their spouses revealed differences on these self-ratings similar to those for college populations of men and women. In this study, the men's overall self-concept emerged higher than the women's.

More husbands than wives rated themselves high on self-confidence, leadership, job effectiveness, and public speaking and writing ability. More men also rated themselves higher on mental and emotional well-being and on physical stamina. Differences favored women on skills that relate to their family roles, i.e., success as a wife and mother, on physical attributes, such as appearance, and on popularity with men and women.

Self-perceptions differ from the perceptions of others. We asked the husbands to rate their wives on these traits. Even though the women rated themselves higher on physical appearance and on popularity than the men rated themselves, husbands tended to rate their wives even higher. The husbands also rated their wives higher than the women rated themselves on such competencies as mathematics ability, success as a wife and mother, and self-confidence. However, women rated themselves higher than their husbands rated them on drive to achieve, stamina, independence, mental and emotional well-being, and athletics. One wonders whether societal stereotypes indicating that these traits are not exhibited as often by women biased these men so they rated their wives in stereotypic ways.

In another analysis, we further estimated the actual agreement or disagreement between a husband's perceptions of his wife and the wife's self-ratings on each trait. Overall, husbands and wives disagreed quite extensively in perceptions. The most disagreement was over physical stamina (66%) and drive to achieve (66%) and the least disagreement was over physical appearance (45%).

In the analyses of education and occupational status and plans the most significant self-ratings were "independence," "intellectual self-confidence," and "leadership ability.". Whether these women were characterized by such traits all along and thus were able to make the break from wife and mother for education or a job, or whether work and recent educational involvement provided experiences that enhanced their self-concepts is hard to ascertain with these data. However, autonomy and self-confidence are important characteristics of career-oriented adult women who decide to pursue educational activities.

Effect of the Women's Movement

How do these adult women view the women's movement? What effect has the movement had on self-assessment, motivation, and clarification of interests and needs?

We asked the women if they had been affected by the women's movement and, if so, in what ways. Their responses from the most frequent to the least frequent were as follows:

Their most frequent response was "it increased my awareness of the various issues, e.g., equality of opportunity, pay, sex roles." (49%)

"It reinforced my views, encouraged me to do what I am doing." (24%)

"I have greater respect for and understanding of other women, including myself." (20%)

"I don't like the extremes of the women's movement."(5%)

"It interferes in the relationships with the opposite sex—is is antithetical to femininity."(3%)

To quote one woman, "The movement has made me aware that I am one of the untapped resources that should be utilized. This means both being given an opportunity and accepting a responsibility."

Another woman said: "The women's movement freed my potential. I realized I had leadership ability. For many years I felt I was a derailed train; now I am on the track."

Another one said, "Before I was not sure about women. I thought they were dull and sneaky, but now I have a high regard for them."

Sixty-nine percent of the women had raised their goals and had become more ambitious as a result of the women's movement: "I feel that I can go in any direction I want." Some women reported that the women's movement had made them feel restless and discontent or that their "marriage had been threatened or dissolved." Whether these outcomes can be viewed as positive or negative, it is hard to say; I am sure it depends on the individual case.

There is some disagreement between the women's and husband's views about how the wives have been affected by the movement. Even though some husbands indicated that their wives have gained self-awareness and increased their self-esteem, a greater proportion believe that their wives' traditional views have been reinforced and that their wives have no respect for aggressive feminists. Similarly, fewer indicated that their wives are more interested in encouraging girls to pursue all kinds of careers or to think girls should be able to join boys' organizations. One wonders to what extent their views and projections interfered with their perceptions of how their wives might actually have been affected by the movement.

A related question was whether the woman had been active in the women's movement. At least one-fifth said that they participated actively. Moreover, there were 7% who said they were members of national women's organizations (NOW, WEAL); 15% said they participated in consciousness-raising groups; 10% had participated in feminist meetings, conferences or demonstrations; 10% belonged to women's caucuses, coalitions or special commissions; and 20% had done community, legal, or political work on behalf of women.

Who were the active women and what were their demographic and personal characteristics? Women active in the movement had done volunteer work in the past. In essence, they had always had an interest in group activities and in "causes." *They were likely to have had group counseling. Their experience with counseling can be interpreted in several ways: on one hand, group counseling may have been important because it provided an opportunity to discuss and share problems, concerns, feelings, and views with other women. It could reflect that women who were searching for a self-identity and a new life style sought out counseling. On the other hand, women who have had a positive experience in counseling might be more likely to become active in the women's movement as a result of that experience. Some evidence supports this latter view, since the "active" women indicated that one outcome from their participation in the programs had been an increase in respect for other women.

The "active" women in the movement rated themselves high on academic ability and had received high grades in high school or college. They viewed their husbands as supportive; they had also had a working mother while growing up. The nonwhite women were most likely to be active in the women's movement.

Reaction of Husband and Family

How do husbands and children feel when the mother asserts herself outside the home? Are they supportive? Do they feel threatened?

A relatively large proportion of the women had been away from school for a long time—almost one-fourth of them for at least 11 years. Thus, the decision to return to academia and to prepare for a career or even to take courses for personal development is not only a new experience for the women but it also affects the whole family. She is satisfying herself not by concentrating on the family alone, but by doing things for herself. As one woman put it, "I really look forward to the mornings of school and to thinking about just me." This new view is bound to create a variety of feelings in the rest of the family. It is a new experience for them to see "mother" or "wife" excited about going to school, or to listen to her talking about her experiences as a student. She is a new person who feels more competent and knowledgeable.

The majority of husbands had positive feelings about their wives' activities. They saw the wife's new role as not only making her a happier, more actualized person, but also as benefiting the whole family intellectually and financially. Husbands believed that as wives increased their earning potential, they would assume part of the financial load. They also reported positive effects on the children, who became more independent and more willing to share household responsibilities. They also became more interested in their school work; mother as a student provided a role model for them.

Of course, apprehensions developed too. Some spouses thought that the marriage suffered and that there were more tensions in the family as a result of the wife's new involvement. In response to an open-ended question, "How do you think your wife's educational plans and/or future work will affect you?"

they indicated from the most frequent to the least frequent the following outcomes:

Make her happier, more fulfilled	92%
I'll benefit from her experience	74%
Improve our marriage; make it a better partnership	58%
Would lessen the burden on me to support the family	41%
Give us less time together	27%
Put strain on our marriage	10%
Make her restless	3%

Husbands realized that it was important for their wives to have a career in addition to the family. Thirty-four percent considered it essential for her fulfillment and another 30% said it was very important. Only 12% considered it unimportant. Moreover, a little over half the husbands believed that both husband and wife should share as breadwinners.

During the study, we interviewed 88 children—50 girls and 38 boys. Although they ranged from 9 to 31 years of age, the majority (73%) were under 18. Children's views about why their mother was going to college differed somewhat from the views of their fathers. Only 29% mentioned "personal growth," while 58% believed their mother went to college to prepare for or to get a better job. To a similar question, 58% of the husbands indicated "personal growth" and 38% to prepare for a job. One wonders whether these differential perceptions result from generational differences in values or whether the children receive different reasons from their mothers for interests outside the home. When I discussed these differences in perceptions, some women mentioned that it is easier to give practical reasons or reasons that indicate benefits to the total family than to give personal reasons—another outcome of the sex socialization process that reinforces the women's role to nurture.

The children unanimously agreed that their mothers were good students. To the question, "How have things changed around the house?" the two most frequent answers were: "I spend less time with her" and "I have more household chores." Few (between 6% and 9%) voiced any disapproval of their mother's working before, now, or in the future.

We asked the children 16 years or older what they might have done differently if they were in their mother's place with her life to live again. Sixty-one percent said that they would have lived differently: they would have gone to school earlier, had fewer children or spaced their children differently, asked their husbands to share more household responsibilities, or married later or not at all. All the responses reflect the known barriers to a woman's educational and occupational development: marriage and children.

If we were to ask the children the same question about their fathers, I would expect that marriage and children would not have been mentioned as barriers to their father's development or self-actualization. I would predict that the children would probably have mentioned aspects of the educational preparation or work and career activities.

SUMMARY

To summarize briefly the highlights of our empirical findings so far: women who participate in continuing education programs are an exceedingly diverse group that does not fit the stereotype of the bored housewife dabbling in a little culture. These women are serious, determined, and very frequently pragmatic in their goals. Those women who enter continuing education with a strong career orientation differ in many respects from the other participants: they express less traditional views about the role of women, are more supportive of the women's movement, and have more self-confidence. Although they are also more likely to be dissatisfied at home, their children and husbands are generally supportive of their work and educational activities. Practically all the women see their continuing education as being highly beneficial both personally and professionally. Many report profound changes in their self-concepts. Although only a minority of these women could be labelled activists, they are uniformly supportive of the women's movement and see it as a positive force in their lives.

Whereas the women's movement has given women the freedom to "be," continuing education has provided the support and training that adult women need to develop their talents and to acquire skills that enable them to enter or reenter the labor market. The same might be said about other campus efforts, such as women's studies, women's centers, and programmatic research.

The very existence of these programs provides a psychological boost to a woman considering venturing from her home. The programs are proof that she is not alone and that she will be meeting and attending classes with women in similar positions with similar concerns. The programs indicate that, as an adult, she can go to college or begin a career; others like her have done it successfully.

The programs offered by continuing education are strongly based on the job market and organized to develop skills for competent performance. Most provide skill-oriented courses, as well as liberal arts curricula, to meet the diverse needs and interests expressed by their clients. Counseling and career guidance play key roles in the educational process.

Time and place constraints have been greatly reduced by restructuring the delivery of courses from, for example, 50 minutes three times a week to a 3-hour sequence once a week, and by using available space in churches and schools to reduce transportation hassles. Admissions procedures and traditional performance criteria have been altered so they are more appropriate for adults.

While many colleges and universities have recognized the demand for continuing education and have developed programs, support is often qualified. The programs are frequently self-supporting rather than university financed; their existence depends on the income from the courses. While this arrangement is good in that a program must meet the needs of its audience to survive, it is unfortunate in that it necessitates a high price for courses and allows little funding for financial aid or program development. Moreover, the programs are not completely autonomous; they depend on the continued support of an administrator in the parent institution. Administrative favor and financial success are two key determinants of a program's continuation.

Continuing education programs for women clearly point out the need for institutional change. Colleges and universities must adopt a more flexible attitude to accommodate individual differences. They must relax nonessential academic regulations and requirements that do not apply to older women returning to school. These programs are in the forefront of higher education innovation, demonstrating how changes can be made with no sacrifice of educational quality. They have tried to remove structural and institutional barriers, as well as to alleviate some of the problems and concerns of the populations they serve. They deserve our support.

REFERENCE NOTES

1. Brim, O.G. Jr. *Selected theories of the male mid-life crises: A comparative analysis.* Paper presented at the meeting of the American Psychological Association, New Orleans, 1974.
2. Mattfeld, J.A. *A decade of continuing education: Dead end or open door.* Mimeographed, 1971.
3. Mulligan, K.L. *A question of opportunity: Women and continuing education.* 1973. (ED 081 323).

REFERENCES

Baruch, R. The achievement motive in women: Implications for career development. *Journal of Personality and Social Psychology,* 1967, *5,* 260-267.

Flavell, J. Cognitive changes in adulthood. In L.R. Goulet & P.B. Baltes (Eds.), *Lifespan developmental psychology.* New York: Academic Press, 1970.

Gass, J.R. Recurrent education—The issues. In *Recurrent Education.* Washington: National Institute of Education, 1973.

Johnstone, W.C., & Rivera, R.J. *Volunteers for learning: A study of the educational pursuits of American adults.* Chicago: Aldine Publishing Co., 1965.

Lowenthal, M.F., & Chiriboga, D. Social stress and adaptation: Toward a life-course perspective. In D. Eisdorfer & M.P. Lawton (Eds.), *Psychology of adult development and aging.* Washington: American Psychological Association, 1973.

Neugarten, B.L. Personality change in late life: A developmental perspective. In C. Eisdorfer & M.P. Lawton (Eds.), *Psychology of adult development and aging.* Washington: American Psychological Association, 1973.

Simon, A. Emotional problems of women—Mature years and beyond. *Psychosomatics,* 1968, *9,* 12-16.

Tough, A. *Why adults learn: A study of the major reasons for beginning and continuing a learning project.* Ontario: Ontario Institute for Studies in Education, 1968.

Women's Bureau, U.S. Department of Labor. *Continuing education programs and services for women.* Washington: U.S. Government Printing Office, 1971.

Women's Bureau, U.S. Department of Labor. *Continuing education for women: current developments.* Washington: U.S. Government Printing Office, 1974.

Strategies for Training Adult Counselors

ELINOR WATERS
SYLVIA FINK
JANE GOODMAN
GAIL PARKER
Continuum Center, Oakland University
Rochester, Michigan

ABSTRACT

Adult counselors can benefit from applied skill training to increase their effectiveness as helpers. This article outlines the eclectic training model developed to train paraprofessional counselors at the Continuum Center for Adult Counseling and Leadership Training. It then describes three major training approaches in use today: Carkhuff's Systematic Human Relations Training, Ivey's Microcounseling, and Kagan's Interpersonal Process Recall; and makes some comparisons among the four training models. The authors conclude that training for adult counselors must be designed so that trainees can identify their own strengths and add new skills to their existing repertoire.

The very existence of this book, *Counseling Adults,* serves to testify to the belief that normal adults, facing the crises and developmental tasks of adulthood, need and can benefit from specialized counseling. If adults are to get appropriate counseling, some adaptations will have to be made in the traditional content and methods of counselor education. Typically, counselor education trains people to deliver vocationally-oriented services to school-age populations or intensive psychotherapy to disturbed people of all ages. Further, such training usually takes place in formal academic and/or practicum settings. This article discusses several less academic approaches used to train counselors to work with adults in a variety of settings. While many of the programs described here were developed to train paraprofessionals, they can and have been used as additional training or "retooling" for

Partial support for this project was provided by the National Institute of Mental Health, Grant No. 3T21 MH 13313-031.

practicing professionals, or as a course or practicum experience in professional training programs.

In the following pages we will present the paraprofessional training program developed at the Continuum Center for Adult Counseling and Leadership Training. We will then briefly describe the more widely known training models developed by Carkhuff (1969a, 1969b, 1972), Ivey (1971, 1974; Ivey, Normington, Miller, Morrill, & Haase, 1968) and Kagan (1972), and discuss similarities and differences among the methods. We have selected these three approaches because they have been used successfully with a variety of adult populations and because information is available on their training methods.

All of the training models described here have some common elements. Although they are in no way atheoretical, they all focus on systematic ways to train helpers to deliver human services to their helpees. The very terms used, helper rather than counselor or therapist, helpee rather than client or patient, suggest that there are fewer differences in status and experiences between the providers and receivers of such services than in more traditional therapeutic approaches. Indeed many of the training models were developed to prepare counselors who are peers of their clientele; that is, indigenous to the populations they serve.

We have concentrated on models which are used to train counselors or helpers who work on a face to face basis with their clients (i.e., not in telephone crisis counseling) and who do affective counseling rather than merely disseminating information or making referrals. All of the models described here use a combined didactic-experiential approach and provide opportunities for trainees to practice the skills learned under supervision of teacher-trainers. All identify certain basic skills which facilitate the development of an empathic, genuine relationship between helper and helpee. The establishment of this basic trusting relationship is now generally considered a necessary but not sufficient step (to alter Rogers', 1957, phrase) in the helping process. A trusting relationship serves as the base upon which later initiative and action steps are built. While various models use different teaching strategies, they all attempt to train helpers who can listen to their helpees, help them identify the thoughts and feelings which underlie their situations, help them explore these feelings, and help them develop appropriate ways to deal with these situations.

THE CONTINUUM CENTER'S APPROACH TO COUNSELOR TRAINING

Before describing the training procedure we use it may be helpful to give some background on the Continuum Center for Adult Counseling and Leadership Training. Its counseling services, both individual and group, are designed to assist men and women in self-exploration, planning and decision-making. Most of the Continuum Center's counseling is done in small groups led by carefully selected and trained paraprofessionals. It is their selection and training which is the focus of this section.

Basic Beliefs

Some of our beliefs about working with adults effect the way in which we train. For example, we emphasize the role and impact of the counselor or helper as a person. This means that helpers must know how to recognize and accept their own feelings and use them appropriately, without imposing them on other people. Frequently we encourage them to consider their own motivations for wanting to help, as suggested by Danish and Hauer (1973). We also believe that in order to be effective helpers, trainees must experience the helping process as helpees. Being in the helpee or client role provides a different, more internalized view of the value of being heard, and of having their strengths and abilities affirmed. This is one of the reasons that participation in a personal growth group, prior to involvement in the training program, is an essential requirement for our trainees. Therefore, in our training we do not bring in outside clients or use hypothetical situations. Trainees take turns being helper and helpee. As helpees they are urged to share real problems or joys, not to play roles.

As a result of our belief that effective counseling is a learnable set of skills and not a mystical process, we try to make everything we do explicit. We give the rationale for activities we use; we describe the verbal and non-verbal behavioral cues on which we base our comments; and we make observations about group processes and norms as they occur, by highlighting interactions among trainers and trainees. Such an approach seems to communicate to the trainees the respect for their intelligence and life experience which we want them, in turn, to impart to their clients.

In our view, not everyone is capable of becoming an effective adult counselor, regardless of the amount of previous training. Therefore, our training program begins with a fairly rigorous procedure designed to screen *in* people with maximum counseling potential and screen *out* those people whose skill level and/or emotional problems might interfere with their ability to function well as counselors within our program.

Selection Procedure

Our paraprofessionals are selected from the client population; sometimes they are self-referred, more typically they are recommended by trained group leaders who see them as sensitive, perceptive, non-judgmental people who are capable of continued growth. In the selection procedure, prospective applicants are asked to write a statement on why they want to be a group leader and what they think they can contribute, to take a small battery of tests, and to participate in a group interview.

The test battery is made up of an adaptation of the Carkhuff Index of Discrimination (1969a, pp. 114-123), an incomplete sentences test, and a critical incident case study to which applicants give a written response. A brief word on the rationale for each of these measures: Carkhuff states as a basic principle of selection "The best index of a future criterion is a previous index of that criterion" (1969a, p. 85). Therefore in selecting potential helpers we look for people who seem to have some initial ability to select a helpful response. The incomplete sentences test is used primarily to screen out people whose personal problems might interfere with their being effective helpers. The critical incident case we present involves a typical situation in which a participant shares intense feelings of depression and frustration shortly before the group is scheduled to break up. In evaluating the responses we look for the extent to which the applicant is able to help the client identify and express feelings, whether or not (s)he deals with the time issue, mentions possible ways of clarifying or working on the problem before the next session, and whether or not (s)he takes note of the rest of the group in the response.

Our primary selection tool is a group interview. This is included to give applicants a sample of our approach to training as well as to enable us to observe how they function in a group situation. In a typical group interview, five or six applicants meet with two staff members. We explain that applicants will interview each other during the course of the session and that we are evaluating their potential helping skills, e.g., their ability to listen and respond to another person, to deal with feelings rather than "data," and to pursue the helpee's interests rather than their own. After the initial exchange, we ask questions of both the interviewer and the interviewee; e.g., what did you learn about this person? What did your helper do that you liked and did not like? We have found that the group interview enables us to assess listening skills, openness to feedback and willingness to take risks. Another criterion we look for in selecting trainees, as well as later in evaluating them, is the extent to which they function at a therapeutic rather than a social level, as suggested by Resnikoff (Note 1). Throughout the interview, trainers give feedback to applicants and encourage them to assess each other's performance. At the conclusion of the interview applicants are asked to set personal training goals for themselves and to predict how they might handle a possible letter of rejection. (Those applicants who are not included in the training are sent individual letters which explain the reasons for our decision and suggest ways in which they can make themselves ready to reapply at a later date, if this seems appropriate.)

Training Design

Our basic training is done in nine six-hour sessions, preferably on a two-day-per-week basis. Because of the highly personal nature of the training, participation is usually limited to 14 trainees. Two staff members work as co-trainers, sometimes assisted by an experienced Continuum Center paraprofessional. The first session is devoted to getting acquainted and goal setting activities and the last day to evaluating and assessing readiness to group lead. The format of the other seven sessions is generally similar, with systematic, cumulative skill practice in the mornings and videotaped small group sessions in the afternoons.

On the first day trainers welcome the group, explain the basic goals and format of the training, and provide a get-acquainted experience. The rest of the day is devoted to videotaping trainees as they engage in a four-minute helping interview. Trainees are paired and designated helper-helpee and each has an opportunity to be videotaped in each role. Helpees are asked to begin the encounter by sharing something about themselves that seems important to them (e.g., a current concern, their reactions to the experience of the morning, their feelings about the training), and helpers are asked to respond in any way they think would be helpful or appropriate. As the tapes are reviewed, trainees are asked to evaluate their own performance as helper and to use this evaluation as a basis for formulating goals for themselves. These behavioral goal statements are then used to develop a "contract" or agreement for each trainee specifying how they propose to work on their goal and how the rest of the group can help them. Another set of taping interviews is done on the last day of training so that the comparisons become a visual record of growth in helping skills, as well as an excellent research tool. More detail on this and other aspects of our evaluation procedure will come later in this article.

Systematic skill training. In our skills training we have adopted the basic format of the Carkhuff (1972) model discussed below. We systematically lead our trainees through the steps of attending, observing and reporting physical behavior of the helpees, repeating helpee statements verbatim, summarizing the gist of helpee statements and adding a feeling word, formulating a response which identifies the major feeling expressed by the helpee with a summary of the content of the helpee's statement, identifying themes in helpee statements and/or discrepancies between helpee's words and actions, and encouraging the helpee to plan action steps to improve his/her situation.

Trainers introduce each skill step by demonstrating an unhelpful and then a helpful example of the skill being taught. This modeling serves several purposes: it humanizes the trainers to have them work in front of the trainees; it is helpful and often amusing to see a poor example and to be able to analyze what makes it poor; and it provides trainees with a relatively clear idea of what is expected of them.

We encourage trainees to adapt the strictly defined model to their own personal styles so that the systematic training becomes an adjunct to their repertoire rather than dictating what must be done. We believe that in training adult counselors it is essential to respect and build upon their existing skills and values and not to assume that they start with a blank sheet.

As indicated above, we combine concentrated skill training in the mornings with simulated group meetings each afternoon of all sessions except the first and last.

Simulated groups. We have built the simulated groups into the training design for several reasons. They provide an opportunity for trainees to practice group leading and to apply the skills they learned in the mornings to a "real" group situation. As group members, trainees have an opportunity to work, albeit somewhat superficially, on some personal issues.

The procedure for each of the seven days is similar. At the end of the morning session trainers announce the names of the four people who will be working as leaders that afternoon. Trainers then meet with the designated leaders to go over the rationale and approach to the exercise they will lead, and to encourage co-leaders to plan ways of working effectively together. This brief meeting also serves as a model of the longer staff meetings for group leaders which precede all regular Continuum Center programs and are a central part of our ongoing supervision. All other trainees have some common experience (e.g., going on a "trust walk," doing a puzzle in groups of five, hearing a lecturette on a particular approach to interpersonal communications) and then an opportunity to discuss their feelings about the experience in a small group. The small group discussions are based on content materials from Continuum Center personal growth or career development programs. Each group, generally composed of five members and two leaders, works for 15 minutes while being videotaped by one of the trainers. After both groups have been taped, the entire videotape is replayed. We have found that the opportunity to see and hear oneself is an invaluable learning tool. In viewing the tapes, trainees can observe individual, dyadic, and group behavior, both verbal and non-verbal. Trainees can see and hear their responses, comment on their accuracy and effectiveness, and suggest alternative responses for themselves. They also get feedback from their peers, who have been members in the groups they led, and from trainers.

This broad range critiquing of the tapes enables trainers and trainees to comment on issues of timing or pacing of responses, to suggest the inclusion of other counseling techniques, and to underline the importance of open-ended questions, and of "what" and "how" rather than "why" questions. (For a discussion of the value of such questions see Benjamin, 1969.) Because of the value of positive reinforcement, trainers stop the tape and comment about effective interventions as well as ineffective ones.

The preceding sections describe the basic format of the Continuum Center training model, but they do not capture the flavor of the training groups. We try not only to teach a common core of skills but also to help trainees incorporate these skills into their personal styles. This means that some of the training time is devoted to helping trainees identify personal issues which may prevent them from fully attending or responding to a helpee with related problems. Trainees are also encouraged to become aware of their strengths and how these strengths can be used or abused.

Since most Continuum Center trainees will work in group settings, trainers highlight group dynamics issues as they arise. We comment on norms which have become established or which may be called into question, on ways of eliciting group support for a group member, and on developmental stages which groups experience. Gazda's (1971) discussion is very helpful here and we ask all trainees to become familiar with his schema.

Evaluation Procedure

As the Continuum Center training model is designed, evaluation is an ongoing process which starts with the selection procedure. Throughout the training program, trainees are evaluated by themselves, their peers and the trainers. While we put considerable emphasis on self-evaluation, trainees recognize that trainers make the final decision as to who may or may not group lead for the Center. Determination of readiness to group lead is based on both skill level and personal factors. With respect to the former, trainees must demonstrate that they have mastered the basic elements of the systematic skill training and have done an adequate job of leading the simulated small groups. On the personal level, they must demonstrate an ability to deal with their own feelings in a way that enhances rather than interferes with their group leading, and a receptivity to learning which includes a willingness to utilize feedback.

Self-evaluation begins when trainees are asked to formulate their own goals in behavioral terms at the first session and continues throughout the program. The motivating value of encouraging students to identify their own educational needs and evaluate their own progress seems particularly relevant in working with an adult population. Support for the importance of the ability to evaluate one's own performance is found in Martin and Gazda (1970). Their study indicated that counselor self-evaluation of live counseling sessions correlated highly with supervisor evaluations. We try to highlight the importance of self-evaluation in several ways. After each simulated group session we ask those who have been group leaders to evaluate their own performance before getting feedback from group members or trainers. Similarly, at the first and last sessions involving one-to-one helping interviews, self-evaluation by the helper precedes evaluation by the helpee, peers, or trainers.

Establishing an atmosphere of group trust and mutual cooperation is essential if constructive peer evaluation is to be given. We try to encourage this cooperation by asking each trainee at the first session not only to formulate personal goals, but also to consider ways in which the group might help facilitate these goals. A list of every trainee's goals and contracts is compiled, duplicated, and given to the entire group so they can remind each other of progress or setbacks in working toward their stated goals.

As indicated above, the entire last day of the training is devoted to evaluation. In preparation for that session trainees write answers to four questions: (1) What did I learn in this training program? (2) How did I do on my personal agenda? (3) How do I assess my readiness to group lead? (4) On what further issues or skills do I want to work? When they arrive at the session they are asked to conduct another four-minute helping interview, with the same helpee they interviewed at the first session. Again, helpees are asked to make an initial statement and helpers to respond in any way they think would be helpful. After all interviews are videotaped, the tape made at the first session is played in its entirety and trainees are asked to take notes on their own interviews. Then the follow-up interviews are replayed one at a time. After each interview, trainees are asked to compare their pre and post interviews, to read the self-evaluations they did as homework, and solicit feedback from peers and trainers. Trainers indicate to each trainee whether or not they think (s)he is ready to group lead. Because of the emphasis on ongoing evaluation, trainee's assessments of their own readiness to group lead are usually consistent with the trainers' evaluations. If trainers believe a trainee is not ready to group lead, they make specific suggestions as to how he or she can work on skills or personal development. While the focus of discussion of changes from the pre-interview to the post-interview is usually on the helper, evidences of helpee growth frequently also emerge, which tend to be very affirming for both trainers and trainees.

As the preceding section shows, the Continuum Center training model combines systematic skill training and practice in leading small groups with considerable attention to interpersonal relationships. The model is designed to prepare paraprofessional counselors to lead semi-structured personal growth groups for relatively healthy adults.

THREE MAJOR APPROACHES TO TRAINING ADULT COUNSELORS

As previously indicated, this portion of the article will briefly discuss the widely used training models of Carkhuff, Kagan and Ivey. Each section will include a brief statement on the derivation of the model, its philosophical base, goals and methods, and some examples of groups with which it has been used. Following these descriptions, we will compare these methods with one another and with the training model of the Continuum Center.

Systematic Human Relations Training

The ground work for Systematic Human Relations Training (SHRT) was laid by Carl Rogers (1957) who identified empathy, genuineness, and unconditional positive regard as the "necessary and sufficient conditions" for client growth. Building on this foundation, Truax and Carkhuff (1967) developed an integrated didactic-experiential approach to training counselors that taught them to communicate the core conditions of interpersonal effectiveness.

In an effort to further systematize counselor training, Carkhuff (1969a, 1969b, 1971, 1972) refined and elaborated on his work with Truax. He identified the core conditions of therapeutic relationships and categorized them under two headings: the facilitative and the action dimensions. The facilitative dimensions are empathy, respect, warmth and concreteness; the action dimensions are genuineness, self-disclosure, confrontation and immediacy. Carkhuff also described verbal and non-verbal counselor behaviors which communicate these conditions; e.g., interchangeable responses and attending behavior. In addition, he specified the following developmental stages which make up the helping process. As the helper communicates empathy, respect, and warmth, the helpee engages in self-exploration. As the helper continues to show empathy, respect and warmth, while beginning to communicate appropriate levels of specificity, genuineness, self-disclosure and confrontation, the helpee reaches a level of self-understanding. Once a relationship has been established, the helper begins to communicate high levels of immediacy and confrontation which facilitates the helpee in taking constructive action steps. This process is recycleable, and ultimately the helper teaches the helpee to be an effective helper who in turn can use this process.

Another basic point made by Carkhuff is that the level of trainer functioning is crucial to the learning of helping skills since the trainers serve as models for trainees. In his view, training, like helping, can be for better or for worse, as trainees move in the direction of their trainer's functioning, just as helpees approach the level of their helpers.

It is by specifying the verbal and behavioral qualities needed to communicate the core conditions, and by defining the helping process developmentally that Carkhuff made the counseling process teachable. His SHRT model teaches the specific skills involved in counseling, one at a time, with each skill building on previous learnings so that ultimately the skills are integrated.

In the first phase of helping, trainees are taught to build a solid relationship base with the helpee. They are taught to emphasize the facilitative dimensions of empathy, respect and warmth in building this base. Initially trainees learn to use attending behavior (e.g., facing the client, maintaining eye contact) and non-judgemental listening as ways of communicating the facilitative conditions. Next, prospective helpers are taught to observe the helpee's physical behavior. They are then taught to make responses that are interchangeable with those of the helpee by reflecting both the content and the feelings of helpee's statements. This level of response does not add to, nor detract from, what the helpee communicates; it conveys clear understanding. Such a response is considered minimally facilitative as it lays a base on which deeper levels of trust are built.

Once an interchangeable base of communication has been firmly established, the helpee will begin to reach plateaus of self-exploration and understanding. It is at this point that the helper will need to formulate what Carkhuff calls additive responses, which encourage the helpee to move to deeper levels of self-exploration. To enable them to make such responses, trainees are taught to implement the action dimensions of concreteness, genuineness and self-disclosure. Sometimes an additive response takes the form of confrontation; that is, pointing out discrepancies between what the helpee wants to do or say and what the helpee is in fact doing or saying.

The final goal of helping is action. Carkhuff has identified several important principles for encouraging helper action (1969a, p. 243). The helper must check with the helpees at all stages of development to be sure that the goals are attainable. In order to facilitate action, helpers are taught to use confrontation and immediacy; i.e., responses which identify interaction between the helpee and helper as they occur.

SHRT is a flexible model and can be modified to meet the needs of a variety of programs. It has been used to train nurses (Kratchovil, 1969), community volunteers (Pierce, Carkhuff & Berenson, 1967), prison guards (Megothlin & Porter, 1969), hospital volunteers (Carkhuff & Truax, 1965), parents (Carkhuff & Bierman, 1970), teachers (Hefele, 1971) and psychiatric inpatients (Pierce & Drasgow, 1969).

Microcounseling

Ivey's approach to training counselors developed out of a desire to teach counselors to demonstrate empathy, respect and warmth through directly observable counselor behaviors. These behaviors are defined in terms of specific response categories and are taught through a series of mini-interviewing situations. Ivey (1974) calls this microcounseling.

Ivey has identified four major skill areas which an effective counselor must have, and a schema to teach them sequentially. The first or basic category of beginning skills includes attending behavior, open invitations to talk and minimal "encourages" to talk. The trainee is taught to show interest and caring by maintaining eye contact, assuming a relaxed, attentive posture and following the verbal expressions of the client. Trainees are also taught to ask open-ended questions and to give non-verbal signs of encouragement. The second group of skills are called selective listening skills, and include reflection and summarization of feeling, paraphrasing, and the summative paraphrase. To acquaint them with this skill, trainees are taught to pay attention to affective verbal and behavioral expressions made by clients, and to rephrase client's words in a way that clarifies meaning for the client. In "the summative paraphrase . . . the interviewer attends to and reflects back to the client the essence of a larger section of the interview" (1971, p. 62). The third category involves counselor self-disclosure. To encourage more openness on the part of the helpee and to foster deeper levels of helpee self-exploration, helpers are taught to share relevant personal feelings and information. The fourth set of skills, which are broader and more complex than the other three, are those of interpretation. In order to successfully interpret, counselors must not only be able to attend, listen to their clients, and express themselves clearly, but also be able to provide their clients with a new frame of reference. In training, counselors are taught to free themselves from a particular discipline and to give a variety of alternative interpretations to a client statement.

The training model as described by Ivey (1974) consists of the following steps. A five minute counseling session between a volunteer client and a counselor/trainee is videotaped. (The client may be either a student volunteer or an actual client.) The trainee then receives written materials describing the skill being taught, and video models of an expert interviewer demonstrating the skill. Trainees also view the videotape of their first counseling session and get feedback from supervisors. Following this, a second five-minute counseling session is videotaped and reviewed by trainees and supervisors. If a trainee has not mastered the skill being taught, the procedure is repeated as the model is predicated on the assumption that trainees cannot progress until they have demonstrated mastery of previous skills. Ivey estimates that the counsel-recounsel session takes approximately one hour, and that a repeat, if necessary, adds another 30 to 40 minutes to the process. One of the most important aspects of the microcounseling paradigm is the use of video feedback which, by isolating and highlighting certain aspects of behavior, helps trainees to concentrate on and master one skill at a time.

Microcounseling was originally developed to train professional counselors and therapists (Ivey, et al., 1968), but it has also been shown to be an effective tool with other populations in various settings. It has been used to train paraprofessional counselors (Haase & DiMattia, 1970); parents as drug counselors (Gluckstern, 1973); camp counselors (Zeevi, 1970); undergraduate psychology students (Ivey & Hinkle, 1968); junior high school students (Aldridge, 1971) and medical students (Moreland, Ivey & Phillips, 1973).

Interpersonal Process Recall

The Interpersonal Process Recall (IPR) procedure is another form of training that employs videotaped feedback extensively as a training tool. Kagan and his associates (1967) originally developed this procedure to help clients better understand themselves; it was then broadened and modified to train paraprofessionals. Rather than teaching discrete skills, Kagan focuses on training the helper to understand the helper-helpee interaction and the effect each has on the other. He believes that while certain skills are important to effective counseling and can be taught directly, such training is only a part of counseling effectiveness. Proponents of IPR believe that an individual's personality dynamics and feelings enter into the counseling process and either facilitate or interfere with that process. To this extent, IPR helps trainees identify the underlying dynamics involved in their interpersonal interactions with clients for the purpose of identifying blocks they may have in their counseling with others. Another goal of the training is to teach students a process for supervising themselves so they may continue to grow independently after the training is over.

IPR is divided into a sequence of learning experiences. The first training unit involves the presentation of some basic skills which are called response modes. Salient characteristics of therapeutic responses are shown on videotape, e.g., affective vs. cognitive responses, open-ended vs. closed questions, direct vs. indirect responses, concrete vs. abstract responses. Trainees are taught how to use these response modes appropriately and are then given an opportunity to practice them by responding to videotaped client statements.

The next unit involves the use of stimulus films which are designed to provoke trainee reactions. Trainees are told to imagine that they are counseling the person on the screen. The issues raised by the film are ones which are often bothersome to beginning counselors; e.g., fear of rejection by clients, fear of approaching clients, or fear of hostility. Trainees are encouraged to talk about their reactions to these films, using the kinds of responses they learned in the first unit of the training. These stimulus films serve several purposes. Trainees begin to identify possible blocks they have in counseling others, and have a chance to practice using the response modes previously learned. In addition, they have an opportunity to talk about their own feelings and thus experience being a counselee.

The next major sequence involves the use of three types of video feedback situations: counselor replay, client replay, and mutual recall with both counselor and client present. Real clients or trainee "clients" can be used. This segment involves a specific type of semi-structured feedback that is unique to IPR.

In the first replay situation, the focus is on the counselor's experience during the client-counselor interaction, and its effects on the counselor. Following the taping of a brief counseling session, the videotape is replayed with the counselor and supervisor present. The supervisor assumes the role of inquirer, rather than critic, and encourages trainees to stop the tape to discuss any thoughts, feelings or images they may have had during the session which they did not share with their clients.

In the next replay situation, the focus is on the client's experience during the previously taped counseling session. The supervisor and the client review the tape while the trainee views this recall session from another room. The counselor/trainee thus hears valuable feedback about the thoughts and feelings the client had during the session and how the client responded to him or her.

In the third replay situation the counselor and the client review the tape together. The supervisor encourages the counselor/trainee and the client to respond to parts of the videotape with the thoughts and feelings they did not share during the counseling session. Hopefully, during this segment both trainees and clients gain additional learnings about themselves and their characteristic ways of interacting.

Throughout this replay process, students are taught to carry out the role of inquirer with each other. In this way they begin to learn to evaluate and supervise themselves and each other. They also gain practice in assertive and confronting behavior which may be useful in counseling.

IPR is a flexible training model which has been used in combination with microcounseling techniques as well as in conjunction with systematic human relations training. It has been used to train resident hall assistants (Dendy, 1971), practicum students (Bradley, 1974), undergraduate students who will teach interpersonal communications skills (Archer & Kagan, 1974) and police cadets (Danish & Brodsky, 1970).

SOME COMPARISONS AMONG THE FOUR TRAINING MODELS

By way of summary, we will highlight some of the similarities and differences in the approaches of Systematic Human Relations Training, Microcounseling, Interpersonal Process Recall, and the Continuum Center model. All of the training programs have an experiential rather than didactic emphasis, which involves systematic skill practice instead of lectures, term papers, and final examinations. In each model the instructor, who is usually called a trainer or supervisor rather than a professor, introduces the trainees to functional helping skills in a sequential manner. Each of these skills is separately demonstrated, in person or on videotape. As part of the skill development, trainees are sensitized to their own as well as their clients nonverbal behavior. In addition to learning how to "read" and use the body cues of their clients, trainees are taught ways of conveying receptivity through eye contact, relaxed body postures, etc. In order to learn each skill, trainees do varying amounts of practicing with each other or a client, and receive immediate feedback from trainers, fellow trainees and/or themselves. The immediacy of feedback is a critical part of these functional training approaches.

Because of the focus on systematic skill development rather than on a psychodynamic theory, all of the training programs can be used across a variety of theoretical approaches. Listening skills, for example, are equally essential for a behavior therapist or a client-centered counselor.

All of the models can be scheduled on a short-term basis as either pre-service or in-service training, and all rely, to varying degrees, on video and audio-tape equipment. While the acquisition of the skills clearly requires that the trainees function well cognitively, as well as affectively, in none of the models is it necessary for trainees to have formal preparation in one of the helping professions.

Along with the similarities, there are differences among the training models which make each unique. Part of the difference lies in the aspect of the helping relationship that is emphasized in each approach. In Carkhuff's SHRT program, the emphasis is on the systematic delivery of facilitative and action-oriented helping skills in a step-by-step prescribed manner. In his microcounseling paradigm, Ivey, like Carkhuff, emphasizes the acquisition of a systematic set of skills. However, he gives more attention than does Carkhuff to the individuality of each counselor, including teaching appropriate ways to use self-disclosure. Kagan's IPR approach differs considerably from SHRT and Microcounseling. Although Kagan teaches specific skills, his primary focus is on helping trainees to understand their own personality dynamics and feelings, and the nature of the interactions between counselor and client in the counseling relationship. The Continuum Center model has a dual emphasis on skill training and the understanding of inter- and intra-personal dynamics. Continuum Center trainees differ from those of the other models in that they are required to have had prior experience as a member of a personal growth group. While many of the trainees in the other programs may have participated in counseling groups, it is not a prerequisite for them.

Carkhuff's training and that of the Continuum Center is done in a small group format. However, Carkhuff gives less emphasis to exploring and using the issues that arise among group members. Such emphasis is important to Continuum Center trainees because they will be working as group, rather than individual, counselors. Ivey and Kagan focus more on dyadic counselor-client relationships than on group interactions.

There are differences, too, in the role of the trainer in each of the models. The SHRT trainer is expected to function at the level of performance to which trainees aspire, just as counselors are expected to set the level for clients. Hopefully, trainers and counselors function as teachers, since Carkhuff sees therapy as training. Ivey assigns a flexible role to trainers, using them to teach skills, to help process video-tapes and to serve as on-the-spot consultants during breaks in actual counseling sessions. Continuum Center trainers model counseling behaviors by demonstrating specific skills, as well as by making therapeutic interventions with trainees when appropriate. Center trainers also provide ongoing evaluation of skill practice and videotaped group leading performances. Kagan utilizes trainers as inquirers who assist counselors and clients, individually and together, to recall the thoughts and feelings they had during their videotaped counseling exchange. In the role of inquirer, the trainer is non-judgmental, focusing on the experience of the people, rather than the correctness of the counselor's interventions.

As mentioned above, all of the training models utilize immediate and ongoing feedback. However, there are differences in their approaches to evaluation. In SHRT, trainees are taught a systematic numerical rating scale for giving each other feedback on the accuracy of their counseling responses. In the microcounseling paradigm, progress is evaluated at each step of the skill training, as trainees are not permitted to proceed to succeeding skill until they have mastered prior ones. Kagan gives considerable weight to self-evaluation and teaches trainees a process of self-supervision. The Continuum Center model utilizes self-evaluation, peer evaluation and trainer evaluation. However, these evaluation procedures are less structured than those of the other models.

WHAT'S AHEAD IN THE TRAINING OF ADULT COUNSELORS?

A number of factors are currently operating which should lead to a demand for increasing numbers of well trained adult counselors. As mid-life career changes, as well as dramatic shifts in family structure, become more common and more widely discussed, adults seem to be more willing to ask for help. This increased receptivity of adults has fortunately come at a time when some new approaches to counselor training have appeared. The training strategies described in this article involve selecting and evaluating counselors on the basis of their interpersonal relationships and demonstrated ability to be helpful, rather than on the basis of test scores or grade point averages. Such an orientation to training is likely to produce counselors who can relate well to adult clients. However good adult counselors need more than the ability to relate well to their peers or to other adults. Hopefully they will also be familiar with some principles of adult development, as well as knowledgeable about vocational development theory and familiar with sources of occupational and educational information. Perhaps some day we can achieve a blending of the best elements of more broadly and theoretically based university courses with short term applied skill training.

REFERENCE NOTE

1. Resnikoff, A. *Interpersonal process recall: A method for training paraprofessionals in helping interaction skills.* Paper presented at the meeting of the American Psychological Association, New Orleans, 1974.

REFERENCES

Aldridge, E. *The microtraining paradigm in the instruction of junior high school students in attending behavior.* Unpublished doctoral dissertation. University of Massachusetts, 1971.

Archer, J. Jr. & Kagan, N. Teaching interpersonal relationship skills on campus: A pyramid approach. *Journal of Counseling Psychology,* 1974, *20*(6), 535-540.

Benjamin, A. *The helping interview.* Boston: Houghton Mifflin Co., 1969.

Bradley, F. O. A modified interpersonal process recall technique as a training model. *Counselor Education and Supervision.* 1974, *14*(1), 34-39.

Carkhuff, R. R. *Helping and human relations. Volume I: Selection and training.* New York: Holt, Rinehart and Winston, 1969a.

Carkhuff, R. R. *Helping and human relations. Volume II: Practice and research.* New York: Holt, Rinehart and Winston, 1969b.

Carkhuff, R. R. *The development of human resources.* New York: Holt, Rinehart and Winston, 1971.

Carkhuff, R. R. *The art of helping.* Amherst, Mass.: Human Resources Development Press, 1972.

Carkhuff, R. R. & Bierman, R. Treatment of parents of emotionally disturbed children. *Journal of Counseling Psychology,* 1970, *17,* 157-161.

Carkhuff, R. R. & Truax, C. B. Lay mental health counseling: The effects of lay group counseling. *Journal of Counseling Psychology,* 1965, *29,* 426-431.

Danish, S. J. & Brodsky, S. L. Training of policemen in emotional control and awareness. *American Psychologist,* 1970, *25,* 368-369.

Danish, S. J. & Hauer, A. L. *Helping skills.* New York: Behavioral Publications, 1973.

Dendy, R. F. *A model for the training of undergraduate residence hall assistants as paraprofessional process recall.* Unpublished doctoral dissertation, Michigan State University, 1971.

Gazda, G. M. *Group counseling: A developmental approach.* Boston: Allyn and Bacon, Inc., 1971.

Gluckstern, N. Training parents as drug counselors in the community. *Personnel and Guidance Journal,* 1973, *51,* 676-680.

Haase, R. & DiMattia, D. The application of the microcounseling paradigm to the training of support personnel in counseling. *Counselor Education and Supervision,* 1970, *10,* 16-22.

Hefele, T. J. The effects of systematic human relations training upon students. *Journal of Research and Development in Education,* 1971, *4,* 52-69.

Ivey, A. E. *Microcounseling: Innovations in interviewing training.* Springfield, Ill.: C. C. Thomas, 1971.

Ivey, A. E. Microcounseling and media therapy: State of the art. *Counselor Education and Supervision,* 1974, 14, 172-183.

Ivey, A. E. & Hinkle, J. Students, the major untapped resource in higher education. *Reach,* 1968, *6,* 1-4.

Ivey, A. E., Normington, C., Miller, C., Morrill, W., & Haase, R. Microcounseling and attending behavior: An approach to prepracticum counselor training. *Journal of Counseling Psychology,* 1968, *15*(5, Pt. 2).

Kagan, N. *Influencing human interaction.* East Lansing, Mich.: Michigan State University, Colleges of Education and Human Medicine, 1972.

Kagan, N., Krathwohl, D. R., et al. *Studies in human interaction: Interpersonal process recall stimulated by videotape.* Educational Publications Services, College of Education, Michigan State University, East Lansing, Michigan, 1967.

Kratchovil, D. Changes in values and interpersonal functioning of nurses in training. *Counselor Education and Supervision,* 1969, *8,* 104-107.

Martin, D. G. & Gazda, G. M. Method of self-evaluation for counselor education utilizing the measurement of facilitative condition. *Counselor Education and Supervision,* 1970, *10,* 87-92.

Megothlin, W. L. & Porter, T. *The effects of facilitation training provided correctional officers stationed at the Atlanta Federal Penitentiary.* Washington, D. C.: U. S. Justice Dept., 1969.

Miller, J. *Microcounseling* (Personnel services review, Series 1). Ann Arbor, Mich.: ERIC Counseling and Personnel Services Information Center, 1970.

Moreland, J., Ivey, A. E. & Phillips, J. An evaluation of microcounseling as an interviewing training tool. *Journal of Clinical and Consulting Psychology,* 1973, *41,* 294-300.

Pierce, R. & Drasgow, J. Teaching facilitative interpersonal functioning to psychiatric inpatients. *Journal of Counseling Psychology,* 1969, *16,* 295-298.

Pierce, R., Carkhuff, R. R. & Berenson, B. G. The differential effects of high and low functioning counselors upon counselors in training. *Journal of Clinical Psychology,* 1967, *23,* 212-215.

Rogers, C. R. The necessary and sufficient conditions of psychotherapeutic personality change. *Journal of Consulting Psychology,* 1957, *21,* 95-103.

Truax, C. B. & Carkhuff, R. R. *Toward effective counseling and psychotherapy: training and practice.* Chicago: Aldine, 1967.

Zeevi, S. *Development and evaluation of a training program in human relations. TEA: Training for effective attending.* Unpublished doctoral dissertation, University of Massachusetts, 1970.

The Lifetime Learning Act: Proposed Legislation

WALTER F. MONDALE

Vice President of the United States

ABSTRACT

A multigenerational examination of learning needs is discussed in terms of proposed legislation which encourages the expansion of lifetime learning options for all citizens.

We have stretched the borders of the life span of the average American . . . from 47.9 years for men in 1900 to 69.5 years for men today; and from 51.1 years for women in 1900 to 75.8 years today.

We have provided a measure of financial security to some 28 million old people in this country through the Social Security system . . . and have tried to cushion those benefits against inflation by requiring them to increase with the cost of living.

Excerpts of remarks delivered at The Center for Research in the Human Aging, Hunter College, New York, April 16, 1975, when Vice President Mondale was the U.S. Senator from Minnesota.

And nearly 22 million Americans now can count on Medicare to help alleviate the health problems of their later years.

We now have zero population growth at one end of the spectrum . . . and a rapidly increasing number of older adults at the other end. This demands that our perception of the whole cycle of human life undergo a radical change. Bernice Neugarten (1975) has coined a useful phrase—the "young old"—to describe what is really a new population group which deserves our attention. These are the people between 55 and 75 years old. As a group, they are getting healthier, and more educated. Many of them are technically retired. But they will increasingly demand more options for personal growth and community service. We have an obligation to provide opportunities to make the existence of Americans of every age meaningful.

I am personally excited and encouraged by a new movement which seems to address many of these needs we are discussing . . . the movement toward "lifetime learning." This is the idea that all of us . . . regardless of age . . . encounter throughout our lives a series of changing demands . . . and that we must shape education in its broadest sense to help us meet these needs.

At one stage of life, the need may be for retraining for a new job; at another stage we may require civic education—how to do our taxes, how to influence the political process. And at another time we may require education for what one distinguished educator has called "the free self"—that part of us and of our time which is not beholden to a job or to other requirements of subsistence.

One of the focal points for this movement toward lifetime learning is my home state of Minnesota. Right now an extraordinary coalition of institutions and individuals is working to build what it is calling an "intergenerational learning society." They have received a little money from the Administration on Aging to move the idea ahead . . . but most of the energy has been generated by committed individuals such as former vice president and dean of Gustavus Adolphus College, Dan Ferber. One of the reasons this idea has progressed is that, for the first time in many years . . . we seem to have educational resources—teachers, dormitories, laboratories— which are not being fully used. These facilities . . . belonging to the University, others in the public schools or private colleges . . . have become a focal point for the "learning society" in Minnesota.

Here are some of the things that are going on:

1. The University is training a corps of personnel in geriatrics and adult education for older persons.
2. Mankato State College has trained volunteers to identify older people in the community and . . . in cooperation with other community resources . . . help provide them with services and activities they seek.
3. The College of St. Benedict is moving older adults right into the dormitories with younger students.
4. The St. Paul Area Technical Vocation Institute is training geriatric assistants for work in nursing homes.

5. The North Hennepin Community College has a "Seniors on Campus" program.
6. The Minneapolis Public Schools have provided facilities and helped organize 33 clubs providing education and other programs for senior citizens.

Planners for the "Minnesota Learning Society" are thinking creatively about the use of other community resources—everything from department stores and churches to banks—as sources of information and education for citizens of all ages. And they have been working closely with many out of state groups on plans for future cooperative efforts.

I will admit that this idea is not the exclusive property of Minnesotans. For example, France, Germany and Belgium all provide paid educational leave for workers. This program is financed through a system of contributions from both employers and employees. In Syracuse, New York, there is an innovative "Regional Learning Service" which helps adults identify their educational needs and goals, counsels them, and identifies the educational resource which can be most helpful to them. And you are probably aware of similar programs that have not come to my attention.

This is a time of severe economic pressures. These pressures are being felt by millions of Americans. We have been constantly aware of them in our recent work on the new Senate Budget Committee. But I sincerely hope that these pressures will not prevent us from moving ahead and trying to act on some promising, hopeful ideas such as the concept of "lifetime learning."

I hope that somewhere in our massive educational establishment in Washington we can start to develop the capability of working toward this goal. We have incredible resources in HEW, in the Administration on Aging, in the National Institute of Education. And I intend to introduce legislation soon which would try to focus some of these resources . . . to encourage some experimentation and some research . . . toward the growth of our country into a "lifetime learning society." The bill has not been drafted yet, and I hope that you will come to us with your ideas on the best way to do it. The concept would be to introduce a "Lifetime Learning Act" which could become a part of the extension of major higher education and vocational education legislation over the next few months.

My bill will establish a program on lifetime learning which would:

1. Coordinate existing efforts in this area by all Federal agencies; and collect and make available information on programs and activities in the public and private sectors.
2. Support research and demonstration projects designed to further lifetime learning.
3. Provide support for training teachers to work with adults; curriculum development; conversion of facilities to accommodate adults; and development and dissemination of television, cassettes and other media appropriate for adult education.
4. Conduct a study of the existing barriers to lifetime learning and how they might be eliminated.

5. Evaluate existing programs—including methods of financing— in this country and abroad and determine whether they can be used as models.

This is a modest beginning but I think it is an important one. Our adjustment to longer life and greater leisure is not going to be an easy one . . . and we owe it to ourselves to make these added days and months productive and stimulating for all of us.

Note: At this time, the bill has been introduced and incorporated into the Higher Education Amendment in the Senate.

REFERENCE

Neugarten, B. The rise of the young-old. *New York Times,* January 18, 1975, p. 29.

Mini-Reviews of Books on Mid-Life

DANIEL SINICK

George Washington University

ABSTRACT

Recent books relevant to the counseling of adults are here briefly reviewed. Relevance was interpreted to eliminate books dealing solely with the years beyond mid-life. Recency is used to include books from 1972 on. These reviews do not cover the entire universe of relevant books, but a world of information awaits psychologists concerned with counseling adults.

Quality of Life; The Middle Years by American Medical Association. Publishing Sciences Group, 411 Massachusetts Avenue, Acton, Massachusetts 01720. 1974. 175pp.

This is the second of three volumes (Vol. I: The Early Years, Vol. III: The Later Years) resulting from three AMA-sponsored "congresses," and contains papers presented orally, some followed by moderated discussion. Unevenly organized, the five parts plus the appendix of "selected papers from Congress I" cover such topics as personal and societal values, roles as workers and parents, and marital crises. Some more masterful than others, authors include Masters and Johnson, Martin Marty, Bernice Neugarten, Lee Salk, and Harvey Wheeler. Scattered shots that hit pertinent targets.

The Coming of Age by Simone de Beauvoir. G.P. Putnam's Sons, 200 Madison Avenue, New York 10016. 1972. 585 pp.

A towering intellectual brings perceptive perspective and literary skill to a vital topic too often treated with little vision and less life. Must aging and dying be dealt with in deadly fashion? Simone de Beauvoir's big book throbs throughout with a sense of the urgency to understand aging and—simply— with sense. Declaring that "old age can only be understood as a whole: it is not solely a biological, but also a cultural fact," she presents material from many sources on both aspects, together with appendices that include one on "sexuality of old people."

Aging and Behavior: A Comprehensive Integration of Research Findings by Jack Botwinick. Springer Publishing Company, 200 Park Avenue South, New York 10003. 1973. 326 pp.

Though oriented to age 65 and up, the book's twenty short and punchy chapters offer plenty of content with implications for earlier ages. Biological, psychological, social, environmental, and sexual factors are covered, as well as simple vs. multidimensional rigidity, cautiousness, memory retrieval, intelligence and problem solving, learning and performance, and operational and conceptual issues in research.

The Psychology of Adult Development and Aging edited by Carl Eisdorfer and M. Powell Lawton. American Psychological Association, 1200 Seventeenth Street, N.W., Washington, D.C. 20036. 1973. 718 pp.

Readers who feel remiss in regard to knowledge of adult development may be reassured by much of this book. Though authored by notables, it is notably modest in its general assessment of the current state of knowledge. One author agrees with another "on the primitive state of knowledge of adult personality," while one editor admits "there is no clinical psychology of old age," despite the use of that term to title a major section of the book. These readings nevertheless constitute a mine of information.

Americans in Middle Years: Career Options and Educational Opportunities edited by Alan Entine. Ethel Percy Andrus Gerontology Center, University of Southern California, Los Angeles 90007. 1974. 54 pp.

This slim publication presents the summarized proceedings of a conference of distinguished participants who discussed two major themes regarding the middle years: "Dimensions and Dilemmas" and "Suggestions and Solutions." This summary whets the appetite for a supplementary conference to explore these issues more fully.

Intellectual Functioning in Adults: Psychological and Biological Influences edited by Lissy F. Jarvik, Carl Eisdorfer, and June E. Blum. Springer Publishing Company, 200 Park Avenue South, New York 10003. 1973. 177 pp.

"The contributions to this volume were drawn from selected symposia of the Division on Adult Development and Aging at the 76th and 78th annual meetings of the American Psychological Association," some of these 1968 and 1970 presentations being updated for inclusion here. Their "clinical applicability" was a criterion for inclusion; life history data and interviews, for example, are presented for their "potential contribution" to practice. Special attention is also given other longitudinal approaches and somatic components of psychological changes in adults.

Late Adulthood: Perspectives on Human Development by Richard A. Kalish. Brooks/Cole Publishing Company, Monterey, California 93940. 1975. 133 pp.

Part of the publisher's Life-Span Human Development Series, this book is more concerned with aging than adulthood. To increase reader concern, the author starts with this consciousness-raising technique: "In the time that it took you to read the first 12 words of this sentence, you have aged . . . ." If this doesn't raise hackles, the persistent reader (reading rapidly to abate aging) finds such topics covered as sensory and psychomotor processes, the changing self-concept, independence, work and retirement, and aging in the future.

Adulthood and Aging: An Interdisciplinary, Developmental View by Douglas C. Kimmel. John Wiley & Sons, 605 Third Avenue, New York 10016. 1974. 484 pp.

"This book begins where child and adolescent development books end," thus filling an aching need. Written by a 30-year-old academic psychologist, it may not achieve the "nontext" flavor he favored but can well serve as a consciousness-raising and content-enriching text. Interspersed among the ten chapters are five "interludes" presenting "actual adults who are living competent and varied lives in the real world." Topics covered include psychosocial processes, identity and intimacy, families and singles, work/retirement/leisure, and dying and bereavement.

The Wonderful Crisis of Middle Age: Some Personal Reflections by Eda J. LeShan. David McKay Company, 750 Third Avenue, New York 10017. 1973. 339 pp.

A popularization by an educator and counselor who has written for *Redbook* and *Reader's Digest,* this frothy book flaunts chapter titles such as "Erich Segal Was a Coward," "The Feminine Mistake" (Get It?), and (Believe it?) "Today is the First Day of the Rest of Our Lives." Beneath the froth are some solid perceptions regarding the possible "Renaissance in our Middle Ages." While she gives much space to women's lib and psychotherapy, she also covers career changes for men, money, and other mundane matters. Suffer the little souffles . . . .

The Physiology of Aging: How It Affects Learning by Huey B. Long. Prentice-Hall, Englewood Cliffs, New Jersey 07632. 1972. 48 pp.

Addressing itself to "adult educators," Long's short but substantive book presents "both public and private" physiological changes and their implications for instructional programs and procedures. Public changes include such visible signs as thinning hair and thickening elsewhere; "private changes include hormone alterations and shrinkage of the brain." (I for one have never seen a brain shrink or heard a hormone.) Sensorimotor, musculoskeletal, and neurological changes are discussed; Long logically concluding that "the changes may not *functionally* affect learning directly, but may contain psychological elements that indirectly" influence behavior.

Four Stages of Life: A Comparative Study of Women and Men Facing Transitions by Marjorie Fiske Lowenthal, Majda Thurnher, David Chiriboga, and Associates. Jossey-Bass Publishers, 615 Montgomery Street, San Francisco, California 94111. 1975. 292 pp.

This hypothesis-creating cross-sectional study, to serve as a basis for a longitudinal study, included 216 transition-facers: 52 high school seniors, 50 newlyweds, 54 middle-aged parents, and 60 preretirees, all four groups about equally divided by sex. Through focused interviews and structured instruments, numerous dynamic variables were tapped, such as psychological adaptation, time perspective, continuity of values, and locus of control. "That the sex of the individual rather than his or stage in life accounts for most of the variation within our sample is well documented . . . ." Provocative conclusions are presented, as well as implications for research and public policy.

From Thirty to Seventy by Henry S. Maas and Joseph A. Kuypers. Jossey-Bass Publishers, 615 Montgomery Street, San Francisco, California 94111. 1974. 240 pp.

Subtitled "A Forty-Year Longitudinal Study of Adult Life Styles and Personality," this report resulted from a treasure trove of records about parents involved in an earlier longitudinal study of their children. Followed up forty years later, the 142 parents yielded a further wealth of data reflecting "diversity and uniqueness," continuities and change during adulthood, sex-context interactions, and disablement/disengagement. Discussion is included of substantive and methodological issues and implications.

The Myth and Reality of Aging in America by National Council on the Aging. NCOA, 1828 L Street, N.W., Washington, D.C. 20036. 1975. 245 pp.

The 8½ x 11 product of an extensive survey conducted by Louis Harris and Associates, this report covers (or uncovers) the public's attitudes and expectations regarding "older Americans" (over 65) and older Americans' attitudes and expectations regarding themselves. Whether the implication is valid that older *Americans* are different or differently regarded and despite the over-65 focus, this material is pertinent to the counseling of younger older persons. Directly relevant is a chapter on preparation for old age.

Normal Aging II edited by Erdman Palmore. Duke University Press, Durham, North Carolina 27710. 1974. 316 pp.

This volume is a sequel to the 1970 collection of reports from the longitudinal studies conducted under the aegis of the Duke Center for the Study of Aging and Human Development (Does aging precede human development?). A team approach produced interdisciplinary studies combining latitude with longitude. Although many of the reports (more in Volume I) deal with aging beyond the middle years, the latter are represented here with respect to such topics as achievement and the self-concept, use of leisure time, and sexual behavior. The editor provides introductory and summary chapters, as well as contributing to several of the reports.

Personality Development: The Chronology of Experience by Leon Rappoport. Scott, Foresman and Company, Glenview, Illinois 60025. 1972. 448 pp.

The perceptive author "singled out what seemed to me to be the most critical problems at each developmental period, looking first at how they present themselves to the developing person and then at how the major theories interpret what is happening." This doubly more personal approach starts where individuals are in the lifespan and infuses the developmental/theoretical presentation with Rappoport's insights. He devotes a full chapter to the period from 26 to 50, as well as one to "the 60's and beyond" (Was he in the missing 50's?), enriching his content with literate writing.

"Adult Development and Aging" by K. Warner Schaie and Kathy Gribbin. In Mark R. Rosenzweig and Lyman W. Porter (Eds.), *Annual Review of Psychology.* Annual Reviews, 4139 El Camino Way, Palo Alto, California 94306. 1975. Pp. 65-96.

Though only a chapter in an omnibus book, this compressed material merits the attention of counseling psychologists. The authors review considerable evidence of the coming of age of adulthood and aging in the psychological literature. Major sections cover methodological issues, cognitive processes, perception and psychophysiology, personality, and attitudes. The 354 references reflect the wide range of recent and relevant writings.

Developmental Physiology and Aging by P. S. Timiras. The Macmillan Company, 866 Third Avenue, New York 10022. 1972. 692 pp.

Since psyche and soma are intertwined, psychological development is better understood in relation to bodily growth—and decline. Psychological equilibrium (balancing, rather than absence, of tensions) is related to physiological homeostasis (again, vectors countervailed rather than a void). Lecture over, here's the author's point: "The adaptive mechanisms necessary to achieve relative physiologic equilibrium are distinctive from one age to another." Developmental differences are dealt with in their many aspects in this two-ton tome, weight being given "factors affecting" this and that—always an aid to understanding.

INDEX